KAFKA

KAFKA

Howard Caygill

KAFKA

In Light of the Accident

Howard Caygill

Bloomsbury Academic
An imprint of Bloomsbury Publishing Plc

B L O O M S B U R Y
LONDON • OXFORD • NEW YORK • NEW DELHI • SYDNEY

Bloomsbury Academic

An imprint of Bloomsbury Publishing Plc

50 Bedford Square	1385 Broadway
London	New York
WC1B 3DP	NY 10018
UK	USA

www.bloomsbury.com

BLOOMSBURY and the Diana logo are trademarks of Bloomsbury Publishing Plc

First published 2017

British Library Cataloguing-in-Publication Data
A catalogue record for this book is available from the British Library.

ISBN:	HB:	978-1-4725-9542-3
	ePDF:	978-1-4725-9544-7
	ePub:	978-1-4725-9543-0

Library of Congress Cataloging-in-Publication Data
A catalog record for this book is available from the Library of Congress.

Typeset by RefineCatch Limited, Bungay, Suffolk
Printed and bound in India

I have so much to do! In my four districts – on top of my other work – people fall off scaffoldings as if drunk, they fall into machines, all the beams topple, all the embankments subside, all the ladders slip and whatever someone passes up falls back and whatever is passed down is tripped over. And what headaches from all the girls in the porcelain factories who incessantly throw themselves down the stairs with towers of crockery.

LETTER TO MAX BROD, SUMMER 1909

A place I have never been before: breath comes differently, a neighbouring star shining brighter than the sun.

17TH ZÜRAU APHORISM

Whither are we moving? Away from all suns? Are we not plunging continually? Backward, sideward, forward in all directions? Is there still any up or down? Are we not straying as through infinite nothing? Do we not feel the breath of infinite space? Do we not need to light lanterns in the morning?

NIETZSCHE, THE GAY SCIENCE, §125

Your Father had an accident there; he was put in a pie by Mrs McGregor.

BEATRIX POTTER, THE TALE OF PETER RABBIT

For Edi

CONTENTS

LIST OF ILLUSTRATIONS

LIST OF ABBREVIATIONS

For ease of reference, citations from Kafka refer first to an available English translation and then to the German edition.

A　　*America*, trans. Willa and Edwin Muir in *Franz Kafka: The Complete Novels*, Vintage Books, London, 2008; *Der Verschollene (Amerika)*, ed. Jost Schillemeit, S. Fischer Verlag, Frankfurt-am-Main, 2003

AS　　*Amtliche Schriften*, hsg. Klaus Hermsdorf, Akademie-Verlag, Berlin

C　　*The Castle*, trans. Willa and Edwin Muir in *Franz Kafka: The Complete Novels*, Vintage Books, London, 2008; *Das Schloss, in der Fasssung der Handschrift*, hsg. Malcolm Pasley, S. Fischer Verlag, Frankfurt-am-Main, 2001

D　　*The Diaries of Franz Kafka*, ed. Max Brod, trans. Joseph Kresh and Martin Greenberg with the assistance of Hannah Arendt, Peregrine Books 1964; *Tagebücher* 1909–1923, S. Fischer Verlag, Frankfurt-am-Main, 1997

L　　*Franz Kafka: Letters to Friends, Family and Editors*, trans. Richard and Clara Winston, Oneworld Classics Ltd, London, 2011; *Briefe 1902–1924*, Fischer Taschenbuch Verlag, Frankfurt-am-Main, 1974

F　　*Letters to Felice with Kafka's Other Trial by Elias Canetti*, trans. James Stern, Elizabeth Ducksworth and Christopher Middleton, Penguin Books, Harmondsworth, 1978; *Briefe an Felice*, ed. Erich Heller and Jürgen Born, S. Fischer Verlag, Frankfurt-am-Main, 1967

NI　　*Nachgelassene Schriften und Fragmente* I *in der Fassung der Handschriften*, hsg. Malcolm Pasley, S. Fischer Verlag, Frankfurt-am-Main, 1993

PREFACE

ear midnight on 29 June 2009 a goods train derailed outside the station of the Italian resort of Viareggio. Its cargo of natural gas exploded causing many deaths and terrible injuries. Among the victims were people sleeping at home, a couple riding by on a motor-scooter, a man walking back from an evening with friends at a bar ... I'd passed through the station a few hours before, but this accident was not meant for me. It provoked a furious outburst of attempts to make sense of it: a terrorist attack, an act of God, negligent maintenance of the track or rolling-stock ... all stories intent on explaining away the accident. Yet none could give any satisfactory reason why precisely those individuals had to be called to their singular fates on that summer's night. None could convincingly point beyond harsh contingency to that semblance of necessity – some hint of justice or at least responsibility – that would lend meaning to the accident.

Waking the next day in a guest house in nearby Montignoso, I saw on the wall a framed photograph of a jetty on Lake Ullswater in the English Lake District. An improbable enough image to decorate a room in an Italian resort, it also had to be the scene of my earliest memory, the jetty from where I fell as a child into the lake and almost drowned. What are the chances of that reminder of a thwarted death by drowning appearing on that far away wall decades later at precisely *that* moment? So small that the highly improbable but evidently *not-impossible* chain of infinitesimal causes that brought me before this image assume the aspect of haunted necessity. And with this a portal opens onto what Kafka described as the 'world of insurance' or that uncanny realm of predictable improbabilities governed by the 'law' of the necessary accident.

This book locates Kafka at the junction of three ways of negotiating the modality of the accident: philosophy, fiction and insurance. It asks what happens to the received ways of making sense of the accident in philosophy and fiction when confronted with the modern 'world of insurance', or the regime of security and the management of chance that provides the infrastructure for the social, economic and political institutions of modernity. It suggests a difficult continuity between Kafka's writing by day as a senior official and theorist in the Workers Accident Insurance Institute for the Kingdom of Bohemia in Prague and his fictional writing by night. And it locates his ambivalent relation to philosophy not only in terms of the old quarrel between philosophy and poetry evoked by Plato in *The Republic*, but also with respect to the crisis of truth and fiction provoked by both the sublime thought of the death of God and the mundane management of the accident by the theory and institutions of insurance. What I hope emerges is a Kafka quite different from the twentieth century's fabulist of the law whose writing dwells in the darkness of domination, a writer of the accident in every sense, a writer of defiant light.

My thanks are due to the audiences who responded to versions of parts of this book and to my friends, students and colleagues at the Centre for Research in Modern European Philosophy, Kingston University, the Department of Philosophy at the University of Paris VIII, IDSVA and to the members of the Digital Cultures Research Laboratory at the Leuphana University Lüneburg who gave me the chance to finish the book and test my translations. Special and personal thanks to my editor Liza Thompson and to all at Parnithos, Molin Nuovo and Regata Run Drive. Finally, my apologies for any errors of fact and interpretation in what follows; had I known where these accidents were to happen I would surely have taken better measures to prevent them.

INTRODUCTION: CHANCE INTERPRETATIONS

While philosophical interpretations of Kafka are legion, few depart from the premise that his writings knowingly address the limits of philosophy. For sure, no other twentieth-century writer has so perplexed the philosophers while eluding philosophical capture. There is an uncanny sense of Kafka leading on the philosophical chase, teasing it to reveal its theological investments and archaic fascination with the law in all its degraded majesty. Kafka knows how to smoke out the 'wizened dwarf' concealed under Benjamin's chess table but not in search of a new ally in an old game but for the sake of completing a defiant enlightenment. This drama plays out in the light of an ontology of the accident[1] and a politics of defiance staged through a reassertion of the truth claims of fiction. It is an anti-theological writing that heeds Nietzsche's declaration of the death of God and his call to tell new stories in an anarchic cosmos without centre or secured law and so infiltrating fiction into the realms of truth and of power.

Franz Kafka's novels, stories, diaries and letters rose to global prominence in the course of the twentieth century. Not only is he one of the most translated, widely read and respected of that century's authors, he is also a point of reference for describing and understanding its disastrous experiments in total domination. There would seem little to connect the experience of an Austro-Hungarian-Prague-German-Jewish writer at the beginning of the century with the maleficent Cambodian Khmer Rouge regime of the 1970s; and yet Prince Sihanouk could find no better word to describe the political terror of the Pol Pot government than 'kafkaesque'.[2] It is no exaggeration to compare the place of Kafka's writing in twentieth century culture with Homer's in Ancient Greece, with both serving as points of cultural orientation and objects of constant citation and criticism. Georg Lukács in *The Meaning of Contemporary Realism* even repeated

Plato's exiling of the poets by expelling Kafka from the ranks of the progressive democratic allies of the proletariat. But the most striking and sustained appropriation of his work has been by philosophy. Philosophy has made an example of Kafka; citations and interpretations of his work by philosophers are ubiquitous, with Adorno, Agamben, Anders, Arendt, Bataille, Benjamin, Blanchot, Butler, Cacciari, Canetti, Deleuze and Guattari, Derrida, Lukács, Malabou, Maldiney, Sartre and Sloterdijk united in little else than this their pursuit of the elusive writer.

The first generation of German language philosophical criticism produced essayistic reflections that are still read and debated within and beyond the reach of Kafka criticism. It also produced an impressive interpretative *summa* – Wilhelm Emrich's *Franz Kafka* of 1958 – still valid as a philosophical introduction to Kafka's work written from the perspective of Adorno's aesthetic theory. In France too the genre of the philosophical essay flourished alongside ambitious philosophical meditations on the significance of Kafka's work. Bataille's journal *Critique* hosted a fascinating series of articles on Kafka in the 1950s at the same time as Sartre paired him with Jean Genet. More recently he has reappeared as a critical political theologian in the Italian language interpretations of Agamben, Cacciari, Calasso and Citati.[3]

Philosophical readers of Kafka rarely ask *why* he works so well as a philosophical example or *why* his writings are able to generate such sophisticated yet radically diverse philosophical interpretations. The failure even to ask points to a systematic underestimation of the philosophical dimension of Kafka's writing and his view of fiction as a philosophical thought experiment.[4] Philosophy indeed touched Kafka in many ways; he was a student and a reader of philosophy and of course an unsurpassed writer of philosophical fictions. While this is recognized by some philosophical critics, most read him first and foremost as a writer of domination and the law. This consensus was expressed most brutally by Brecht who in conversation with Benjamin insinuated 'Disciple Kafka's' proximity to 'Jewish fascism',[5] or in a more measured way by Canetti in his widely cited comment, 'Of all writers, Kafka is the greatest expert on power (*Macht*)' (*F* 64).

Yet the view of Kafka as a fabulist of power and domination should not be accepted too uncritically.[6] With respect to Canetti's observation, attention to the character of his *expertise* should not be distracted by too exclusive a focus on power. Not only was Kafka's 'expertise' more pronounced in the field of domination (*Herrschaft*) than power (*Macht*), it was also oriented more towards defiance than obedience.[7] Kafka's expertise in the investigation of the conditions of possibility of domination is less salient than his renewed wonder at the eruption of defiance in the face of it. Kafka is the rare case of a writer who frees defiance from *dis*obedience by pursuing an understanding of it unrefracted by any prior opposition to law. Contra Canetti, Kafka never concedes the primacy of power nor the normative value of obedience, and his 'expertise' consists in identifying power and domination as *reactions* to unpredictable, incalculable and even *accidental* outbursts of defiance. For him it is less a question of defying the law than of seeing law as a response to real, imagined, feared or anticipated defiance. The accidental character of defiance – its being *before* the law – nevertheless possesses its own, uncanny necessity that attends its eruptions without tying it to any discernible conditions of possibility. This necessity cannot be approached through any transcendental analytic of domination but only through fictions of defiance. The terms of Canetti's appreciation repeat the theological capture of Kafka's writings by bringing them under the sign of submission or vain resistance to inscrutable power and law. It entirely misses the philosophical character of Kafka's work and its attempt to think defiantly without and beyond the law.

Wilhelm Emrich's reading of Kafka follows Adorno's alignment of the critique of modernity with a theory of the avant-garde. Departing from a diagnosis of the ills of modernity framed in terms of 'a breach between the individual and the universal' (Emrich, 2) – with 'universal' standing for the ethical and political life of a community or latterly nation-state[8] – Emrich assigns avant-garde art the task of inhabiting and exposing this breach. Echoing Adorno's 'Notes on Kafka', he approaches Kafka's work in terms of 'an absolute enigmatisation with reference to the universal of this century' (Emrich, 3), one with aesthetic and political import. Kafka and other avant-garde artists host the promise of an experience beyond the diremption of individual and universal. His work does not just mirror and confirm power as Canetti believed, but points beyond it to an emancipation encrypted in the retreat of philosophizing into fiction. In Adorno's idiom, the failure to realize philosophy by actualizing freedom forces it to take refuge in fiction: the 'clear-sighted critical knowledge of the inescapable conformities of an era that no longer tolerates any universal existence that is meaningfully free of purpose … forced Kafka to the poetic form of his empirically incomprehensible world of animals and concrete things' (Emrich, 267). From this point of view the philosopher can only escape the predicament of domination and the conformities and disciplines investing labour and the exercise of modern government by emigrating to fiction; the free, philosophical life can only be imagined, can only be justified aesthetically through the invention and elaboration of enigmatic fictions. Nevertheless, at the limit of his negative dialectic Emrich too effects a dialectical reversal by proposing that 'Kafka's writing can be understood as an uninterrupted wrestling to overcome the lawlessness of the human world ... and to gain an inviolable, true, universally binding system of administering justice' (Emrich, 39) but one understood in opposition to the 'inconceivable chaos of multifarious focal points and movements' (Emrich, 39). For Emrich's qualified Hegelianism, Kafka's fictions testify to a future *Sittlichkeit* where freedom and law align without domination, one intimated in a realm of fiction that has immunized itself against labour and domination but also it seems against the chaos, chance and defiance that attend but might also undermine them.

The emergence of Kafka's fictional writing from a philosophical context informed by the study of Nietzsche refracted through the phenomenology of the Prague Brentano school should not be understood too quickly in terms of a retreat to the enigmatic. We shall indeed see an anti-Platonic movement engaged in Kafka's work, one that rescinds the banishment of the poets or fiction from the *polis* in the name of domination and the law by their return in the name of defiance.[9] Making this possible is Kafka's reflection on the *accident* as a momentary suspension of necessity that paradoxically possesses its own necessity.[10] And he arrived at this reflection not by retreating from modernity as Emrich believed, but by fully immersing himself in it at one of its most sensitive points: the management of chance and the accident through the institutions of insurance. And he does so not as an expert in power, but as one who works at the limits of law and domination exposed by the accident – as an official in the Worker's Accident Insurance Institute.

Kafka's efforts to find a medium equal to thinking chance and accident led to an anarchic thought with scarce sympathy for the laws of fixity and continuity. His writing is less a secured retreat than a landscape formed, traversed and unsettled by the fault lines of truth, fiction, power and defiance.[11] Kafka was not an orator in the fashion of the ancient *polis* but an inhabitant of the modern site for the exercise of power, a bureaucrat who during the working day wrote strategic policy and theoretical reflection using a legal and technical vocabulary drawn from the lexicon of modern legal-rational domination. A large part of his professional role as *concipist* or legal writer in the Workers Accident Insurance Institute consisted in *writing the accident* – literally preparing reports on accidents, interpreting accident statistics, adjusting risk classifications and attempting to foresee and prevent accidents where- and whenever possible.[12] His profession was dedicated to translating the faltering, unpredictable and uncertain language of chance and accident into words of power and so bringing unpredictable events under institutional regulation. Yet such translation secretly depended on fiction since the accident by definition eludes easy capture by the normative discourses of law, statistical analysis and technical efficiency that were officially at Kafka's disposal.

Kafka's ability to negotiate the intersection of legal, technical and fictional writing was recognized and valued by his colleagues; he showed pride in his words of power, his 'office writing', especially his contributions to the published Annual Reports of the Institute. These form a discrete *oeuvre*, widely distributed and read in their time – certainly more so than his fiction – and notable for the precision of their technical, juristic and even philosophical reflections on the accident and its tormented relationship to law. Their speculative quality distinguishes them from the dictated memoranda and internal documents that made up his more everyday work for the Institute. The quality of his regular contributions to the Annual Reports between 1908 and 1917 made him 'one of the most important contributors to the Institute's journal' (*Amtliche Schriften*, 27) as well as its leading theoretician. He forwarded copies of his official writings to friends and even his fiancée Felice (see the letter dated 30 v 15) and one can only imagine the surprise of Franz Blei – the editor of the *fin-de-siecle* literary journal *Hyperion* where Kafka made his fictional debut – upon receiving a copy of 'The Scope of Compulsory Insurance for the Building Trades'.[13] The impersonality of these writings, and the pseudo-, crypto-, allo- and ano- nymity required by such products of a complex and highly regulated bureaucratic *Apparat*, complement but also contrast with his fictional writings.[14] His words of power depended on a relationship between truth, fiction and domination whose balance and intensity varied according to occasion and that became a major theme of his fictions.

The borders between thinking, administration and fiction are neither fixed nor well defined but subject to sudden and unpredictable realignments: Kafka does not subsume them under law or the universal but instead contemplates them in the light of defiance and the accident. This entailed his carrying the technical analysis of the modalities of the accident developed by insurance into fiction at the same time as demonstrating how fiction had always already been present in such analysis. In insurance theory, accidents are a systemic property manifest in the relatively stable number of accidents befalling a given population over a given time. Yet beside the actuarial necessity that makes it possible to calculate and administer the incidence of accidents, insurance must also confront the singularity of the accident experienced by its victim. The tension between the stable population of accidents and the devastating impact of their singular incidence opens the fictional space of Kafka's insurance work as well as the uninsured space of his fictions.

The two aspects of the accident – statistical regularity and singular incidence – have their fictional analogues in Kafka's recurrent figures of landslides and falls. The landslide figures the systemic properties of the accident: a certain number of accidents are waiting to happen to a given population over a given period of time; they approach like a slow landslide. The fall figures singularity or the individuated accident, the experience of being, fearing to be or having been the unhappy one in the wrong place at the wrong time, transfixed in the path of the landslide. The two figures constitute a tension that describes a major fault line in Kafka's fiction and insurance work.[15] The impersonal statistically probable accident must manifest itself in singular and intimately devastating fates: while a certain number of immigrants to the USA will fail, a certain number of suspects will be arrested and a certain number of employees hired by mistake, it is the individual fates of Karl Rossman, Josef K. and K. that interest Kafka in his fictions. For fiction can individuate systemic properties and explore the complex reactions – evasion, guilt, defiance, rage and resignation – provoked by falling under the accident. With the signal exception of defiance, all these reactions concede the necessity and even justice of the accident and strive to lend its individuation the semblance of truth and necessity.[16]

The borders between fiction, the philosophical protocols of truth and the official words of power are porous and shifting in Kafka. The critical technique commonly used to manage this anti-Platonic hybrid of poetry, truth and power combines stylistic and chronological criteria. Kafka's move from stories and novels to parables and aphorisms during the winter of 1916–17 has been viewed in terms of the increasing prominence of philosophical concerns in his writing. Yet this forgets that Kafka's fiction emerged from the matrix of philosophy *and* insurance and was concerned with truth and specifically the tension between truth and power. His are fictions of the accident in search of philosophical consistency rather than narratives of accidental vicissitudes befalling already constituted consistencies such as family, law, state and religion.

Kafka could not insure even his own work against the hazards of chance, survival and interpretation. The chapter of accidents surrounding the editing, publication and interpretation of his three abandoned novels is cautionary in this respect. The legal and economic constraints that led Kafka's friend and editor Max Brod to publish his abandoned novels in a different order to their composition[17] created the impression that his first novel, *America* (*Der Verschollene*), largely written during the autumn of 1912 but published last in 1927 followed both *The Trial* (published in 1925 but written during autumn and winter of 1914–15) and *The Castle* (published in 1926 but written during 1922). This editorial accident conditioned the powerful and still influential redemption narratives of Arendt and Benjamin that maintain Kafka wrote a *trilogy* culminating in *America*, whose brutal final chapter, 'Nature Theatre of Oklahama' (written alongside *The Trial* and 'In the Penal Colony' during the autumn of 1914), is held to provide an implausibly *redemptive* finale to Kafka's entire *oeuvre*.[18] Walter Benjamin unwittingly read *America* against the chronological grain as the culmination of a redemptive history in which the protagonist 'K' of the 'first' novel gradually assumes his full name, becoming Josef K in *The Trial* and finally Karl Rossman in *America*, a progression through an attention to names that inexplicably overlooks the significance of Rossman's entry into the exterminatory 'Nature Theatre' under the assumed name of 'Negro'. Hannah Arendt too accepts the published ordering of the novels in setting the development of Kafka's work within a political narrative that raises the 'Nature Theatre' to the status of a political utopia.[19] Her reading of Kafka in terms of a distinction between the Jew as 'pariah' and 'parvenu' not only justifies the political possibilities of the 'self-conscious' or rebellious pariah but also the utopian realm of constructed citizenship – 'a new possibility of authentic life' (Arendt, 117) she sees 'tentatively' described 'at the end, the happy ending of *America*' (Arendt, 108). The chronological assumptions underpinning these philosophical critiques were the result of an editorial accident and the false sense of security given by Brod's edition to interpreters working on a very hazardous textual site.

One way of partially insuring a philosophical reading of Kafka against such accidents is to attend to the century of remarkable historical scholarship setting Kafka within specific urban, religious, political, philosophical and cultural contexts. Another is to heed Malcolm Pasley's advice to the 'hasty interpreters and doctrinal exploiters of Kafka' (Pasley 1995, 210) to respect the letter of Kafka's texts and manuscripts as established by the scrupulous work of his editors. Hence the effort in this book to give due attention to historical and philological issues that may try the patience of some philosophical readers but probably without fully convincing the cultural historians and editors of Kafka's work of the probity of the outcome.

Kafka exegesis of the past two decades has indeed been notable for its sophistication and quality. It has been enriched by the contributions of new historicism and cultural studies, with illuminating individual studies of Kafka's clothes (Anderson 1992), photography (Duttlinger 2007), cinema (Zischler 2003), deportation (Müller-Seidel 1986), gender and race (Boa 1996), travel (Zilcosky 2003), religion (Mosès) and politics (Löwy 2004, Casanova 2011). One of the major inspirations for this work were the theoretically open and sophisticated inquiries of Stanley Corngold who, while supportive of cultural analyses of Kafka's texts, pursues his own neo-gnostic interpretation whose learning and subtlety set a standard for philosophical and theological exegesis. Corngold taught the current generation of readers that there can be no barriers between the theological, literary and institutional Kafkas: the author of *Lambent Traces* and the translator of Kafka's short stories is also an editor of the English translation of the *Office Writings*. The latter body of work, first published in the East German edition of Klaus Hermsdorf in 1984, is proving increasingly significant for the more innovative currents of Kafka criticism most notably in Benno Wagner's iconoclastic and inspirational work on the 'poetics of the accident' (Corngold and Wagner 2011). Wagner situates Kafka's narratives within a poetics of accident indebted both to Nietzsche and the discourse of insurance 'that serves as a hidden link between the potential narrative fascination of the accident and the alienation potential of statistically conceived humanity' (Wagner in Koch and Wagenbach, 114). Wagner's work freed philosophical readings of Kafka from the Hegelian philosophical premises of Emrich's interpretation, and his steady insistence on the significance of Nietzsche's *Also Sprach Zarathustra* to Kafka's official and fictional work provides a gratefully acknowledged condition of possibility for the reading ventured in this book.[20]

My approach towards a philosophical Kafka begins by showing some of the accidents surrounding Kafka's emergence as a writer and then moves to his writing of the accident. There it joins the recent work of Paul North in emphasizing the importance of Nietzsche for the atheological timbre of Kafka's thought and writings that increasingly marks a major rift between twentieth- and twenty-first-century Kafka scholarship. It then considers the centrality of the image in his writings and his engagement with photography in both his insurance and fictional work. Finally, after analysis of the themes of defiance and domination in Kafka's fictions, I arrive at some thoughts on the affinities between the lights of defiance, truth and the accident.

1 WRITINGS

Accident narratives

The heap of words left by Kafka's writing – stories, novels, aphorisms, letters, official reports, memos, messages, diary entries and even notes to his carers after TB took away his ability to speak – has been assiduously quarried for almost a century. More than any other writer, his words have been sifted, separated, collected, dispersed, titled and retitled; they have been set and reset into patterns, ranked in hierarchies, reduced to their elements with their *disjecta membra* variously reconstituted. Work on his words began with Kafka himself and continued through generations of editors, critics, exegetes and interpreters. There exist innumerable permutations of his short stories, fragments, poems, novels and novellas in German and in translation whose morphology is shaped by currents of criticism whose tendency often finds confirmation in the textual body they helped form.[1] Yet there remains something *accidental* about the patterns emerging from the swirl of Kafka's words, a *clinamen* that defies any tendency towards a settled *oeuvre* with secured interpretative protocols.

The role played by chance and accident in the bare survival of Kafka's writings cannot be underestimated. Kafka notoriously gambled on the destruction of his work: from the outset he was the author of works he preferred personally not to publish. The infamous testamentary instruction to Max Brod to destroy his manuscripts was not an exceptional measure but a late manifestation of a consistent stance.[2] There are references to destroyed works and the routine self-destruction of his writings as early as 1903 in his correspondence with Oskar Pollak, along with two parables – among Kafka's earliest surviving fictions – that address the theme of leaving his writings to the care of others.[3] They reveal Kafka as an author of abandoned works, not just interrupted, left unfinished or otherwise destroyed, but *abandoned* to chance and the care or neglect of others. While his *Diaries* survived due to the care of his Czech translator Milena, other texts were not so fortunate. His posthumous appearance on the Nazi's 'List 1 of harmful and undesirable writings' not only put his published writings at risk, but also provoked the Berlin Gestapo to raid his last partner Dora Dymant's apartment to confiscate any papers remaining in her possession. And by a slender chance, Max Brod left Prague just before the Nazis entered the city carrying with him the manuscripts that form the basis of our current editions of Kafka's work.[4]

Any attempt at understanding Kafka should be vigilant to the ways his surviving words have been cut, carved and shaped into blocks pre-adapted to fit existing and emergent interpretative structures. This holds not only for the major division of his writing according to day and night – office and fiction – but also for the nomadic distribution of the fictions across letters, diary entries, novels and short stories. Caution is also advised when approaching the critical reception of his work – as already seen in the case of the interpretations of the 'trilogy' – but more saliently with the critical significance lent to his story 'The Judgment' written during the night of the 22–23 September 1912 and widely assumed to mark a watershed in his writing.

Accepting 'The Judgement' as the inaugural moment of Kafka's mature authorship relegates his earlier fiction – 'Description of A Struggle', 'Wedding Preparations in the Country' and the collection *Meditation (Betrachtung)* – to the realm of juvenilia. This grievously underestimates these writings conceived from the outset as philosophical fictions or 'meditations'. It also poses difficulties for explaining Kafka's subsequent repudiation of the style of 'The Judgement' in the aphoristic or short philosophical texts of 1917 with their relative indifference to such themes as judgement, guilt and punishment also wanting in the stories comprising *Meditation* not to mention the abandoned 'Description of a Struggle' and 'Wedding Preparations in the Country'.[5] These may be described as philosophical accident narratives that refuse the logical and narrative coherence offered by the juridical and familial scenarios of 'The Judgement' and its successors and instead pursue an asymptotic coherence among the multiplying accidents that befall them. By fusing juridical and familial logics in 'The Judgment' and its successor stories, Kafka contains the possibilities opened by the accident narrative, imposing an external coherence difficult either to sustain or escape.

Orienting Kafka's achievement according to 'The Judgement' not only obscures the philosophical dimension of his fiction but also reduces its motivation to an obsession with law, domination and punishment. Kafka certainly considered collecting 'The Judgement' along with 'Metamorphosis' and 'The Stoker' under the title *Fathers and Sons* or in a later configuration with 'In the Penal Colony' as *Punishments*, but these planned collections should be approached as variations on a theme that was by no means his *only* theme. The first collection, with the addition of the later 'Letter to my Father', presents Kafka as *the* writer of filial claustrophobia and subjection to paternal law, while the second makes him a writer of law, domination and punishment. But privileging such themes and sequences over others including travel, urban experience, insurance theory and the philosophical fragments and meditations condemns the latter to the critical margins. Indeed, the prominence given to intersecting family and punishment sequences in the reading of Kafka is rarely challenged but is nevertheless based on tendentious assumptions that in foregrounding the themes of domination, obedience and punishment create the illusion that these represent the main or even sole concern of Kafka's writing.

It is necessary to resist the occlusion of the philosophical accident narrative by too exclusive a focus on the fictional unfolding of juridical and familial logics. The latter do not make sense without the former, and represent particular responses to the predicament of the accident. The difficult alignment of accident and familial logic is a structural element of 'Wedding Preparations in the Country', whose hero Raban pursues an ever deferred passage from the accidental encounters of urban experience to the congealed familial world of the fiancée waiting in the country. By tarrying with Raban's increasingly asymptotic passage towards familial consistency, 'Wedding Preparations' defers the encounter central to 'The Judgement' and succeeds in evading the punishment scene as the only escape from familial logic. Locating 'The Judgement ' with respect to the writings that precede it makes it possible to identify the juridical and familial narratives as repressive *responses* to the predicament of writing the accident. This breaks the critical enchantment with the sequence opened by 'The Judgement' and followed by 'The Metamorphosis' and points to another sequence that moves from 'Description of a Struggle' through 'Wedding Preparations in the Country' and *Meditation* to *America* and beyond. According to this revisionary sequence, 'The Metamorphosis' is less the 'triumphant synthesis' of reflections on 'the nature of life in the contemporary urban and industrial world' and 'a group of psychological and moral relationships arising from family relationships' described by Ritchie Robertson (1985, 85–6) than the tormented attempt to come to terms with being a family accident victim.

The move towards the more aphoristic philosophical style found in the Oktavo notebooks of 1917 and the Zürau Aphorisms extracted from them and especially in Kafka's second published collection of stories *A Country Doctor* makes more sense as a return to the concerns of his first collection

Meditation than an extension of the sequence opened by 'The Judgement'. *Meditation* not only participates in the sequence of texts rooted in the accident narrative, but also anticipates the question of the relationship between fiction and philosophy explicitly posed by Kafka's work after 1917. It testifies to the elusive and intangible relation between fictional and philosophical expression motivating his move from formal philosophizing to fiction. Both forms of expression emerge in his night writing, but the borders separating truth and fiction remain porous and shifting, as does their complicity with the day's words of power. By focusing on the accident narrative, it becomes possible to see how Kafka from the outset pursued a consistent (and anti-Platonic) effort to 'think through images' and to appreciate how the kind of familial/juridical fiction he explored in 'The Judgement' represents a special case or even a deviation from this kind of thinking.

An assessment of the case for Kafka's return to explicit philosophizing in 1917 provides some criteria for understanding the neglected *Meditation* as a collection of philosophical fictions. The development of Kafka's authorship during 1917 has been the subject of a subtle debate on the relationship between the 'philosophical' aphorisms Kafka wrote in 1917–18 (and prepared for publication in 1920) and the notebooks he kept at his sister's home in the village of Zürau while convalescing after the onset of tuberculosis. Reiner Stach in his biography makes a lucid case for regarding these texts as marking a transition from the fictional towards the philosophical, claiming that fragments such as those Brod entitled 'The Silence of the Sirens' and 'The Truth about Sancho Panza' are 'no longer really narrative; they are experimental setups, trains of thought derived from and shaped into images' (Stach 2013, 201, 229). For Stach, these experiments inspired by Pascal's *Pensées* and Nietzsche's aphorisms constitute 'acts of reflection' or *meditations* that attain 'formulations that appear to operate at the outer limits of human cognition and several steps beyond in the clear, rarified zone between knowledge and wisdom' (Stach 2013, 201, 230). The writings of 1917 and the sequences they inaugurate dissolve the distinctions between truth and fiction – philosophy and literature – into thought experiments not so distant from those pursued by Kafka's contemporary Ludwig Wittgenstein.[6]

Stach's use of Martin Greenberg's now classic distinction between Kafka's early 'dream' and later 'thought stories' commits him to a particular view of the role of 'reflection' in the early diaries and fictions.[7] Corngold had already given this view a neo-gnostic inflection by reading the 'thought stories' as 'lambent traces' or purifications of the divine sparks from the materiality of the created world: 'I refer to Kafka's readiness to lend his stories the tension of the gnostic world view, in which the created world consists of debased images of a transcendent source that has nonetheless left lambent traces in the mind' (Corngold in Preece, 96). Yet already in *Meditation* the lines between dream and thought are more finely drawn than these distinctions admit, and point less to the gnostic remotion of divinity from creation than the Nietzschean proclamation of the death of God.

The debate concerning the transition of 1917 also addresses the form and character of Kafka's fictional philosophizing. In a study of Kafka's aphorisms, Richard T. Gray showed how aphoristic expression's figural rigour and un-Platonic attention to singularity was ideally suited to staging the tension between the fictional and the philosophical.[8] These formal properties also made the aphorism an apt medium for narrating the accident and reflecting on its peculiar modal necessity; for while not empirically contingent, its necessity nevertheless remains intangible and requires the space of the fictional to find expression. Philosophizing by means of the aphorism is certainly anti-Platonic, both in terms of ancient precedent and contemporary use, but this does not make it empirically or pragmatically oriented according to a 'practical logic' as Corngold believes when he writes, 'Thereafter, Kafka does not think of writing as a type of philosophical reflection; instead it constitutes "a way", a practical orientation' (Corngold in Preece, 97). Writing aphoristically is not just a matter of practical orientation but the presentation of a necessity of the contingent that is distinct from empiricist and transcendental argumentative protocols and that draws explicitly on the resources of fiction.

The kind of philosophical fiction made possible by the aphorism exploits the tension between singularity and necessity characteristic of the accident narrative. It is a vehicle for the practice of 'meditation' that departs from the peculiar necessity of the accident. Such exploration of the fictional and philosophical space of the accident and its necessity also characterizes Kafka's *Diaries* which began under the auspices of this pre-defined practice of philosophical meditation.

The *Diary* that Kafka began in 1910 and continued until shortly before his death (the last entry is from 1923) served as a laboratory for observation, elaboration and philosophical reflection. In keeping a diary, Kafka participated in a broader cultural trend to which Victor Klemperer's diary is justly regarded as the most fitting monument.[9] At the same time as Kafka began to keep a diary, other theoretically inclined diarists such as Georg Lukacs and Walter Benjamin were also reflecting on the possibilities of the genre, and like him regarded it not only as a place of inwardness and solitary conversation but also a site for disclosing the necessities informing the accidental events of their everyday lives. Kafka's programmatic statement in spring 1910 that the diary was a way of 'talking to himself' after five months of life in which he 'could write nothing of which I could be satisfied' (*D* 12, 6) agrees with the first criterion, but its emphasis on the meditative technique of recording incidental events – descriptions, reported and imagined speech, thoughts, dreams, situations – in search of their necessity also points beyond it.

In his diary, Kafka scrutinized the accidents he lived, observed and recorded through fragmentary narrative descriptions that sometimes metamorphosed into stories that out-grew the limits of the diary form. There are many examples, one of the first being the repeated variations from late spring 1910 of the 'Little Dweller in the Ruins', a fugal meditation upon the mantra 'When I reflect, I must say that my education has in many respects damaged me a lot' (*D* 15, 8) that gathers all the bad educators who through commission or omission contributed to ruining him. Another important example are the variant endings of 'In the Penal Colony' recorded in the diary entries of the summer of 1917, themselves meditations on the meaning of that incomplete and evidently incompletable story.

The diary became a quarry from which Kafka and following him Brod extracted fragments in the guise of free-standing stories. Yet the practice of philosophical fiction or meditation did not emerge, as Brod and successive critics believed, from Kafka's practice of keeping a diary but chronologically predated and philosophically motivated his diary practice. The fragments recorded in the diary were already informed by a technique of reflection close to philosophical meditation. It is for this reason that Kafka's first book, *Meditation*, is of singular importance for his authorship, testifying to the fictional/philosophical practice that served as a condition of possibility for the diary and the stories that emerged from it. Most of the narratives of *Meditation* predate the diary and were produced under quite different auspices. By mistakenly tracing the origin of the stories that make up *Meditation* to Kafka's diary, Brod made the first of his many editorial misjudgements and perhaps one of the most unobtrusively consequential.[10] For most if not all of these stories were written, even published, before Kafka began to keep a diary. It is telling that half of the 18 stories making up the final version of *Meditation* published by Ernst Rowohlt Verlag in 1912 have no manuscript provenance either in the *Diary* or elsewhere.[11] Of the remainder, one survives in manuscript as a supplement to a letter sent to Hedwig Weiler in October /November 1907, two are extracted from the first version of the 'Description of a Struggle' project, another two from the second version and only four from the notebooks making up the *Diary*. What is more, the latter group, dating from 1911 and 1912, appear to be fair copies of existing manuscripts transcribed in the diaries as part of Kafka's editorial preparation for assembling the final collection of stories. Brod is thus entirely mistaken in tracing the *Meditations* to the writing regime Kafka pursued in his *Diaries* after 1910; the latter *emerged* from the philosophical fictions or exercises in 'aesthetic apperception' Kafka pioneered in the texts making up *Meditation*. To confuse them with the diary practice not only blurs their differences from the writings associated with 'The Judgement' and the diary regime but wholly underestimates their philosophical motivation.

Rather than a new beginning, 'The Judgement' represents a specific variant on the crossover between philosophical fiction and accident narrative ventured in 'Description of a Struggle', 'Wedding Preparations in the Country' and *Meditation*. It emerges from internal tensions traversing these writings, but is by no means their definitive resolution. The tensions in question are salient in the two versions of Kafka's earliest surviving project, 'Description of a Struggle'. The overlapping words of truth, power and fiction that inform the dissolving landscape of the first draft of 'Description of a Struggle' contrast radically with the affirmative account of aesthetic apperception that motivates the second draft. The latter advanced Kafka's knowingly anti-Platonic programme of thinking through images inspired by the powerful thought/image narrative that is Nietzsche's *Also Sprach Zarathustra* while transforming its love of chance into a narrative of the accident. Between the drafts of the two versions of 'Description of a Struggle', Kafka moved from a nihilistic narrative dissolution to an affirmative Nietzschean meditation in the form of a parable of eternal return that was extracted to open the *Meditation* collection. The place occupied by 'The Judgement' in this practice of meditation would be complicated by the impact of Yiddish theatre, but we will begin with the interweaving of truth and fiction around the accident in the first of Kafka's many explicit accident narratives, the 'Little Car Story' of autumn 1911.

My Little Car Story

Departing full of good intentions for their 1911 summer vacation in Switzerland and Paris, Kafka and Brod also embarked on a joint-authored novel, *Richard and Samuel*, inspired by their travels. Kafka disliked the project from the outset,[12] but dutifully pursued it during the autumn while nursing a new passion for Yiddish theatre.[13] His rancour exploded in the diary entry of 5 November that records 'the bitterness I felt yesterday when Max read my little car story at Baum's' (*D* 104, 173). His assessment of the story reads like a mechanic's report on an ailing vehicle. It has trouble starting, the engine is out of tune and the story keeps spluttering to a halt: 'There are only disconnected starts that come through, disconnected starts for example all through the car story' (*D* 105, 173). And when the little car story eventually does begin to motor, the steering turns out to be badly awry: 'every little bit of the story runs around homeless and drives me away from it in the opposite direction' (*D* 105, 173). Kafka ruefully contrasts his errant ride with 'something large and whole . . . well-shaped from beginning to end' (*D* 105, 173), but his failure to start, finish or even go in the right direction mirrors the story itself, which breaks off with a policeman failing to pull together in his notebook the threads unravelled by an accident between a car and a baker's tricycle witnessed by Kafka on the morning of Monday, 11 September 1911 on Place de L'Odeon in Paris.[14] But it should not too quickly be dismissed as an inaugural failure, preceding by a year the publication of *Meditation* and the triumphalist composition of 'The Judgement'.

On the threshold of his published authorship, the story of an accident that starts badly only to crash ingloriously into itself has played a minor role in narratives of Kafka's beginnings. It is called to mark a transition from the paratactic assembly of epiphanies characteristic of his 'early style' collected in *Meditation* to the (relatively) more continuous narratives of his novels following 'The Judgement'.[15] This assessment seems to echo Kafka's own contrast between the story's staccato character and his desire for something continuous and 'well shaped'. Yet it overlooks his sharp self-criticism of it as a 'sleepy imitation of Max [Brod]' (*D* 105, 173), whose stories pursued continuity at all costs. The aspiration to a 'flowing narrative' in the little car story is rejected by Kafka as a contrived 'see-sawing' that fails to keep the story on the road. The fragment has also been read in terms of a self-identification of the writer with the figure of the hapless policeman,[16] but if this is so, then it becomes a parable of the difficulty of writing the accident. For the story is an explicit accident narrative that tells of the failure to narrate a single accident witnessed by the author in the context of the looming catastrophe that is traffic.

It is wholly consistent with the accidents that befall Kafka's texts that the diary entry passing for the 'Little Car Story' is probably not the unfortunate story read by Max Brod at Oskar Baum's *soiree*. The entry relating the accident of 11 September in the travel diary was probably a draft for a version subsequently worked on with Brod. The diary entry for the next day – 12 October– records 'Yesterday at Max's wrote on the Paris diary' (*D* 73, 57) and was later glossed by Brod as 'Preliminary work on the novel *Richard and Samuel*', and the shared authorship probably explains why Brod read the story at Baum's and why Kafka thought it conceded too much to Brod's style. It also suggests that the story read aloud that evening was an elaborated and extended version of the surviving diary entry. Given the brevity of the diary entry – it is only three printed pages long – Kafka's complaint that it proceeded like a 'dancing course' through its 'first quarter of an hour'

(*D* 105, 173) points to the existence of an extended and elaborated version that took over 15 minutes to read. Thus what has been taken to be the transitional 'Little Car Story' is probably but the travel diary entry that preceded its elaboration into a now lost final version.

The travel diary version begins with some helpful advice from the author who is, of course, an accident prevention specialist: 'Motor-cars are easier to steer on asphalt surfaces, but also harder to bring to a halt' (*D* 462, 789). A car has indeed run into a tricycle ridden by a baker's boy, leaving it with a buckled front wheel. The baker's boy and the gentleman driver meet in the road to discuss the accident. For the baker's boy the accident threatens his entire livelihood, while for the gentleman driver it is at worst a minor inconvenience. Kafka's testimony moves from tragedy – complete with protagonists, mime play and chorus – to comedy in the travails of a perplexed policeman. The driver first mimes the accident for the benefit of the growing crowd, putting the blame firmly on the boy who 'monotonously stretches out his arms uttering his protests' (*D* 463, 790). The crowd/chorus debate the issue and the extent of the damage, arguing among themselves and relating to newcomers what has happened. In the course of discussion the driver concedes some share of responsibility for the accident – 'not all the blame, both to blame, therefore neither, such things just happen, etc' (*D* 463, 790) – and the contours of the event blur as the accident slips into oblivion: 'Newcomers now have to guess at what really happened' (*D* 464, 791). With the emerging consensus that there is no serious damage and the chorus of spectators 'already conferring together over the costs of repairs' (*D* 463, 790–1), the until now self-governing anarchic crowd/chorus arrives at the idea of a *deus ex machina* and decides to appeal to external authority and call a policeman.

For the gentleman driver 'such things just happen', for accidents are inevitable in busy traffic, but for the boy it represents a singular and potentially catastrophic event. He cannot afford to split the difference with the driver and as his protest begins to falter, 'subdued by his respect for a car-owner but inflamed by the fear of his boss' (*D* 462, 789), he seizes on the appeal to law and goes to fetch a policeman who will make the official report that will satisfy the boss (and perhaps his insurance company) as to the course of events and the degree of responsibility. The driver remains talking quietly with the eyewitnesses awaiting the officer's arrival to 'bring the whole matter to an immediate and objective conclusion' (*D* 464, 792). The gendarme's efforts to translate the accident into legal narrative begin badly and get worse. De-accelerating from an already slow start, the event evades the officer's entropic attempt to write the accident: 'The policeman pulls out of his notebook, with the speed of a building worker, a worn, dirty but blank sheet of paper' (*D* 464, 792). His slowly noting down the name of the bakery and carefully checking it against the tricycle defeats any expectation that he will promptly conclude the episode and initiates the protracted aesthetic pleasure of enjoying the asymptotic 'details of the statement-taking' (*D* 464, 792). Everything conspires against the completion of the legal accident narrative and even the policeman begins to flag; he's made a mistake, he's written the wrong thing in the wrong place, he's run out of page and doesn't know where to go on – in short, the policeman encounters writer's block and surrenders to inconclusive even comic *thaumatezein* as 'his astonishment with it is repeatedly renewed. He has to keep turning the paper around over and over again to persuade himself of having incorrectly begun the statements' (*D* 465, 792). It is hard to imagine the policeman ever concluding his accident report, and so Kafka abandons both him and his story by observing that 'the calm the whole affair acquires in this way is not to be compared with that earlier calm which it had achieved solely through the parties involved' (*D* 465, 792). The delicate irony conceals a critique of law and even a veiled reference to the Parisian crowd during the Paris Commune: Kafka's reaction to reading Sarcey's *Le Siège de Paris* earlier in his travel diary refers to an analogous 'calm' in the Paris Commune following the French surrender in 1870; by chance, this is followed by an entry referring to 'stories about old women who were run over by automobiles' (*D* 451–2, 770). Read in this perspective, the story contrasts the 'earlier calm' achieved by the parties and the crowd with the 'calm' secured by the intervention of law and the state in the person of the policeman. But 'My Little Car Story' is not an encrypted anarchist manifesto since the policeman intervenes initially in the interest of the weaker party to the dispute; the story, in short, is also a parable of accident insurance.

Kafka was forced to take a professional interest in car accidents after the Austrian legislature passed a law in 1908 introducing compulsory car accident insurance and making his Institute responsible for it. Kafka's anonymous commentary in the Institute's Annual Report – 'Inclusion of Private Automobile Firms in the Compulsory Insurance Programme' – records his organization's dismay at a measure that 'presented the Institute with a new and difficult task' (*OW* 80, 177). In order to treat automobile accidents as industrial accidents, the legislator defined the owner of a car as a 'firm' – with the peculiar consequence that an individual owner of a car had to be treated as if they were a company. Kafka protests in the name of the Institute that this expedient will lead to administrative confusion and enormous costs in time and money for the Institute. He also discerns a problem of legal principle, since actuarial statistics for the accidents of individual driver/firms will necessarily individuate risk in a context of civil liability: 'Nor do these new "firms" fall under the usual terms of collective insurance; rather, the circumstances approach those of individual insurance, since the automobile firms generally have only one insured person (though without providing the institute with the advantages of individual insurance) so that each firm represents an individual risk, without any possibility of an internal counterbalance within the firm' (*OW* 81, 178). In the usual case of an insured firm, the predicted incidence of accidents could be approximated over time by the differential performances of individual firms within a given risk assessment. In the case of individual insurance, this statistical counterbalance could not be relied upon since insurance in this individual case is far more vulnerable to chance and responsibility far harder to calculate than in the case of collective coverage.

The complex narration of the accident on Place de l'Odeon exemplifies the difficulty of managing automobile accident risk. To the indifferent car owner the accident was an annoying contingency or statistical inconvenience, while for the delivery boy it was an industrial accident with potentially grave consequences for his livelihood. The story narrates both perspectives punctuated by the efforts of first the Parisian crowd/chorus and then the policeman to do impossible justice to the accident as both a routine statistic and an occupational misfortune. Both statistical and individual aspects of the accident are an inevitable by-product of traffic that generates a quota of accidents with unpredictable consequences for its singular victims. Kafka worked and dreamed at the intersection of the two, with statistical inevitability figured as avalanches and landslides and its singular manifestation as a fall, whether from a tricycle, wall or building. The accident manifests as both a landslide in the cosmic catastrophe that ends the first version of *Description of a Struggle* and as singular catastrophe in the case (*Fall*) of Josef K; it also appears in the approaching rockfall that threatens the workers' coffee break in 'Accident Prevention in Quarries'; and finally, what else is *America* if not a report on the fall of Karl Rossmann, buried under the slow-moving landslide that is the USA?

Kafka's work in industrial insurance brought him into daily, professional contact with accidents, issues of liability and accident statistics. His use of accident statistics from various branches of industry shows awareness that accidents occur in a population with predictable regularity. Their predictability holds only for the population but not for the individuals who compose it. The industrial system generates a statistically regular number of accidents, but the individual incidence of these accidents is not easily predictable. In the course of his career Kafka devoted his attention increasingly to accident prevention, in order to reduce the risk of accidents, but was continually faced by the problem of liability or *Schuld* for events such as the accident in the 'Little Car

Story'. Many of his official writings present industrial insurance and the work of the Institute as mediating not only between the interests of the workers and the employers – balancing liability – but also between responsible and irresponsible employers. An important part of Kafka's professional role consisted of grading companies according to their statistical record of industrial accidents and so determining their financial contribution to the common pool. Issues of intent and negligence were not directly relevant to the work of the Institute, whose role was to distribute the *Schuld* of the accident *rates* among all the parties. Indeed, the pursuit of individual guilt or liability would obstruct its work by distracting it from managing a statistical population of accidents and diverting its attention – like that of the hapless policeman – towards the intractable problem of assessing the intent and negligence of individual perpetrators and victims.

Kafka thus worked with a systemic understanding of *Schuld* as a statistically predictable and definable property of a system or *Apparat*, applying it in his work to branches of industrial production and transport. In a sense his insurance work was parallel in its method and guiding intuitions to the contemporary sociology of Emil Durkheim, whose study *Suicide* focuses less on individual suicidal intent than on differential statistical suicide rates. Durkheim even spoke of 'suicidal waves' sweeping European societies with almost predictable regularity and carrying away their quota of vulnerable individuals. The prognosis of the sociologist, however, can only extend to the inevitability of a determinable number of suicides; it cannot predict who the individuals destined to make up that population will be. Similarly, it is rare in Kafka's *official* writings for the impact of statistical rates on individual fates to be given extended consideration as in the case of the baker's boy, although at an early stage of his career his work did involve negotiating with individual employers and victims of industrial accidents. A notable exception, and perhaps not to be included as part of his official writings, are the newspaper articles on psychiatrically damaged soldiers published in 1917, where Kafka's recommendations for rehabilitation show a full and sensitive appreciation of the individual consequences of what would in other contexts appear as statistical casualty rates.

It is in his fiction that Kafka explores the question of the incidence of statistical regularities on individual lives. His fiction is a catalogue of the accidents befalling his protagonists: literally so in the case of the hunter Gracchus who falls off a cliff, the ape Rotpeter captured by the entertainment industry in A Report to an Academy, the travelling salesman who wakes to find himself metamorphosed into an *Ungeziefer* or K. who arrives on snowy night at the village below the Castle, apparently summoned by an administrative error for which no one wants to admit responsibility

(*Schuld*). These accidents befall an individual, selecting him or her without sufficient reason but always according to a necessity captured in statistical regularities. There is a necessity to the chance accident, but one that should not be sought in the intentions or negligence of the individual whom it happens upon – they are the victims, or the chosen ones, of a systemic property. The individual stories Kafka tells in his fictional world individuate the statistical patterns of the world of insurance; they explore the singular impact on his character's lives of having been accidented.

Many of Kafka's fictional characters remain blocked in an inappropriate pursuit of *Schuld*, seeking the guilty person, intent or act of negligence responsible for their misfortune and not understanding the random necessity that has called them to individuate a systemic property. The hunter Gracchus is condemned to wander the earth between life and death not because of any guilt associated with the accident that befell him, but because of his unrelenting search for the truth of his accident in terms of guilt. His quest leaves him distracted by detail; he tells us he fell off a crag in the Black Forest, adding the unnecessary detail 'which is in Germany'. The same plethoric detail released by distraction in the face of the accident undid the policeman as he strove both to describe the accident on Place de L'Odeon and assign responsibility for it.

A certain insensitivity to the vagaries of the accident narrative chronically afflicts the critical assessment of Kafka's stories. Emrich's analysis of the compendium of accidental perceptions and actions that befell Raban on his reluctant journey to the country in 'Wedding Preparations in the Country' emphasizes how 'The phenomena appear and disappear without leaving a trace. It is a matter of the profusion of all Being itself that has as yet not been subjected to a centralising idea or a compositional structure' (Emrich, 27). Emrich sees the accident narrative as describing a chaotic state preceding the advent of a 'centralising idea' or 'structure' – a law in short – that might organize it. But it is precisely this subjection to a law that is in question, and to pursue it under the guises of guilt, meaning and responsibility is what undoes Kafka's characters, and critics. Raban, for example, shelters from the Prague rain before setting out on his ominous, unannounced weekend visit to his fiancée 'in the country'. He accidentally meets the glance, perhaps, of a lady across the street. In the first draft, the accent falls on the uncertainty of his perception – perhaps she was watching the rain and not him: 'She did it casually, and, besides, perhaps she was merely watching the rain coming down in front of him or the little commercial sign fixed to the door above his hair' (*NI* 13). In another attempt at the same passage, the accidental character of the glance is underlined by emphasizing the lady's absence of intent – whether to look or be looked at: 'Without meaning to, she seemed estranged from all the passers-by, as if because of a law' (*NI* 52) Emrich observes perceptively that 'By "law," the young Kafka hence understood nothing other than the force of collectively anonymous, unknown occurences, hidden from the will and the "intention" of the individual' (Emrich, 132), but does not take the next step of seeing the 'as-if' of 'law' and lack of intent as marking the peculiar necessity of the accident. He does link this 'law' to the one guiding the officials of the Castle, anticipating Foucault by noting that the Castle administers a population and not individuals, applying a statistical law 'that compels them to behave indifferently toward the "I" of "personal" existence and, what is more, even to guard themselves against this personal existence, since it would "practically disrupt" the official organisation' (Emrich, 133), but without drawing any broader conclusions. He is in fact describing the property by which individual accidents merge into the necessity of accident rates – Kafka's narratives, however, linger on what is not completely absorbed, with the singular fates that try to live with what has befallen them.[17]

Another underestimation of the accident narrative is provided by Ritchie Robertson's analysis of the alleged fault lines of *America*. He sees these not only in the stylistic distinction between the first six chapters of the novel written in the autumn and winter of 1911–12 and the 1914 'Nature Theatre of Oklahama', but also within the six chapters themselves. Robertson believes the novel is vitiated by a failure to achieve a 'necessary connection' between 'action and description', and after describing a series of inconsequential, accidental events and relations concludes, 'Later, Karl's work as a lift-boy is described in detail, but there is no *necessary connection* between the nature of his work and the events that *befall* him. Robinson could still have turned up drunk and got Karl into trouble, no matter what job he was doing. In short, Kafka has not succeeded in integrating his two main themes. The novel falls apart into description and action' (Robertson 1985, 62, my emphasis). Kafka's performance is implicitly judged according to the criteria of law and necessity – the accidents that *befall* his hero lack causal necessity and the narrative remains inconsistent. Yet it is precisely these 'failures' that characterize the accident narrative Kafka was pursuing, one whose very success consists in failing Robertson's critical criteria.[18] Description must be exceeded by action, for were they to coincide their integration would provide a total causal and moral explanation of what remains inexplicable.

The 'Little Car Story' performs the impossibility of even fully describing an event let alone assigning causal responsibility for it. If it had been completed as a continuous, integrated whole then it would have subsumed the individual accident under the consistency of law and satisfied the critical strictures of Emrich and Robertson. The policeman would have completed his report and assigned full causal responsibility. But this would have left no place for an accident nor for its singular impact. The 'Little Car Story' narrates the fault line between the necessary accident and its contingent incidence, between traffic and a delivery boy on his tricycle.

Landscapes and landslides

Precarious landscapes feature in both drafts of Kafka's earliest surviving work, the abandoned *Description of A Struggle* that would become the quarry from which he mined some of the stories for his first collection, *Meditation*.[19] It survives in two variants – Version A in the 'Black School Exercise Book' that occupied Kafka over the winter of 1907–8 and Version B from 1909–10 – both exploring radically different responses to Nietzsche's announcement of the 'death of God'. Nietzsche's parable of the madman in *The Gay Science* dwelt on the catastrophic gravity of the death of God and the unsettling of hierarchical principles or guarantees of truth at the same time as rescinding Plato's decision to expel the poets from the *polis*. It was the task of future philosopher-artists to contain the nihilistic consequences of the event by telling new, post-metaphysical stories and inventing new truths.[20] *Description of a Struggle* assumes this task, with Version A telling a catastrophic story of nihilistic collapse following the destruction of divine truth by human desire and invention, while Version B tells of a new truth to be found in *poiesis* or 'aesthetic apperception'.[21] Both depart from a condition or *doxa* where events and perceptions are accidental, no longer possessing any intrinsic necessity, and go on fictionally to explore the end of an old narrative of truth in lawless cosmic catastrophe and ruin (Version A) or the embarkation (in Version B) upon an interminable and disoriented journey not to the Platonic city of the philosophers, nor to the city of God, but to the city of the mad. Yet however different their stories about truth, both versions stage the return of the poet to the *polis* and fiction to philosophy in order, in their very different ways, to take up Nietzsche's challenge to justify life aesthetically.

Both versions begin with two companions leaving a party for a walk through snowy moonlit Prague, crossing the Danube to the Laurenzburg park. The first chapter of both versions relates the events of the walk, while the second unfolds two very different philosophical allegories concluded in Version A by a short third chapter that tells of the companions' resumed conversation beside a garden house in the park. In Version A the first two chapters are given titles and subtitles: 'Description of a Struggle' for Chapter One, and the philosophical 'Diversions or the Proof that it is impossible to

Live' for Chapter Two. The most significant differences between the variants are found in the philosophical allegories of Chapter Two: Version A's proof of the impossibility of living is divided into four sections: 'Ride', 'Walk', 'The Fat Man' and 'Downfall of the Fat Man', with the third section subdivided into four sections with the headings a) 'Address to the Landscape', b) 'The Beginnings of a Conversation with the Beggar', c) 'Beggars Story' and finally d) 'Continuing Conversation between the Fat Man and the Beggar'. In Version B the section headings are removed and the story of the Fat Man and his protagonist's role in the beggar narrative replaced by a very different philosophical dream allegory that would later become the opening story of the *Meditation* collection, 'Children on a Country Road'. In this version the beggar narrative is extended and presented as the experience of the narrator rather than the Fat Man, while the debates and conflicts of Chapter Three beside the garden house in the park in the first version are deleted.

The epigraph to 'Version A' evokes a cosmic sabbath – a Nietzschean 'great noontide' – set in the arena of an 'enlarged sky' stretching from 'distant to more distant hills'. The sun is at its zenith and equidistant with respect to the faraway hills while the sky stretches out between them. Clothed humans (*Menschen*) pass through this arena or 'nature theatre', strolling at their leisure as if in a park. There is an air of suspension as the walkers sway on their way under the fasting sky.[22] The story itself though begins by inverting all the values announced in the epigraph: midday is replaced by midnight, summer by winter, and the open-air park by a claustrophic salon take the place of humans in nature (*Menschen*) by people in society (*Leute*) aimless strolling by oriented movement (exiting from the salon) and the loose swishing garments of strollers by the contrained folds of the hostess's skirt. The protagonists of the struggle set out for a walk towards the park of the epigraph, but now deserted at frozen midnight and approached not through the bright solar zenith but through diverse lighting regimes – lanterns, moonlight, streetlights – interrupted by bursts of erotic desire.

'Description of a Struggle' confronts truth with fiction on the terrain of desire, exploring the degree and the ways in which perception is shaped by what is absent or, more precisely, by what can never be made present. The confrontation of philosophical and fictional orders of truth and desire is staged through a staccato sequence of erotic scenarios. The irruption of events defying the rational/juridical order of sufficient reason are framed erotically and evade attempts at capture or displacement through narrative elaboration. The narrative of the first chapter in both versions is a catena of such events and elaborations, with precise phenomenological *descriptions* of unaccountable events being elaborated by fictional attempts to justify and give them meaning, even if only in terms of lies and dissemblance.

After an Aristotelian delineation of the place and time of the action – a brightly lit salon at midnight – the observing and narrating 'I' introduces himself as a tipsy voyeur sat at a tiny table sipping his third glass of benedictine and surveying the little store of pastries he had 'sought out and piled up' (*S* 9; *NI* 54). His ostentatious absorption in his quarry of confectionary masks other interests, including his precise observation and enjoyment of the ascent and descent of the 'dainty folds' of his hostess's tight skirt as she bows to her departing guests.[23] The narrator's erotic revery is interrupted by the entrance of a 'new acquaintance', a dishevelled and excited young man, himself fresh from an erotic conquest in the room next door. The observer's anxiety about being observed – a recurrent trope in the first chapter – is activated when his companion begins excitedly to narrate how he '– kissed – her – on – her mouth, her ears, her shoulders' (*S* 10; *NI* 56). Seeing that the young man is beginning to attract attention, the narrator implements the drastic escape plan of feigning a prior agreement with him to walk up the Laurenziberg. This first of many embedded fictions in the story removes the companions from the bright lights of the salon only to deliver them into the rough hands of a maid with a lantern who guides them down dark stairs to the door and moonlit street waiting outside. The orderly retreat is unexpectedly derailed as the drunken maid embraces and kisses the young man, letting him go only upon receiving a coin from the narrator.

The exit from the salon corresponds to a radical shift in lighting regime as the protagonists move from the artificial glare of the salon down the lamplit stairs to a 'deserted street' lit by an enormous moon set in a slightly clouded 'extended sky' reflecting off the snow. The change in lighting regime accentuates aural perception – ringing footsteps, low whistling – but with a few significant exceptions visual perception remains clear and distinct, in apparent conformity with Cartesian principles of certainty. Version A's 'The moon was clear, one could see distinctly' (*NI* 58) is enhanced in 'Version B' by 'The air was clear there, I could distinctly see his legs' (*NI* 125), both emphasizing the clarity and distinctness of perception. The change from the 'clear moon' as a source of light to the 'clear air' as its medium accentuates the continuity between aural and visual perception in the later version – consistent we shall see with a new emphasis on aesthetic apperception in the second version – while the change from the impersonal third to the first person along with the focus on a discrete object of perception – the companion's legs – emphasizes the intentionality of the perception. Both descriptions of the quality of the perceptual field provoke references to being watched as the walk to the Laurenziberg mutates into a bid to escape fixation as the object of a gaze and to open a space for fictional desire.

The maid's apparently unprovoked embrace on the doorstep provokes but the first of the erotically motived crises of perception that punctuate both versions of 'A Description of a Struggle'. Shuffling through icy, empty streets 'evenly lit' by hazy moonlight, the narrator suddenly makes a wild triumphant leap, shouts out a name and throws his hat in the air while slapping his companion on the back. Then, unnerved by his companion's indifference to his eruptive and apparently unmotivated display the narrator withdraws his hand – 'seized by shame' in version A – and places it in his coat pocket.[24] Ashamed but also irritated by the refusal of complicity, the narrator plots his retreat. His disappointment at the non-event of their escape from the salon modulates into an auto-erotic revery in which he secretly slips into his house by a side passage to enjoy watching his companion walk unwittingly past. But a sense of lassitude overwhelms him as he contemplates the hours he must spend alone after his companion has passed, observing only himself and the walls of his apartment in the mirror. His home becomes an enchanted cave, with specular auto-erotic desire literally warping perception. The erotic undertow of the description of lighting his lamp, sitting back in his armchair and passing the hours contemplating the painted walls in the warped reflection of 'the gilt framed mirror hanging on the rear wall' is intensified in Version B. In Version A the specular scenario provokes a fatigue that brings on a desire to slump into his bed, while in Version B the erotic affect is accentuated by tingeing description with reflection. The room is warm, he slips into his armchair and reflects, with pleasure but also anxious apprehension, 'Beautiful prospects! Why not? But what then? No then' (*NI* 126). Indeed, in Version B the time of self-contemplation is extended almost infinitely in the circuit of the mirror reflecting the lamp shining off the chest of the narrator and the passage of time measured not by visually perceived movement – his visual enjoyment of his own reflected chest is almost a *nunc stans* – but in terms of the cooling of the room as the hours pass.[25] In Version B, fatigue is detached from the revery, but both versions share the effort to resist falling asleep.

It appears that the companion has also been lost in erotic revery, trying to make sense of his encounter with the housemaid. The companions replay the encounter in analytical key, inquiring into the identity of the passionate doorkeeper. In the initial description of the descent of the staircase the narrator described the maid as 'beautiful', with a 'naked neck' dressed in 'loose clothing', with 'red cheeks' and 'half-open lips'. This eroticized perception is amplified in Version B when the young man tries to interpret the embrace; the narrator refers to her 'red hands' with 'rough skin' that confirm her status as a housemaid but concedes 'in that lighting one couldn't distinguish everything' (*NI* 127). Under such conditions of imperfect perception the narrator must resort to narrative in order to secure meaning – but this is a sexualized, class narrative in which confirmation of the maid's status and sexual availability is confirmed not by sight but by touch and by reasoning through analogy to her similarity with the 'elder daughter of an officer of my acquaintance' (*NI* 127).

The even lighting of the moonlit walk gives way to darkness and a parallel obscuring of thought; while the companion rehearses aloud his explanation to his girlfriend for having left the party for a walk with a stranger, the narrator's clarity begins to blur and waver – 'the Moldau and the part of the city on the other bank shared the darkness. Just a few lights were burning there and played with the eyes' (*DS* 14, 63). The narrator imagines the young man describing his new companion to his girlfriend Annie as a strange combination of Harlequin and a tree, clad in patches of yellow leaves lying flat because of the absence of wind. He imagines his companion alluding to the cosmic dimension of his homo-erotic unrest, especially the way in which it shapes and threatens his sense of being in the world: 'To me it was as if the rigid dome of the starry sky rose and fell with the breaths of his flat chest' (*NI* 62). In Version A the rise and fall catastrophically ruptures the 'rigid dome' – anticipating the catastrophic cosmic landslide to come later in the story while also opening up the consolatory vision of an infinite number of future landscapes: 'The horizon broke off and under enflamed clouds apparently endless landscapes appeared, so as to make us happy' (*NI* 62). Confronted with the break-up of the horizon and the prospect of new landscapes offered by his companion, the young man hastily retreats to heterosexual intimacy: 'Good heavens, how I love you Annie and your kiss is dearer to me than a landscape. Let's not talk about him anymore and love each other' (*NI* 62).[26]

As the companions lean over the railings contemplating the river, the narrator breaks the silence by reflecting how night has the strange property provoking memory. He recalls sitting by a river one evening with head laid on his arm contemplating the cloudy hills of the other bank, listening to a violin. He remembers how on both banks trains passed with 'shining smoke'. In Version A the narrator admits that he inhibitedly sought to invent behind these words 'love stories in remarkable settings' (*NI* 64), a reflection replaced in Version B by 'Oh, I could tell much more' (*NI* 131). Version A describes the young man's earlier intimation that an adventure (*Abenteuer*) would happen this day, while in Version B the same sense is evoked in the words 'something will happen today. And it did too' (*NI* 132). The evocations of a past perception and a past, fulfilled prediction of the future lead into a subtle parody of 'The Moment' in Nietzsche's *Also Sprach Zarathustra*. The motley narrator bends himself over and mimics a hunchback but his gesture is neither understood nor appreciated by the young man and leads only to an accident as the distracted narrator trying to escape his companion trips over a step and falls into the darkness. The piano in a nearby wine bar stops playing and a man and a woman look out but do not see anything. In the meantime the narrator is inventing a story to explain the accident – 'it was the ice' – a (false) narrative subsequently confirmed by the companion who comes back for him. He continues to invent – the reason he gives for going down the alley was that he saw a cat – and with this the two companions cross the river to ascend the Laurenziberg. The account of their adventure shifts to a different key when in Chapter Two the companions' ascent takes an unexpected turn that prepares for the philosophical allegories of the 'fat man'[27] in Version A and the 'Children on a Country Road' of Version B.

The second chapter begins with the narrator forcibly mounting his companion and riding him out of nocturnal Prague 'with good speed deeper into the interior of a vast but still unfinished region [*unfertigen Gegend*] where it was evening' in Version A (*NI* 73) or 'arriving fast enough at the interior of a vast, but still unfinished region' (*NI* 140) in Version B. In Version A the penetration of the unfinished region continues 'with good speed' while in Version B the ride is complete, 'arriving fast enough' at the region; in Version A the time of day – evening – is emphasized while in Version B all reference to it has been erased. In both versions the region surrounds a steep, rocky country road up which the narrator is riding and accompanies the explicit shift of the narrative into the realm of reflected desire. The step from descriptive to creative narration is announced by the claim that since riding the steep rocky road gives the narrator pleasure, 'I let it become even rockier and steeper [*ich liess sie noch steiniger und steiler werden*]' (*S* 21; *NI* 73, 140). The region of realized desire remains unfinished and untrue – for as the landscape accommodates itself to the narrator's desire, it also points beyond itself. Indeed, it seems that the rider's desire feeds on an insurmountable limit or absence thwarting its satisfaction. This becomes evident as the narrator escalates his demands on the region, intensifying his desire by imagining ever more extravagant obstacles. The narrative is now driven by the question of whether resistance is interior to desire and projected onto the limits of the region or whether the region has properties that structurally exceed the desire of the narrator. Version A conducts this inquiry in a landscape beset by winds and landslides, with fiction serving to defer the realization of truth as coming catastrophe and oblivion, while Version B seeks a point of suspension or still point of 'aesthetic apperception' amid signs of imminent catastrophe. While Version A offers clear proof of the 'impossibility of living', Version B seems to suggest that life is possible, but only in the moment of suspension that is fiction.

With Chapter Two, Kafka enters an uncanny, incomplete region where resistance to fiction is both essential to desire and the repeated occasion of its ruin. The opening paragraphs of 'the ride' replay the scenario of the two companions but setting it earlier in the evening (Version A) or in a suspended present (Version B). The ride is impelled forward by raising and overcoming obstacles, primarily the resistance of the companion to being ridden, making overcoming a spur to the narrator's pleasure whether through pulling his mount's hair from behind (Version A) or gripping his collar (Version B) and slapping his head in order to force him to a livelier trot. Since overcoming this resistance gives him satisfaction, he escalates it by making his companion 'even wilder' by letting 'a strong headwind blow against us in strong gusts' (*S* 21; *NI* 73, 141). This wind, making its first appearance in Kafka's work, denotes an exterior resistance that the narrator unsuccessfully tries to incorporate and overcome in fiction. Yet in Version A it is clear that the winds are not internal to some dialectical scenario of the narrator's desire – the poetic figure of a limit he proposes triumphantly to overcome – but the harbingers of a coming catastrophe or landslide that will carry away both unfinished region and its narrator.

As the ride approaches its point of ecstasy – tempered by the narrator's prudish reminder that he is of course riding on the *broad shoulders* of his companion – its rhythm intensifies and the rider almost strangles his mount in the effort to lean back and enjoy the spectacle of this new region to the full.[28] He contemplates clouds 'weaker' than him that are driven along by the wind without offering any resistance, and the realization of his strength in opposing the winds provokes a spasm of joy: 'I laughed and shuddered with high spirits' (*S* 21; *NI* 73, 141). The wind that billows his coat like a cloud could not slow him down 'but gave me force' and by opposing only made him stronger. He comes back to himself – to 'reflection' (Version B) – when the sky is gradually blocked out by the crooked branches of the trees 'that I let grow along the side of the road' (*S* 21; *NI* 73, 141). Still imagining himself in control of the landscape that is now closing in on him, he rails (in Version A) against the heterosexual lovers whose stories he cannot share, or in Version B against the Nietzschean 'Last Men' whom he does indeed join for a stroll in the mountains but who can no longer feel the resistance of the wind since 'it blows through the holes left open by us and our limbs' (*NI* 142).[29] He joins the latter in remaining unaware of the catastrophe that is blowing up for them out of paradise and that now forcibly begins to impress itself on the narrator's attention. But before proceeding deeper into the 'unfinished region' he must leave his wounded companion/mount – 'having no further use for him' (*S* 22; *NI* 74, 142) – to the tender care of some fictional vultures, peremptorily summoned out of nowhere.

Having abandoned his spent mount, the second section of Chapter Two, 'The Walk', continues the exploration of the 'unfinished region' on foot. Without the mount to focus resistance, the region itself seems just for a moment to give unimpeded shape to the narrator's desire. Unenthused by the prospect of walking an uphill path, the narrator lets 'the way become increasingly level and finally in the distance to slope downhill into a valley' (S 22; NI 74, 142). The passive formula used until now to describe the response of the unfinished region to his desire is now replaced by a reference to an act of the will – 'the stones disappeared according to my will and the wind lost itself in the evening' (S 22; NI 74, 142, reference to the evening deleted in Version B). At this point the narrator attempts to abolish the figures of resistance evoked during the ride: first the mount, then the stony ascent and finally the wind. Anticipating the momentary satisfaction of the builder of the burrow in the later story – whose security is fugitive for the same reason as the fugitive satisfactions of the narrator – the walker of 'Description of a Struggle' dares to complete the unfinished region by imagining himself in a realm of pure and seemingly unimpeded, realized desire: 'As I like pinewoods, I walked through pinewoods and as I like looking silently at the stars so the stars came out slowly and peacefully for me in the extended heavens just as they usually do' (S 22; NI 74, 146, with variants). Yet there is a hint of trouble at the edge of the region that will undo the narrator's security of enjoyment. It is announced in the return of the winds: 'I saw only a few stretched clouds that a wind blowing only at their height pushed through the air' (NI 75), testifying to a continued resistance but at great height and distance. In Version B this defiant climatic phenomenon provokes the 'astonishment of the walker' (NI 143), but in both versions it is a source of disquiet and a harbinger of catastrophe for the human walking seemingly secure through his human world.

The narrator cannot rest but must continue with his efforts to shape the region; he 'lets emerge' a 'high mountain' whose heights, covered with brushwood, border on the heavens. Yet even this is not immune to the defiant high altitude winds: 'I could distinctly see even the tiny branchings on the highest branches *and their movements*' (S 22; NI 75, 143, my emphasis). Consistent with the earlier joy at resistance, the narrator tries to make the evidence of something *that is not him* causing movement on his mountains into an occasion to assert his cosmic power, becoming a small bird on one of the distant bushes who 'swaying forgot to let the moon rise' (S 22; NI 75, 143). The return of the swaying motif alerts us to its significance as a point of intersection between power and powerlessness, provoked in this case by the uncontrollable high winds. Although subject to the resistance of these distant winds, the little bird nevertheless believes itself to have the cosmic power to keep the moon waiting behind the hills 'apparently enraged on account of the delay' (S 22, 75/143). But the ineluctable rising of the moon is announced by a 'cool shining light' that once again poses a limit to the narrator's world-contructing imagination; he had been looking elsewhere and as the moon stepped up to challenge him he looked with 'troubled eyes' at the steep path that led directly to a frontal confrontation with the terrifying moon. The confrontation of cosmic force and human will played out between the rising moon and the ascending narrator results in the dissolution of the narrator and his world; progress slows as his powers wane with growing fatigue and he can only keep himself conscious and awake by clapping his hands.

The dissolution of the world and the threatened extinction of the narrator is staged through the undoing of the unfinished region by a cosmic landslide. Before the imminent catastrophe – 'as the path threatened to slip away from under my feet and everything as tired as I was began to disappear ...' (S 23; NI 76, 144) – the narrator attempts to escape the end of his world. He fades out the stars and has the adversary moon sink 'feebly in the sky as if in troubled water' (S 23; NI 76, 144). But with the onset of darkness accompanying this last exercise of his waning powers, the mountain disappears, the path crumbles away and the narrator *listens* to the landslide that is coming to sweep away both him and his world: 'out the depths of the forest I heard the approaching crashes of falling (Version B, *plunging*) tree trunks' (S 23, NI 76/144). For security he grasps a tree trunk that is itself 'already swaying without wind' (S 23; NI 76, 144) and slips into a dream, inventing in extreme adversity a companion, this time a 'squirrel' who sits on the end of the trembling branch riding the wild movements of the tree.

At this point Versions A and B diverge radically. Version A stages the catastrophe in the oneiric encounter with the philosophical 'fat man', while Version B narrates a dream – the story 'Children on a Country Road' – that secures the swaying world in a perpetual aesthetic present. The dream of Version A begins with the vision of a brightly lit landscape extending from the light dancing off the waves on a wide river to 'meadows' on the far bank, 'which merged into bushes behind which, at a great distance, one saw bright rows of fruit trees leading towards the green hills' (S 24; NI 77). But something *sounds* wrong about this idyll: the scintillating waves are 'noisy' but more disturbing are the sighs and the sobs accompanying this landscape. The narrator's first response is to stop his ears 'against the fearful sobbing' (S 24; NI 77) and to imagine himself in the idyllic landscape of fruit trees further up the bank; 'here I could be content. "For here it is solitary and beautiful"'(S 24; NI 77). To block out the sound of suffering marring the idyllic landscape, the narrator has to suppress the memory that even in utopia there will always be struggle and a feeling of forsakenness – in order to live a future life. And he almost succeeds: 'Thus I played with my life to come and tried stubbornly to forget. I looked blinking at that sky of an unusually happy colour. I had not seen it like that for a long time and was moved and recalled specific days when I had also believed to see it in this way' (*S* 24–5; *NI* 77). With this intimation of a new light – a light full of promise recalling the rainbow skies of the Noachite covenant after the flood – the narrator lets his hands fall from his ears.

The sound of sobbing returns and the glimpse of utopia unravels with the arrival of the ever ominous wind and a distinct change of climate: 'It grew windy and a large heap of dry leaves, which I had not seen before, flew up rustling. Unripe fruit from the fruit trees thudded madly on the ground. Ugly clouds came out from behind a mountain. The waves on the river creaked and receded from the wind' (*S* 25; *NI* 78). The wind confirms the aural reminder of the suffering that accompanies beauty by blowing up the dead leaves lying beneath the fruit trees that attest to the suffering and death of seasons past and then blowing down the unripe fruits that will litter the ground in an allegory of futile fertility. The river now reveals itself as a stage prop in this nature theatre by 'creaking' (*knarrten*) under the pressure of the opposing wind. With this confirmation of why the unfinished region must always remain so, the narrator prepares 'to turn and leave this region and go back to my former way of life' (*S* 25; *NI* 78). Yet he is deterred less by the reassertion of the large, abstract philosophical question of the possibility or impossibility of living than by surprise at what he now sees taking place before his eyes and the pragmatic question it provokes of why 'even in our time' 'prominent people are carried across a river in such a difficult way' (*S* 25; *NI* 78). He is referring to the unlikely Buddha-like figure carried on a bier by four naked attendants who has just come into view crossing the river.

The fat man (*der Dicke*) is a burst of autumnal yellow in the brightly lit but beset late summer landscape. Jaundiced with folds of fat hanging 'like the hem of a yellowish carpet' (*S* 25; *NI* 79), he seems oblivious to the world and insensible to the thorns of the bushes through which he is carried. But in reality he is quite the contrary of indifferent; he is *too* sensitive. He presents the polar opposite to the world-creating persona of the now dreaming narrator, one painfully conscious of the incursions the world makes on him. In place of the narrator's letting the landscape emerge according to his will, the fat man laments in a 'low voice' irresistibly recalling Brando's Mr Kurz in *Apocalypse Now*: '"The landscape disturbs me in my thought"' (*S* 25; *NI* 79). It does so by making his reflections *sway* – ever Kafka's figure for the struggle between external pressure and internal resistance – but with the fat man figured in terms of an uncompromisingly modern simile: '"It lets my reflections sway like suspension bridges in a raging current"' (S 26; NI 79). The swaying suspension bridges that both defy and bow to adverse winds and currents figure the fat man's inversion of the insatiable desire responsible for the incomplete state of the region. With him it is not that the achievement of stable presence is disrupted by the dissatisfaction provoked by ever renewed desire as earlier with the narrator, but because the landscape is itself dissatisfied and calls on the fat man to complete it through contemplation. Paralleling the gesture by which the narrator tried to block out the sound of the landscape, the fat man tries to block out its mundane appearance and to enjoy its ideal aesthetic image in place of reality: 'I close my eyes and say: you my green mountain by the river with your stones rolling against the water, you are beautiful' (S 26; NI 79); but it 'is not satisfied; it wants me to open my eyes to it' (S 26; NI 79). The reason for this demand, and for the fat man's resistance, is already hinted at in the aesthetic image itself: the moment it would perpetuate is ineluctably becoming, not only the river but the landscape itself is in perpetual flow; Kafka figures this as a landslide with *stones rolling against the water*. As in Zarathustra's 'Yes and Amen Song', the fat man's joy wants eternity, but this landscape says *Vergeh* – it is a river of stones rolling into a river of water, a mountain passing like a cloud – it disrupts the contemplation of the aesthetic image that would please by showing the 'attainable in a beautiful overview' (S 26; NI 80).

The fat man regards the incomplete landscape with what Nietzsche called the 'squint-eyed' gaze of *ressentiment* and the spirit of revenge. The mountain's non-human duration is an affront to him and he is incapable of loving it; he regards this call from beyond the human as threatening and predatory and so in need of constant propitiation: 'mustn't we keep it friendly towards us, so that we can keep it all upright, this mountain that has such a capricious partiality for our brain pulp? It would cast its jagged shadow on me, would shove me aside with its silent and terrible bleak walls ...' (S 26; NI 80). Unlike Zarathustra, the fat man is not well disposed towards life and eternity, but is assailed by them; the mountain, even just its shadow, blocks his path and threatens to obstruct his disinterested satisfaction. And it turns out that not only the mountain has this effect, but 'everything else' too: the fat man regards the whole world – 'so vain, so importunate, so vengeful' (S 26; NI 80) – as existing only repeatedly to hurt him. His resentful plea, 'please, mountain, flowers, grass, bushes and river, give me a little room to breathe' (S 26; NI 81), coats the landscape in 'a curtain of fog' that reduces its bright colours to the uniform grey of a 'humid cloud'. The shape and colour of the unfinished region glimpsed across the river literally *slips* away in a rapid landslide of the surrounding hills: 'Although the avenues held firm and seemed to protect the width of the street they were quickly overrun' (*S* 27; *NI* 81), leaving only a halo irradiating the grey indifference – 'a softly transparent edge into whose shade the country sank deeper while all things lost their beautiful definition' (*S* 27; *NI* 81).[30] The slippage of the region into a sequence of contrasting greys and finally darkness clouded over the vision of the fat man and his bearers and initiated the catastrophe. Walking into the now 'unruly river', the four bearers are swept away by the rising flood to be drowned in silence by a 'low wave that swept over the heads of those in front' (*S* 28; *NI* 83). This accident in the river, however inevitable it might seem, provokes a meteorological epiphany or illumination of the accident that points to the intangible necessity that attended it.

The wave that drowned the bearers now carries away the fat man, who sweeps down river like a golden Buddha on a raft, clearly visible in the slanting rays of the evening sun that 'broke out of the rims of the great cloud and illuminated the hills and mountains at the limits of vision while the river and the region beneath the cloud lay in indistinct light' (*S* 28; *NI* 83). The accident of death by drowning illuminated by a breakthrough of the sun from behind the clouds is given a consistently resentful interpretation by the fat man as he hurtles downstream. Appealing to the narrator not to save him, his last words are a shriek of *ressentiment*: 'This is the water and the wind's revenge; now I am lost. Yes, revenge, for how often have we attacked these things' (*S* 28; *NI* 84). The fat man goes under imagining himself a victim of nature's just vengeance.

Kafka uses the fat man's obstinate downgoing as a cue to move to the narrative of the beggar – for it is both he and the fat man who are being revenged by the landscape for their attacks on it whether through sound or vision, through the singing of the sword, the flash of symbols, the splendour of trumpets and the 'leaping blaze of drums' (*S* 28; *NI* 84). Kafka emphasizes the fat man's identification with the very landscape avenging itself upon him by sending an impossible mosquito through his body – 'A tiny mosquito with outstretched wings flew through his belly without reducing its speed' (*S* 29; *NI* 84). This is followed by a genealogical narrative of how the fat man came to his current state of philosophical *ressentiment* through his conversations with the beggar who tells a love story set in a church after the death of God that is full of bright colours and affirmations of finitude and living differently. The fat man cannot follow him to this point of affirmation and breaks into tears. He cannot bear to sway and while the beggar says 'We build war machines that are really useless, towers, walls curtains of silk and we could wonder a lot about this if we had time' (*S* 45; *NI* 109) he cannot accept that

'We hold ourselves in the balance, we don't fall, we flutter, even though we may be uglier than bats' (*S* 45; *NI* 109). He cannot accept the beggar's claim that 'we are already on this earth and live according to our agreements' (*S* 45; *NI* 109) and cannot bear to think that to flit like a bat in the gloaming is just as permanent or impermanent as being a tree trunk buried in the snow. The fat man, still sobbing, cannot follow the beggar to his post-metaphysical conclusion that 'We can't have been talking about the heavenly light because we are standing in a dark hallway' (*S* 45; *NI* 110), nor his claim, anathema to a metaphysician, that 'we don't want to achieve any goal or truth, but just jokes and entertainment' (*S* 45; *NI* 110). The philosopher mourning and the drunken beggar celebrating the death of God step out together and the beggar 'blew away a few bruised little clouds so that the now uninterrupted surface of the stars offered itself' (*S* 46, NI 111). The fat man, however, steps back from the light of the stars visible in daylight, and, taking to his bier, submits himself to the vengeance of nature and the landscape at sunset.

The last section of Chapter Two in Version A brings the catastrophe provoked by the fat man's longing for revenge, the arrival of the landslide that has been threatening the narrative from the outset. The narrator explains that the fat man is not drowned in the river like his bearers but engulfed by a landslide of the world that carries away even the river in a cosmic act of revenge: 'Then everything was gripped by speed and slipped into the distance. The water of the river was dragged towards a precipice, tried to hold back, rocked about a little on the crumbling edge but then crashed in clumps and smoke' (*S* 46; *NI* 111). Reality itself begins to slip over the precipice, stretching and warping the unfinished landscape and carrying with it even the narrator and any previous aid to orientation: 'Meanwhile the banks of the river extended beyond measure and for sure I touched the metal of a minute signpost in the distance with the palm of my hand' (*S* 46; *NI* 111). The growing dislocation of the senses beginning with sound and vision and now touch is accompanied by a remarkable description of the warping of the narrator's body and the slippage of his proprio-perception along with the cosmic worldslide. His body, like the fat man's, is revealed to be part of the very landscape avenging itself upon him and participates in the act of revenge by stretching in vengeful desire until it exceeds the limits of the unfinished region: 'But my legs, yes my impossible legs lay on the wooded mountain and put the inhabited valleys into the shade. They grew, they grew! They already towered into the space that no longer possessed any landscape and already their length exceeded my range of vision' (*S* 46; *NI* 112). But then he says no, he is really very small, and Chapter Two in Version A closes with the cry 'I'm rolling – I'm rolling – I'm an avalanche in the mountains' (*S* 46; *NI* 112), so echoing the cosmic disorientation evoked by Nietzsche's madman announcing the death of God to his murderers, an avalanche falling on itself and appealing to impossible 'passers-by' to tell him how big he really is, to measure his arms, his legs ...

While the dream in Version A rolls towards catastrophe in a paroxysm of philosophical *ressentiment* against the existence of limits of experience, Version B affirms the aesthetic image in a manner inconceivable to either the fat man or the Version A narrator. Speaking in the name of the failed philosophical project of grasping eternity, the fat man wills the end of the world at the hands of infinity rather than renounce his ambition to grasp and hold it. The narrator of 'Children on a Country Road' that replaces the 'Fat Man' narrative in Version B would on the contrary perpetuate the journey towards an incomplete and incompletable horizon by telling stories to prolong the day rather than succumb to the night. Version B *affirms* the aesthetic image as an unrealizable desire for eternity in place of Version A's preferring to end the world rather than give up on ever grasping it. The melancholy catastrophe of Version A and the dream of a boy happily running the wrong way for all of the day and all of the night in Version B tell two different stories, but they also stage the unequivocal farewell to a certain philosophical past and a wry welcome to another, different philosophical future.

Aesthetic apperception

Version B of *Description of a Struggle* pursues a very different strategy that approaches the anti-Platonic thinking through images that Kafka described as 'aesthetic apperception' or meditation (*Betrachtung*). The delicately poised opening story of his first collection *Meditation* – 'Children on a Country Road' – is a manifesto for this style of philosophizing and was extracted from the section of Version B that replaced the narrative of the passive nihilism of the fat man. Even given this provenance, the story has attracted little comment beyond being regarded as a charming even nostalgic childhood idyll,[31] and its claim to inaugurate a new style of thinking utterly overlooked. This of course is part of the critical underestimation of *Meditation* that is a specific consequence of the significance attributed to 'The Judgement'.

This term 'aesthetic apperception' is drawn from a response Kafka jotted down to an article by Max Brod, 'Zur Aesthetik', published in the weekly magazine *Die Gegenwart* late February 1906. The philosophical context of this contribution and Kafka's response have been carefully described by

Arnold Heidsieck who locates it with respect to Brod and Kafka's interest in contemporary phenomenology and philosophy of mind, and in particular the work of the Brentano group active in the University of Prague, the activities of the 'philosophers' club' at the Cafe Louvre and the philosophical Salon hosted by Frau Berta Fanta in which both friends participated.[32] Brod's essay on aesthetics marked his break with this group by his appeal to a traditional 'Herbartian' view of apperception. In this view, apperception consists of 'the admission of new ideas into consciousness through assimilation, as well as the conscious reproduction of repressed ideas' and serves to keep 'the constant struggle among accumulated as well as new ideas – their combining and reinforcing, counter-acting and impeding – in a state of equilibrium' (Heidsieck, 16). The apperceiving consciousness experiences this struggle in terms of pleasure and displeasure, with pleasure provoked by the reception of new ideas into consciousness and displeasure with their repression and exclusion. Brod's essay locates this equilibrium in terms of individual thresholds for novelty – with the attachment of new to existing ideas provoking the feeling of pleasure.

Kafka's ironic reflection on Brod's article locates aesthetic pleasure less in novelty and disinterested absence of will than in fatigue. However, his approach has implications that exceed the immediate philosophical context of the physiology of perception carefully reconstructed by Heidsieck.[33] As a way of framing the distinction between realized cognitive ('scientific') and unrealizable aesthetic apperception he develops the strategy of the philosophical fiction pioneered by Plato in the *Republic*'s allegory of the cave but disowned later in the dialogue.[34] He philosophizes by telling a story, imagining himself a stranger in Prague: 'Let's say I'm a person without any sense of direction and come to Prague as a foreign city. I just want to write to you, but don't know your address, so I ask you, you give it to me and I apperceive it and need ask no more. Your address is something "old," it is thus we apperceive in science' (*NI* 11). If he wishes to write a letter, he need only *know* the address – there is little novelty or pleasure to be had in writing the address on an envelope. If, however, he wishes to pay a visit, 'then I must at every corner and crossroads ask and ask, I can never avoid a passer-by, an apperception here is absolutely impossible' (*NI* 11). Not only is the disoriented friend constantly distracted and unable to fix his knowledge of the way to his friend's address in an reliable apperception, but trying to make sense of the constant novelty posed by every street corner and every passer-by eventually fatigues him: 'What is possible is that I get tired and go into a cafe that is on my way and rest there, it's also possible that I'll give up on the visit, for this reason I have still not apperceived' (*NI* 11). Aesthetic pleasure consists of growing tired of pursuing a goal and being diverted into a place of suspension or relaxation, here a cafe, in other places a fictional world. Put more formally, aesthetic as opposed to cognitive apperception is always a task, a state that can be approached, held in supension, but never accomplished. It gives each cognitive decision – necessary at each new corner and at every crossroads – an affective charge, but one which is eventually fatiguing and can lead to the overall goal being abandoned or deferred. There does not exist a clear and consistent trajectory – address or logic – that can be attained, but only a search that may be suspended and perhaps resumed later.

Kafka used the term *Meditation* (*Betrachtung*) for this movement towards an ever interrupted state of aesthetic apperception and as the title for his first collection of stories. The latter incorporated and extended Kafka's first literary publication, a sequence of eight short prose pieces[35] published under the title *Betrachtung* in the January-February 1908 edition of *Hyperion*.[36] The *Hyperion* stories relate experiences of the anxiety of possibility and are firmly located in a metropolitan ambiance that provokes fantasies of trying to make sense and give coherence to fatigued distraction and accidental encounters. On 27 March 1910 a smaller selection of stories was published in the newspaper *Bohemia*[37] as *Betrachtungen*, adding 'Reflections for Gentleman Jockeys' to the stable, with the final collection published in book form by Rowohlt in 1912–13. For the latter, and after having been persuaded by Max Brod to assume the obligation to publish a book, Kafka painfully added a further nine stories to those already published including prominently 'Children on a Country Road'.[38] By an accident of fate his meeting with Brod at his home on the evening of August 13th 1912 to agree the final order of the stories in *Meditation* coincided with his first meeting with his future fiancée Felice Bauer, affording us a description of he and Brod spreading out the manuscripts of the stories in the 'piano room' after dinner and deciding to open the sequence with 'Children on a Country Road' and to end it with the dark tale of haunting, 'Unhappiness'.

The importance of this ordering becomes clear when we examine the first manuscript version of 'Children on a Country Road' in Version B of 'Description of a Struggle'.[39] In Version B the story that ends by evoking the sleeplessness of urban fools begins with the narrator falling asleep in the face of the landslide threatening the unfinished region or landscape: 'I slept, and with my entire being entered into the first dream. In it I tossed and turned in such anguish and pain that the dream could not bear it, but did not dare wake me either; for, after all, I was sleeping only because the world around me was at an end. And so I passed through this profoundly torn dream and returned as if saved – fleeing sleep and dream – into the villages of my *Heimat. I heard the wagons passing the garden fence . . .*' (*NI* 145).[40] For the *Meditation* collection, Kafka deleted this framing dream-narrative that situated it within the nightmare of the end of the world, leaving it as a detached but enigmatic narrative: he will make only one further significant cut towards the end of the story. The story or his dream within the dream is a *therapon*, or healing vision, but one still touched by the horror it would escape. In it the healing light is accompanied by other sensations such as sounds and the touch of the omnipresent and ambivalent wind, blowing from the end of the world that we saw haunt 'Description of a Struggle'.

'Children on a Country Road' is a meditation, an exercise in aesthetic apperception or thinking through images that departs from sensation in search of an impossible, hence exhausting, consistency. But it has the peculiar character of resisting capture by apperception – the dream is in flight from 'sleep and dream' – it is a dream of not-dreaming, but one always threatened by sleep and entry to a third and perhaps more terrible oneiric state. It is thus attended by an enormous fatigue born of the effort to stay awake: indeed the dream is made up of strategies for staying awake as long as possible, preferably but impossibly forever.[41] The dreamer who cannot bear to awake from the dream of not being asleep thus joins a band of children who also do not want to go to bed. And in this dream he is repeatedly woken up on the point of falling asleep, called back to the sweet dream in which he seems free of both sleep and dream. And when the other children must finally go home to bed, he will have to leave the village and keep walking, forever, to stay awake and not abandon this for another, perhaps worse dream. It is the foolishness of security – later the foolishness of the creature who dug an impregnable burrow but had to stay awake to guard it, or the foolish prudence of those sleepwalkers who keep moving in order not to awake from the dream of being awake.

The story is striking for the privilege it lends to sound and touch over vision. The story opens with sounds – 'I heard [*Ich hörte*] the wagons passing the garden fence' – and continues with the sounds of heat – 'how the wood of their spokes and shafts creaked in the summer heat' (S 27, 379). We hear of labourers laughing and in the middle of this carefully described soundscape there is a moment of unsure vision as the wagons passing on the country road are seen but then not-seen through 'gently moving gaps in the foliage' (S 27, 379). The near invisibility of the sources of the sounds behind the hedge warns of the invisible forces already at work in this story – the summer heat and the wind that is already rustling the foliage. The breeze and the return of the labourers locates the perception towards evening, but it is so far without an apperceiving subject. The dream framing of the story in 'Description of a Struggle' Version B identifies the place as the 'villages' of the dreamer's childhood, and this seems confirmed by the next sentence that finds the dreamer at momentary rest on a little swing in his parents' garden. The swing is crucial for the disruptions that follow, for as the dream child starts to swing, his surroundings seem to swing relativistically with him; he swings between moving with respect to the garden and the garden moving with respect to him. The alternating movement of the dream-swinger modulates into a swaying of the narrative voice between the first and third persons.

The first-person narrator swings in and out of his own story. His disappearance is announced by means of a pun; the story swings from the first person '*Ich hörte*' listening on this side of the fence to the impersonal third person '*Vor dem Gitter hörte es nicht auf*' – 'Over the fence it never stopped' (*S* 379, 27). The first paragraph uses the verb *hören*, 'to hear', in the first-person imperfect; the second uses '*aufhören*', 'to stop', in the third-person imperfect. The two sides of the fence in the two sentences are tied by the pun on *hören* that enables the point of perception to swing between the first and the third person. The movement is then held – as if the child leant back on the swing at its most extreme point – in a moment of suspension that Kafka calls an *Augenblick* or blink of an eye which is filled by children running by, wagons slowly passing and darkness falling on the flowerbeds. Then, following one of Kafka's very rare uses of the semicolon, the first person returns to *see* – '*sah ich*' – a gentleman stroller with a stick meet two girls arm in arm by the side the road: the visual detail suggests that the 'I' has swung back and was able at the other extreme point of his swing to look momentarily over the hedge.

This is followed by another moment of suspension – this time described as an *Atemzug*, a drawn breath – in which the child stops swinging and leans back to watch a flock of birds fly up 'as if in a spray' (Ronald Spiers' inspired translation). Although the subject of perception is now stationary, perception itself continues to swing until the 'I' is no longer sure whether it is the birds who are rising or he who is falling: 'I' watches them 'until I no more believed they rose but that I fell and holding on to the ropes out of tiredness began to swing a little' (*S* 379, 27). The description is accompanied by a growing sense of fatigue not at all characteristic of the tireless Cartesian subject but for Kafka an essential feature of incompletable aesthetic apperception. But as the 'I' swings more strongly, the air grows cooler – not because of the evening breeze, but because of the motion of the swing – and vision blurs as the soaring birds are transformed into 'trembling stars'.

The faint trembling light of the stars then changes into the shuddering candlelight by which the tired child, 'often' with both arms on the table, bites into his bread and butter. The omnipresent and seemingly friendly 'warm wind' billows the curtains and again, 'often', someone outside would hold them still in order to see and speak with the child indoors. The use of 'often' and 'usually' describes an action at once specific and typical, suggesting that in this dream *Heimat* the same events repeat eternally, driven by the omnipresent wind blowing, as we saw in Version A, from some distant future catastrophe. So 'usually' the candle was quickly blown out and 'usually' the midges would go on circling in the dark smoke, still unaware that the light was spent and in a holding pattern as yet unscattered by the wind. The swarm theme that began with the birds and then moved to the stars now arrives at the midges before finally settling on the gang of kids running and playing along the country road. The swaying between presence and absence we saw earlier on the swing returns as the eternally repeated question from the window prompts an absent gaze as if looking 'at a distant mountain or at mere air' (*S* 379, 28). Then, if one of the questioners would jump up at the window sill announcing the arrival of the others, and it seems as if in this suspended dream *Heimat* one of them always would, the 'I' would always rise sighing to join them.

The sigh is met with reported speech, the first of five speech acts in the story that form a chorus of questions sometimes with responses, sometimes not. The first and the last instances of speech differ from the others in coming from outside the world of children, that is from outside the endless dream. The first sequence of questions are in the voice of a child at the window who has succeeded in stopping the dreamer falling asleep over his *Butterbrod*, but they are addressed less to the child than to the dreamer of the end of the world who has taken refuge in this memory of childhood: 'No, why are you sighing so? What has happened? Is it some accident that can never be put right? Will we never get over it. Is all really lost?' (*S* 379, 28).[42] The sigh or audible expulsion of breath marks a point of contact between versions A and B, with the sigh of the fat man initiating the catastrophic dream sequence of the first version and the answers he gives to unspoken questions. In Version B the questions interrupt the typical/singular narrative of the dream and potentially awake not only the child dozing over the supper table but also the one who dreams of the child forever awake at that table. For these questions respond to the sigh of the dreamer who would stay awake and not to that of the dreamt child who would prefer to sleep; they nevertheless have the potential to provoke an apperception that would tear the fabric of the dream. The answer then must come from nowhere (there is no place for a philosophical fat man in Version B), so the response is reported not as a speech act but as an impersonal statement of fact tied to the first-person plural: 'Nothing was lost. We ran in front of the house' (*S* 380, 28). 'We' can be as well the band of children as the dreamer joining them for an evening gallop.

Now follows the second sequence of questions, spoken this time by voices punctuated by abrupt dashes in the manuscript, subsequently tidied up with the orderly inverted commas of reported speech in the published version.[43] This time the questions are posed by the gang who it seems have always been waiting outside, forever ... "Thank God, here you are [seid Ihr] at last!" – "You always come [du kommst] so late!" – "What me?" – "Right You, stay at home if you don't want to join in." – "No mercy!" – "What? No mercy? What are you talking about?"' (S 381, 28; see also NI 146-7). The punctuation is important at this point since it marks a transition from the first-person singular to plural: it reports the 'We' talking to itself. The 'I' merges into the 'We', the dreamer into the dreamt, and then the 'We' impels itself headlong into the longed-for perpetual evening where 'There was no day or night time' (S 380, 28) – just perpetual twilight. The 'We' runs in ordered formation, waistcoat buttons clacking and breathing fire like fabulous beasts. They are a troop of cuirassiers who run down the alley leading from the house to the country road and some will always run into the darkening ditch that parallels the road and emerge the other side onto the raised field path and look around 'like strangers', splitting the We. The We responds by breaking into speech, again with minimal punctuation in the manuscript: '"Come down!" – "Come up first!" – "So you can throw us down, no fear, we're too sharp for that." – "You're too afraid, you mean. Just come, come!" – "Really, of you? You want to throw us down? What must we look like to you?"' (S 380, 28). And so trench warfare breaks out, the We attacks and repels itself only to fall back into the ditch or grave of the third-person impersonal where 'Everything was equally warmed, we didn't feel warm, we didn't feel cold in the grass, one just grew tired' (S 380, 29). The resolution of the We's conflict into the equanimity of das Mann fallen in the warm ditch is attended by the fatigue threatening the dreamer with sleep and with it the passage into another, perhaps worse dream.

The ditch suddenly assumes disquieting complexity as the tired dreamt child narrated in the third person assumes first a foetal position – 'a hand under the ear' – and then repeats the moment of birth: 'Then one wanted to throw oneself towards the air with the arm held across and legs bent only to fall for certain into a deeper ditch' (S 380, 29). Yet this is a birth or leap into a grave – a Graben – the word is repeated twice and qualified by the adjective 'deeper' on both occasions. The dream child wishes to be reborn to death and then be reborn repeatedly – 'And one wished this would never cease [Aufhören]' (S 380, 29). In short, the text enters another moment of suspension, this time swinging between birth and death or the womb and the tomb. Luckily this moment of suspension headed towards dreaded sleep is disrupted by the other children jumping over the ditch between field and the country road and the spectacle of the soles of their shoes flying past in the air is enough to rouse the third person out of the ditch and back to life.

The child just metamorphosed into a tearful foetus lying on his back looking up at the night sky is pulled back *in extremis* from serious sleep in the last grave – *im letzten Graben*. At this most remote point of existence/non-existence 'one' could see the moon rising, and the light of the passing mail coach. A wind begins to blow – it could be felt even in the grave/ditch and was heard to 'rustle the nearby woods' (S 381, 29). The threat posed by the wind and the motif of the rustling, waiting woods made 'one' less keen to be alone. The revery in the womb/grave is then broken by a call to assembly from above, from the country road, a call that summons first all the children and then specifically the second-person familiar, the one who was absurdly playing unborn/dead in the ditch. The hour is late, the post-coach has passed, this is no time to fall asleep, everyone has to move: 'Kommt!'

The gang runs homewards, anxious at the onset of night and bunched together holding hands running downhill. The descent anticipates a later story in the *Meditation* collection – 'The Wish to be an Indian' – in which speeding against the wind the rider loses all sense of terrain and even of the horse – a child indeed whoops like an Indian- and they all gallop, but in this version the wind comes from behind and gives them wings. But just like the Indian in the later story, speed becomes stasis – 'we were in such full stride that even overtaking we could fold our arms and peacefully look around us' (S 381, 29–30); if in 'The Wish to be an Indian' speed no longer leaves any space or time for contemplation, here the flying child borne by the wind can look around and meditate like a pre-figuration of the fat man floating on his bier. Their career comes to a stand at the bridge over the brook, a location related in the second-person plural but attended by a moment of dispersal and assembly: if some children overshoot the bridge in their gallop and others pull up before it, all will nevertheless join in a moment of suspension figured by the water below rippling endlessly over stone and root oblivious to the lateness of the day. The children wait, and in this world not one of them would have jumped up on the parapet, but there was just no reason why you should not have done so.

This time the moment of suspension and the eternal return of nature figured by the ripples in the river is interrupted by the lights in the carriages of a distant passing train whose windows, although too far away to see for sure, 'were certainly left open' (S 381, 30). The children accompanied the passage of the train with a popular song sung at high speed, with waving arms, the kind of scene witnessed by the passing travellers in 'Wedding Preparations in the Country'.[44] The singing, which seems to have been both salute and an invocation to the 'distant travellers', was of course inaudible to them in their far away and noisy train but for those singing the mixing of the voices felt like 'being caught by a fish-hook' (S 381, 30). Yet the train passes by, all seems well and the forest is 'behind us'; back in the village the grown-ups are still awake and mothers are making beds. Everything was being prepared for sleep in the villages of the *Heimat*, but bedtime for the gang meant it was time for the dreamer to move on: '*Es war schon Zeit*'. In the darkness the I separates himself for the last time from the We, kissing goodbye to his neighbour, and shaking hands with three companions; he too sets out on the way back – '*den Weg zurückzulaufen*' – but for this child it was not to be the way home. When out of sight of the others, he abandons the country road and the children on their way home and takes the path across the field towards the wood.

At this point, Kafka makes a significant change in the published version of the story, which up to now, apart from the deletion of the opening framing narrative and the changes in punctuation, has remained extremely close to the manuscript. In both versions the dream child runs *back* into the wood; he has done this before, but in the first version the phrase 'I turned off and ran along the field paths again into the wood' (*S* 381 30) continues 'and further. I hurried through the great forests, once the light of the sun, now that of the moon, once on the back once on the face [*und weiter. Ich eilte durch die grossen Wälder, einmal das Licht der Sonne, einmal das des Mondes, einmal auf den Rücken einmal in Gesicht*]' (*NI* 150). Why should Kafka delete this sentence in the version published in *Meditation*? Perhaps because it interrupts the stasis of eternal return that characterizes the childhood idyll, for the dreamer in the first version not only returns to the wood but 'goes further'? He sets out on a journey through 'great forests' analogous to the one through the 'deeper graves' earlier in the story, his hurrying figure touched on face and back by the light of the sun and the moon. But maybe another reading is possible – in the first version we are implicitly told why he will never arrive at the longed-for city in the south: the sun on his back and then on his face means he is travelling from east to west, running in the wrong direction if his goal is the city to the south. However much he hurries he will – like most of Kafka's travellers and messengers, like aesthetic apperception itself – never arrive but remain suspended in a fatigued present. In the published version the deletion does not so much seal the stasis of eternal return as leave open the possibility – for better or worse – that the dream child might just arrive at the city of the south.

This leaves just the last episode of reported speech that closes both versions of the story; spoken in the village from which the child is escaping: it tells of the city to the south for which he is with sun and moon and day and night *sleeplessly* striving in the first version. In this version the traveller is already one of the insomniac fools who inhabits the city of the south, mentioned at the beginning of the speech. It is a speech cited in a peculiar way by Walter Benjamin in his celebrated but misguided *Jüdische Rundschau* essay: 'There are some people there! Just think, they don't sleep!' 'And why not then? Because they don't get tired (*müde*).' 'And why not then?' 'Because they are fools.' 'Don't fools get tired?' 'How could fools get tired!' (*S* 382, 30). For Benjamin this dialogue refers to a clan that 'reckons with the brevity of life in a peculiar way', whose spokesmen are the students devoted to study and achieving cognitive apperception. But this interpretation focuses too narrowly on sleep, overlooking the dialogue's is concern with fatigue. What is important is that the city dwellers do not get tired, the fools cannot sleep because they do not get tired. Leaving aside Benjamin's focus on sleep, we can infer from this dialogue that wisdom lies in fatigue, and fatigue we have seen is characteristic of aesthetic apperception. Fatigue is precisely the sign of an inability to arrive at a destination – of remaining suspended between oblivion and apperception.

Yet the story has also been one of a dream within a dream that resists the onset of sleep and the entry to another dream world. The exit from the dream of the end of the world was the entry into a dream of stasis and membership of a mobile band of children running up and down the same country road every night resisting bedtime.[45] When they could no longer resist, it was time for the dreamer to leave and to find another way of staying awake. In this way the city in the south might indeed be the 'utopian prospect of perpetual motion in perpetual rest' described so perceptively by Ronald Speirs: 'Such a place would be one of unending movement but also one where movement is indistinguishable from rest, since the "fools" who live there never become tired' (Speirs in Lothe, 211). The fools are fellow inhabitants of the dream of not sleeping and not having to dream. Yet their world is under threat, since the 'villages of my Heimat' are less the villages of my childhood than a fictional scene of aesthetic apperception where worse dreams can be held off. Yet the village is on the main road and railway line, mail coaches and trains pass according to rigid schedules and the *Heimat* is inextricably tied to the tireless city. And there are the sounds and the winds that like the disquieting whistle in the burrow intimate the coming catastrophe, threatening the oneiric securities of rustic oblivion and childhood with the wide-awake knowledge and apperception of the city of the south where this dreamer at least will hopefully never arrive.

Judgements

Kafka's reputed breakthrough story 'The Judgement' (*Das Urteil*) is a far less sophisticated performance than 'Children on a Country Road'. It does not sustain the disinterested distance from the logics of cognition and action required of an aesthetic apperception or meditation. It is a work of insomnia that stages an awakening to the law of the father in the passing of a sentence and its execution. It is hard to share the almost universal critical enthusiasm for this story or to restrain the suspicion that it represents a narrowing of the range of aesthetic apperception achieved in *Meditation*.[46] Its first enthusiastic critic was of course Kafka himself, who in an entry dated 23 September 1912 immediately following the story in his notebook refers to writing it in 'one sitting during the night of the 22nd–23rd, from ten o'clock at night to six o'clock in the morning' (*D* 212, 355). In the light of morning Kafka found 'The confirmed conviction that with my novel-writing I find myself in the shameful lowlands of writing. Writing can only be done in this way, only with such coherence, with such complete opening of body and soul' (*D* 213, 355). Yet it seems he prizes more the event of writing than its product. For with the same breath that praises the singularity of 'The Judgement', Kafka also reflects on its *relation* (i.e. its non-singularity) to Freud, Brod, Wasserman, Werfel and to his other work, notably 'of course also my "The Urban World"' (*D* 213, 355).

The view that 'The importance for Kafka of writing his first great story "The Judgement" cannot be overestimated' (Corngold 2004a, 13) is in danger of becoming a critical prejudice, for it *can* and *has* been systematically 'overestimated'. Examined more closely, the terms by which Kafka expressed his own high estimation of writing the story do not justify regarding it as the Archimedean point from which to assess his entire authorship or its interpretation. But it is nevertheless held to mark a brave new beginning, overcoming and resolving past failures and looking 'back to many attempts to find the themes and forms that he could acknowledge as his children' and 'forward to a time of despondency' (Corngold 2004a). It has come to serve as a point from which to measure progress and regression in Kafka's writing, a form of critical gold-standard.[47] Yet we do not need to confine our critical judgements of Kafka within what Corngold describes as 'the circle of "the judgement"' (Corngold 2004a). Indeed we might even see it as foreclosing on the possibilities open to a fiction in search of a radically new coherence, what we have called the philosophical accident narrative and Kafka himself called 'aesthetic apperception' or 'meditation'.

The prominence of 'The Judgement' is complicated by its place in narratives of Kafka's rediscovery of his Judaism through his fascination with Yiddish theatre during the autumn of 1911.[48] A powerful statement of this position was proposed by Evelyn Torton Beck (1971), whose arguments are endorsed by Robertson (1985, 34) and most recently by Corngold (2004a). Yet hers is in many respects a problematic critical narrative both for understanding Kafka's work and the place of 'The Judgement' within it. It rests on the premise, clearly stated by Beck, that 'The Judgement' 'came only after years of artistic failure' (Beck, x), thus consigning 'A Description of a Struggle', 'Wedding Preparations in the Country' and *Meditation* to the realm of failed juvenilia. These allegedly unhappy experiments join the novel *America* in the 'lowlands' of failed efforts to achieve or sustain the intensity and technical prowess said to have been glimpsed in 'The Judgement'.

Beck's case for the importance of the Yiddish theatre for 'The Judgement' rests largely on the circumstantial evidence that connects the themes, characters and style in Jacob Gordin's Yiddish play *God, Man and the Devil* (1900) with the expressionist dramatic technique and domestic content of Kafka's story.[49] Her account of the connection between play and story does not emphasize how far Gordin and his plays were untypical of the popular Yiddish theatre – he was known above all for his adaptations of classical drama by Shakespeare and others into Yiddish, and *God, Man and the Devil* was a loose adaptation of some elements of Goethe's *Faust*. It is unlikely that Gordin's classical dramas would have been performed in the cramped Cafe Savoy by Yitskhok Levi's itinerant troupe, even if Gordin's plays stood for the highest aspirations of the Yiddish theatre. And while it is true that *God, Man and the Devil* possesses a sub-narrative of family conflict between father and son, its larger moral criticism of the pursuit of wealth through industrial production focuses on the causes and consequences of an industrial accident.

In spite of the importance of Gordin's play for her claim that Kafka's writing was catalyzed by the dramaturgy and themes of the Yiddish theatre, Beck's account of his encounter with *God, Man and the Devil* is itself unusually accident prone. Not only does she overlook the significance of the industrial accident that is central to the play, but also underplays the fact that the play's relegation of the domestic world of the family in favour of the public world of industrial production compromises any case for its direct influence on the claustrophobic father–son conflict of 'The Judgement'. But there are also other difficulties surrounding her account of the role of Gordin's drama. In analysing Kafka's contact with the play related in the *Diaries*, Beck mistakes the date, reading 16 October 1911 for 26 October 1911, an insignificant detail were it not symptomatic of a deeper problem with her reading. She cites the passage 'Thursday. All afternoon yesterday Levi read from *Gott, Mensch, Teufel* by Gordin and then from his own Paris diaries' (cited by Beck, 71) in support of her claim that Kafka not only saw the plays many times but additionally 'mentions hearing private readings of these plays by his friend, the actor Yitskhok Levi' (Beck, 71). In fact Kafka mentions only having heard this one play, but more seriously there is no evidence that he ever saw it performed. Levi read it to Kafka as a demonstration of what the Yiddish theatre could be, as a play whose length and complexity exceeded the powers of his own modest company. In her appendix 2 that lists the plays Kafka saw or read, she includes *Got, Mentsh, un Tayvel* by Jakov Gordin on 26 October 1911, the date Kafka heard Levi *reading* the play. By misreading the dates, Beck seems accidentally to have added a performance of the play to the repertoire at the Cafe Savoy, but unfortunately the evidence does not support the view that Kafka ever saw this play or that it was ever performed in Prague.

This creates difficulty for Beck's reading of 'The Judgement' and consequently her case for the impact of the dramaturgy of Gordin's play on that story and later *America*. She *imagines* how this play might have been staged at the Cafe Savoy: 'The improvised staging at the Savoy probably placed the angels who were to be "in the air" on pedestals, dressed in the long white robes traditionally associated with angels in the Yiddish theatre ... Could this elaborate, no doubt intentionally ludicrous allegory of the heavenly spheres have suggested the idea of the Nature theatre to Kafka?' (Beck, 126). Gordin's Yiddish version of the Prologue to *Faust* is certainly a tempting precursor for the nature theatre, except that it seems very unlikely that Kafka ever saw such a tawdry staging or that it had any impact on his later vision of the 'Nature Theatre'.

The reliance on *God, Man and the Devil* as key evidence for the influence of the Yiddish theatre on Kafka's 'breakthrough' to a dramatic style oriented towards domestic conflict does not completely compromise the argument, but it does put a question mark beside it. In the play, God allows the devil to tempt the scholar Herchel by the acquisition of industrial wealth that severely disrupts his familial and other relationships. The emphasis on temptation through industrial profit adapts a traditional theme to modern circumstances, thus framing an allegory of modernity. However, by focusing on the disruption of family relations, Beck's account understates what would most have fascinated Kafka, namely the pivotal role played by an industrial accident in the action of the play. Herschel witnesses a fatal industrial accident involving the son of his friend Khatshel, and the revelation of the price paid by others for his personal wealth is emphasized in Khatshel's speech of reproach that prompts Herschel to commit suicide and thus attain redemption. At the centre of the play is a narrative of the accident revealing the truth of capitalist wealth acquisition that provokes the sense of guilt that justifies God's confidence in the scholar Herschel. In comparison with this event, the tensions between Herschel and his father along with his other family tribulations seem strictly incidental.

If Gordin's Yiddish theatre can be discounted as a prime inspiration for 'The Judgement', the relationship Kafka himself noted with 'The Urban World' is also open for re-evaluation. It is not entirely implausible to read

'The Urban World' as a draft for 'The Judgement': both focus on conflict between father and son and both accord a pivotal role to the 'friend'; but they differ in that Oskar, the hero of 'The Urban World', succeeds in escaping the scenario of parental judgement and punishment that fatally envelops Georg Bendemann in 'The Judgement'. The evasion of the logic of parental domination through escape into the city with the support of a friend in 'The Urban World' is a far more sustained act of aesthetic apperception than the unequivocal final judgement and sentence according to the same logic in 'The Judgement'. Unlike Oskar, the city cannot save Georg from judgement; while gazing out of his window he misses the chance to escape his fate offered by 'An acquaintance who greeted him crossing the street' but to whom he 'barely responded with an absent smile' (S 80, 51). Instead of descending to the street and joining his acquaintance he fatefully turns towards his father's bedroom. The light of the sunny spring morning is extinguished as he enters the dark room where his invalid parent sits lost in the past and the darkness deepens until the moment of sentencing when the father becomes incandescent with 'radiated insight' and the light of the law in all its obscene necessity flares up to consume the hapless son.

In a letter to his fiancée Felice Bauer, whom he met a month before writing 'The Judgement' and to whom he dedicated the story, Kafka offered a very different account of its genesis than the one noted in his diary the morning after: 'when I sat down to write ... I meant to describe a war; from his window a young man was to see a crowd advancing across the bridge, but then the whole thing turned in my hands into something else' (Letter to Felice, 2 June 1913, 392).[50] Some traces of its genesis as a story about urban insurrection persist in the final version, but they mainly serve to interrupt the relentless narrative of domination, judgement and submission. These textual insurrections are associated with the pen friend in St Petersburg to whom Georg has just belatedly announced his engagement. Georg and his father initially struggle over whether the friend exists – the son assuming the father has 'forgotten' the existence of the friend – and then against the father's redefinition of the friend in terms of the logic of the family as a substitute for Georg: 'He would have been a son after my own heart' (S 85, 56). Georg's proof of the existence of the friend consists in citing the description of a scene from the 1905 Revolution told by the friend and subsequently repeated by the father:

If you think back you'll remember. He used to tell us unbelievable stories about the Russian Revolution. How he saw, for example, on a business trip to Kiev a priest on a balcony cut a broad bloody cross on the palm of his hand that he raised and called on the crowd [*Menge*]. You've told that story yourself now and again.

$$(S\ 83,\ 55)^{51}$$

This story of defiance – of the crowd's defiance of urban order and the priest's defiance of the crowd – quickly reduces to a fable of paternal domination and an apparent failure of filial defiance. Gray's reading of it in terms of an aporia of conformity and defiance – mapped across the characters of George and the Friend[52] – confirms this view of domination even more terribly, with the father reaffirming his domination by condemning his son for not being sufficiently defiant, unlike the friend in St Petersburg. Paradoxically, here the successful defiance is that of the father, who defies his son's bid to define him as a helpless geriatric and rises up to condemn his conformist son to death, a sentence whose legitimacy his son duly confirms by immediately executing it.

There is something stifling about a narrative that departs from the epiphany of an insurrectionary crowd only to be captured by a logic of familial domination and failed generational defiance. The 'urban world' into which Oskar escapes the sphere of parental domination is reduced in 'The Judgement' to the arena of Georg's execution. The city cannot save him from his father's sentence of death by drowning; holding on to the side of the bridge 'he spied through the railings a motor-bus that would easily drown out his fall, calling softly: "Dear parents, I really did always love you," he let himself drop' (*S* 88, 60). Under cover of the noise of the passing bus, Georg Bendemann ensured that no one would be disturbed by the mawkish last words of his 'reactionary suicide' or surrender to familial domination.[53]

The passage of the 'almost infinite traffic' with which Kafka ends the story has provoked fascination, largely because of associations of *Verkehr* with sexual intercourse (*Geschlechtsverkehr*). It has some other strange qualities that underline the uncanniness of its appearance at the end of the story. The sudden surge of 'almost infinite traffic' is puzzling, literally coming out of nowhere on the quiet spring Sunday morning in Prague so carefully established at the outset of the story. From the story's idyllic beginning we might expect the Sunday morning bridge – the site of execution – to be deserted except for a few strollers walking their dogs: instead there is a flash flood of traffic. Kafka stresses this sudden, infinite surge by conjoining the *Augenblick* or instant with the *geradezu Unendliche* in which the instant and the infinite cross over at the moment of execution/suicide. Hanging on to the edge of the bridge, Georg is literally suspended between the flow of traffic above and the bisecting flow of the river below him. The instant is *almost* replete, as is the moment of death by *Apparat* in the 1914 story 'In the Penal Colony'. The indifferent flows that extinguish the individual mark a limit point of domination, one in which individuals – to use Durkheim's formulation – are compelled voluntarily to take their lives. The differentiated pedestrian city into which Oskar escaped in 'The Urban World' is reduced in 'The Judgement' to a spectral surge of traffic that smothers all trace of the victim – pushing him discreetly aside in just the way Kafka described the fate of Karl Rossman in *America*.[54] But the closing tsunami of traffic that sweeps over the bridge also substitutes for the image of an insurrectionary crowd surging over the bridge at the origin of the story: Kafka transforms the defiant upsurge of the insurrectionary crowd into an irresistible and murderous wave of domination. Georg's attempt at self-affirmation through letter-writing and speech is drowned out by the roar of traffic and the 'No!' of the father. He falls, carried away by an avalanche of traffic that came suddenly out of nowhere to push him into the river and have him swept helplessly away like the 'fat man' in 'Description of a Struggle'.

Kafka's attempt the day after to situate his story with respect to other works and writers continued in his efforts to publish it as part of a themed collection. In letters to his publisher Kurt Wolff on 4 and 11 April 1913, Kafka proposed to publish it alongside 'Metamorphosis' and 'The Stoker', claiming the stories 'belong together, both inwardly and outwardly. There is an obvious connection between the three and, even more importantly, a secret one, for which reason I would be reluctant to forgo the chance of having them published together as a book, which might be called *The Sons*' (*L* 96, 116). Kafka returned to this project in a letter of 15 October 1915 but now considers placing 'The Judgement' alongside 'Metamorphosis' and 'still another novella' ('In the Penal Colony') in a collection entitled *Punishments*. While admitting 'a certain unity' between the stories, he is nevertheless far from enthusiastic and effectively withdraws the proposal. From this it may be deduced that 'punishment' is not the 'secret connection' that unites 'The Judgement' and 'Metamorphosis' (and by extension, 'The Stoker'). If not punishment, then the secret connection might be the peculiar connection of law and the accident. This is strikingly the case if 'The Judgement' is read as an accident narrative in which the death sentence, according to paternal law, is executed almost by accident through the suicide of the son. We shall see a similar movement in the chapter of accidents that is 'The Stoker' and in the most famous industrial accident in literature that befalls the Officer 'In the Penal Colony'.

One of the unintended consequences of exaggerating the significance of 'The Judgement' is the retrospective (and prospective) orientation of Kafka's writings away from modern experience understood under the sign of the accident towards the domestic familial sphere and law. This afflicts the critical assessment of the work, especially in the comparison of 'The Judgement' with 'The Urban World', regarded by Beck as a failed precursor that did not free itself from the alleged limitations of Kafka's early writing.[55] In spite of the clear statement of intent in the title – the story is about the 'urban world' – Beck approaches it solely as a failed family drama, describing its content in terms of the eternal student Oskar M's conflict with his father and a comic visit to his friend K. Because it is supposed to be 'transitional', Beck allows its strength in an 'economy of detail' absent in 'Wedding Preparations in the Country' and the reduction of the experience of the 'urban world' to the limited world of family apartment and the apartment of his friend.[56] In this view the open sequence of accidents that comprises an urban experience in search of a logic that is 'Wedding Preparations in the Country' is succeeded by the reduced but almost inescapable logic of law and the family. The narrowly avoided road to the limited perspective of 'The Judgement' opened in 'The Urban World' is praised as an artistic success rather than the failure to confront the emancipatory potential of the urban world with respect to familial and other logics of domination.

Beck's description of 'The Urban World' and its perceived failure to attain full dramatic expression focuses on the second of the three scenes that make up the story, namely the encounter in the family apartment with the hostile father. The relief from the logic of the family represented by Oskar M's earlier walk home through the city in the first scene and his efforts in the third scene to get his friend out of bed and dressed for a walk are described as 'wordy discussion'. But this underestimates the force of the first scene or description of the 'urban world' and Oskar M's passage through it on the way to the family apartment. For Beck this merely 'sets the stage and mood' for the encounter with the father, but perhaps it meant more. Oskar is in an empty square in the middle of a snowstorm, dressed for the weather and lost in thought. He turns away from the empty square and with a dancing motion heads home. Once there and confronted by his father he cannot wait to escape back to the 'urban world': 'Thereupon Oscar pressed his shoulder against the door – it opened easily – as if he were trying to break it down' (*D* 43, 118–19). The entire thrust of the narrative is directed towards escaping the brutal simplicity and closure of domestic logic into the complexity of the urban world that is open to accident and adventure. Oskar's dancing motion exemplifies this complexity, serving as an embellishment of the linear route home. 'The Urban World' is perhaps less an example of artistic failure and immaturity than the attempt to discover a logical sequence that escapes the strictures of family, debt and obligation. It is an allegory of escape from a domestic logic of family guilt into another logic that affirms the aleatory experience of the urban world. Perhaps it is 'The Judgement' that fails, for after transforming the insurrectionary crowd into deadly traffic its only escape lies in the suicidal execution of the logic of paternal domination. City traffic is the avalanche that carries George Bendemann away and not the solvent capable of dissolving the fixed and exterminatory law of the father into an array of unpredictable accidents.

2 ACCIDENTS

The world of insurance

In mid-August 1907, Kafka reported to Brod from his annual vacation in Triesch – motor-cycling, swimming, nude sunbathing and the company of two 'bright' and 'extremely Social Democratic' girls, Agathe and Hedwig Weiler.[1] It is to Hedwig that he announced his decision to pursue a career in insurance, writing on 19 September, 'In the coming weeks I must study insurance incessantly, but it is really very interesting' (L 32, 45). After securing a post in the private insurance company Assicurazioni Generali,[2] he writes again to Hedwig describing an office revery 'of one day sitting on chairs in distant countries looking out of office windows at fields of sugar cane or Mohammedan cemeteries; and while the world of insurance interests me greatly my present work is depressing' (L 35, 49). The contrast between the world of insurance and the daily work with the Assicurazioni Generali confirms Kafka's fascination with the theory of insurance expressed in the earlier letter. He soon left the world of private insurance for a career in worker's accident insurance with The Workmen's Accident Insurance Institute for the Kingdom of Bohemia in Prague.

Kafka's career in the Institute has been meticulously described by Klaus Hermsdorf in the introduction to his 1984 Berlin edition of the *Office Writings*, and later by his collaborator Benno Wagner in the 1999 Fischer Verlag Frankfurt edition and Princeton English translation. It began with a vocational course at the Prague Commercial College and then his first day at work on Thursday, 30 July 1908 as Assistant Secretary *Aushilfsbeamter*, the latest addition to a staff of over 200 specialist officials and support workers. Kafka began his generalist training in the 'Technical Insurance Section' of the Institute, responsible for collecting and interpreting accident statistics and setting premiums, moving on to the 'Accident Section' in

April 1909. There, from working largely with statistics and populations, Kafka was suddenly confronted with actual accidents and their individual victims and called to produce the detailed descriptions of circumstances, responsibility and degree of compensation for industrial misfortunes.[3] In September 1909 he returned as a trainee (*Anstaltspraktikant*) to the 'Technical Insurance Section' on the eve of the structural reform of the Institute by its new director Robert Marschner.[4] In April 1910 Kafka's position as a technical legal writer or *concipist* was confirmed and his professional profile established for his remaining years with the Institute.[5] He was a key contributor to Marschner's reforms, taking charge of the 'Appeals Department' now part of a single 'Firms Department' (*Betriebsabteilung*) formed in March 1910 out of the merger of the technical, insurance, control and finance departments. His department was responsible for dealing with appeals by firms against their risk classification and thus their insurance rating (reviewed in five-yearly cycles), and required of its officials, and above all its leading official, considerable legal, technical and statistical expertise. Kafka's working life was thereafter spent administering §18 of the 1887 National Insurance Act, which gave businesses the right to appeal against the risk classification assigned them in the quinquennial exercise.

Apart from drafting the legal documentation necessary for contesting appeals against the Institute, Kafka's role also extended to other areas. While in the 'Accident Department', Kafka was responsible for four districts in northern Bohemia – Reichenberg, Friedland, Rumburg and Gablonz – the most rapidly industrializing region in the Austro-Hungarian Empire with textiles, machine production, glass and stone quarrying.[6] He represented the Institute in important legal hearings and was active in promoting safety at work (foreseen by the 1887 Act as an important factor in reducing industrial accidents and thus ultimately insurance premiums).[7] He was also a regular contributor to the Institute's Annual Reports submitted to the ministry in Vienna and widely distributed to its clients and an interested public. As a professional writer he had a wide range of duties, ranging from speechwriting for the senior officials of the Institute, presenting its work to a broader public in newspaper articles, drafting the Institute's Annual Reports and preparing the briefs for complex legal cases. However, the core of his role was risk classification and accident prevention, duties that placed him, as Wagner has shown, on 'the junction' between the Foucauldian norms of discipline and regulation constitutive of the modern nation-state.[8]

Kafka's work in risk classification consisted of establishing and then policing the framework according to which insurance premiums varied according to the statistical mapping of accident risk.[9] Premiums varied according to the risk level of a branch of industry, the accident statistics for a particular firm over the previous five years and their safety standards. In theory the system provided an incentive to individual firms to reduce their accident rates and raise their levels of safety by rewarding more safety conscious firms with lower premiums. In reality it encouraged corruption while provoking constant conflict around the interpretation of accident statistics and industrial safety measures. Kafka's role was not entirely restricted to managing routine bureaucratic traffic but extended to researching and writing legal, technical and theoretical contributions for the Annual Reports.[10] The annually produced articles from 1907 to 1915 (with the addition of the Institute's 25th anniversary special issue)[11] were characterized by an exegetical precision and quality of reflection that makes them a discrete but critically underestimated part of Kafka's published *oeuvre*.[12]

Kafka's contributions to the Institute's Annual Reports form a corpus that combines legal and technical expertise with theoretical and political reflection. They begin with a discussion of the changing legal definition of the accident and its consequences for social insurance in the 1907 report – 'The Scope of Compulsory Insurance for Building and Related Trades' – that was followed by reflections on insurance premiums in mechanized agriculture and motor cars in the 1908 report.[13] The Annual Report of 1909 finds Kafka contributing to the Institute's accident prevention agenda by addressing the hazards of wood-planing machines,[14] an article he followed up in the 1910 report.[15] The 1911 Annual Report contains summary notes on accident prevention and meetings with employers, among other points such as announcing the extension of accident insurance to quarries. The model of brief reports is repeated in 1912 and 1913, with articles on meetings with employers, fixed rate insurance and accident prevention in agriculture and in quarries. The 1914 Annual Report represents Kafka's *tour de force* in the genre, containing not only a statistical financial report, a masterly announcement of new categories of firms liable to compulsory insurance and a preliminary report on the impact of the war, but also Kafka's extraordinary article 'Accident Prevention in Quarries' discussed extensively below. The 25th Anniversary Issue finds Kafka reflecting on periodic revisions of risk classification and reviewing the changing jurisprudence of the building trades and accident prevention. The series terminates in 1915 with Kafka's last reflection on risk classification and the war, along with his thoughts on insuring barrack construction, the problem of sabotage and the impact of the war on accident prevention work.

The most interpreted of the contributions to the Annual Reports are 'The Scope of Compulsory Insurance for the Building Trades', published in the Institute's Annual Report for 1907 and the contributions to accident prevention in planing machines. In the former, Kafka elaborates a theory of the accident and its ambiguous relationship to the law that sets out from an analysis of the conflicting implications of decisions taken in the Administrative Court modifying the definition of insurance coverage laid down in the 1887 Law. At issue in the article is the project of extending social insurance to as many branches of industry as possible, in this case to workshop labour. The law governing workshop insurance of 1889 was ambiguous but subsequently clarified by a 1906 Administrative Court decision that extended coverage to all production sites. After lobbying by employers, the Administrative Court retreated from this decision at the same time as draft legislation for comprehensive social insurance was submitted to the Reichsrat. Kafka's anonymous contribution to the Annual Report defends the principle of extended coverage in terms of comprehensive legislative reform and pointedly not by a return to the 1906 judicial status quo.

The report begins by tracing a conflict within the building industry concerning compulsory insurance coverage to a distinction between two types of accident risk – '*die differenzierung zwischen zwei ganz verschiedenen Unfallsgefahren*' (*OW* 55, 107) – risk/danger (*Gefahr*) in the workshop and risk/danger on the building site. This distinction of accident risk according to location is subsequently described in terms of 'spheres of risk' (*Gefahrensphäre*).[16] Having made this distinction within the genre of accident risk, Kafka then traces the ambiguities of the jurisprudence surrounding the 1887 Act to different definitions of the accident in the conflicting Administrative Court decisions of 1906 and 1908. For instance, one of the more damaging innovations introduced by the Administrative Court consisted in making accidents themselves 'accidental'. Instead of seeing that accidents were a statistical constant and basing the case for compulsory insurance on this perception, the Administrative Court argued that accidents were introduced to the workplace as if by chance and that it was this risk that needed to be covered by insurance. The Court replaced the sheer statistical necessity of accidents 'in general' by 'particular risks' associated with 'particular circumstances'. In Kafka's words, the Administrative Court justified trades' obligation to insure their activities 'not on account of the risk essentially [*an sich*] bound up with their activities' that is to say, because of the accident danger inherent to any activity, but rather 'on account of the particular dangers [*besonderen Gefahren*] incurred by the introduction of particular circumstances [*besonderer Verhältnisse*], such as the factory conditions of the firm, the use of motors and the undertaking of construction works' (*OW* 56, 109; translation modified).

Kafka insists on a distinction between the danger 'in itself' of the accident and the apparently contingent accidents attending particular circumstances; as an inhabitant of the world of insurance and an adept in insurance statistics, he was familiar with the peculiar logic by which accidents obey rules and are in some sense necessary.

Kafka also points out that one of the consequences of the new jurisprudential definition of particular accident risk led to situations in which 'the worker in the same firm owned by the same employer is insured in one instance and not in another' (OW 59, 118–19). This led not only to litigation on behalf of employees – litigation that threatened to become infinite as the risk of each particular activity became contestable – but also to widespread dissatisfaction: 'For a certain period workers had the reassuring certainty of being protected by insurance from the consequences of all possible industrial accidents, this will now no longer always be the case. And the workers must, when as the most concerned laymen they reflect on the matter, conclude that it is contingencies [*Zufälligkeiten*] rather than principle that dominate the world of insurance [*Versicherungswesen*]' (OW 60, 118). The disaggregation of the statistical population of accidents into a series of discrete accidents and risks threatened the very project of managing accident rates rather than individual accidents. The solution was to consult with employers to determine whether exposure to or protection from the consequences of accidents was itself a matter of accident or of 'principle'. Kafka concludes his report by returning to the 'common centre' of all the questions of social insurance: 'only the broadest possible generalisation of insurance can satisfy the intent of the legislature (to grant the benefit of insurance to as many segments of the working population as possible) and the interests of the those most closely affected – the workers, the employers, and the Institute' (OW 69, 138). Thus the object of a new law should be the population of accidents as a statistical regularity rather than the risk and the event of individual accidents. Only in this way could accidents be brought under law, and insurance given an appropriate 'principle', a juridical approach framed in terms of individual intent and negligence threatened to atomize the entire sphere of accident insurance.

The legal expertise displayed by Kafka in the 1907 report is joined by technical expertise in the famous articles on safety measures in the use of wood-planing machines. This expertise was not plucked from the air: in a letter to the Management Committee of the Institute dated 7 October 1909, Kafka claimed that his office work required 'a comprehensive knowledge of mechanical technology' and requested leave of absence to attend Professor Mikolaschek's lectures in the German Technical University four mornings a week (Kafka 1984, 124). His technical expertise allowed him to assess technological risks and to advocate prevention by informing employers and workers about recent technological developments in their fields of production. To this end he introduced visual material into the Annual Reports, drawing on established practice in German industrial safety literature sponsored by the state, employers and organized labour.[17] Kafka's contribution to the Annual Report of 1909 graphically contrasts the accident risks of square and cylindrical shaft lathes. The former were high-risk propositions, vulnerable to slips of the hand and the sudden irregular movements of the wood being planed. In these circumstances, the probability of an accident is high: 'This jumping up and sliding back of the wood could not be predicted or prevented, since it happens when the wood is in certain places misshapen or gnarled, when the blades do not spin quickly enough or slide out of alignment, or when the pressure of the hand on the wood is unevenly distributed. Such an accident cannot take place without several finger joints or even entire fingers being severed' (*OW* 110–11, 196). It is inevitable that this technology will provoke a relatively uniform but high number of accidents; what remains unknowable is precisely whom they will befall and when. The round lathes, on the contrary, are less accident prone, generate fewer accidents and represent a lower risk to the population of workers using them.

Kafka's accompanying line drawings are set within the text and carefully cross-referenced to relate to each other. Text and image work together to portray the irresistible arrival and aftermath of an accident. In spite of the technical context and iconography, word and image conspire to enhance the sense of danger posed by the coming accident. The first image (Fig. 1) represents a hand entering the aperture of a dangerous square shafted lathe, frozen at the instant before it is severed by the blade. The accompanying text notes that these lathes rotate at around 3,800–4,000 cycles per minute and with this impressive statistic in mind, the reader who looks at the image of the fingers in the lathe knows that they cannot possibly be withdrawn in time to avoid the accident about to take place. The image of the shirt-sleeved arm and hand entering the lathe is invested with the technical information that this blade is moving at a speed far beyond the response of human reflexes. The accident has yet to happen but it is as if it has already happened: the worker's fingers are doomed.

The second image (Fig. 2) is shown directly after, evoking the uneven wood or unsteady grip that make the hand slip into the aperture. It is a complex image (only partially reproduced in the translated *Office Writings*) juxtaposing two large injured left hands with a sequence of one left and six right injured hands – all severed from their bodies like anatomical

FIGURE 1 Square-shaft wood-planing machine with hand from 'Measures for Preventing Accidents from Wood-Planing Machines', 1909.

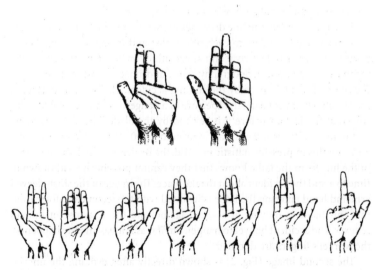

FIGURE 2 Rows of injured fingers from 'Measures for Preventing Accidents from Wood-Planing Machines', 1909.

specimens. The text has just explained why accidents with the square-shafted lathe are inevitable, and the image gives us a corresponding population of injured hands, telling us that the necessary accident has struck all of these hands, with different but related injuries. The image tells us that it is not the accident that is singular – it is always the same and decreed by dangerous technology – but only its incidence on the unfortunate hands that it strikes. The image presents variations on an ineluctable accident. The first of the upper two hands has a thumb severed at the first joint followed by the path of the blade written in severed finger joints with the fifth finger completely severed. The second larger hand has the first, fourth and fifth fingers severed at the first joint – both hands show abrasions and cuts. There follows a sequence of seven variants of disfigurement, all manifestations of the same genre of accident. The serial image prompts its viewers to imagine how the accident struck these various hands – whether the wood slipped or the hand was tired – as well as the suffering bodies that have been abstracted away from these broken hands, but whom Kafka surely met while working in the 'Accident Office'.

The sequence of injured hands is followed by a repeated pairing of images of the round lathe and endangered fingers: the first represents the shaft separated from the lathe on an abstract shaded background widely used in machine drawing, the other the vulnerable sleeved hand of Figure 1 – miraculously still intact – slipping in the same direction but now without the threatened deadly contact with the right-angled blade (Fig. 3). Accidents still happen with circular shafts – worker fatigue and irregularities in the wood are still factors – but their effects are confined to cuts and grazes which, Kafka assures employers, 'need not even interrupt work' (*OW* 113, 199). There follows a reference to an image of four intact right hands with minor abrasions (Fig. 4) – the first on the thumb, the second on the tip of the third finger, the third on the upper third, fourth and fifth fingers and finally cuts on the tips of the second, third and fourth fingers. The contrast with the mutilated hands of the prior sequence is deliberately emphasized and visually aligned with the images of circular shafts. The image sequence ends with a reconditioned shaft evidently posing only minor risks to its operators.

Kafka's use of visual imagery in conjunction with text creates an imaginary field in which the accident appears in its peculiar conjuncture of chance and necessity. This is emphasized by the statistical populations of injured hands that obey the principle of the identity of indiscernibles: while the injuries differ, they remain recognizably members of the same family of accidents. The gap into which the first hand slipped haunts the sequence of accidents that the roster of mutilated hands encouraged their viewers

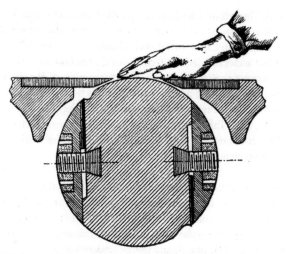

FIGURE 3 Round-shaft wood-planing machine with hand from 'Measures for Preventing Accidents from Wood-Planing Machines', 1909.

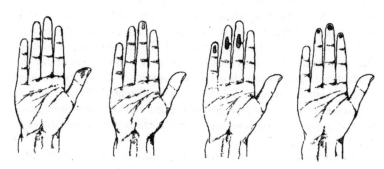

FIGURE 4 Row of grazed right hands from 'Measures for Preventing Accidents from Wood-Planing Machines', 1909.

to imagine. This strategy, raised to consummate heights in the article on accident prevention in quarries from the 1914 Annual Report, has other features that will also recur. One is the attention to sound that emerges in the closing lines of the report. What begins as an account of the economy of the cylindrical shafts – they encounter less air resistance and expend less energy – modulates into an evocation of the soundscapes associated with the two technologies. The cylindrical shafts 'run much more quietly' and, Kafka adds, 'there can be avoidance of the shrieks emanating from the old square shafts – shrieks that literally announced their danger.' (OW 115, 201). Here the coming of the accident is announced in aural premonition – the shriek of the lathe precedes that of its victim. The diminution of the premonitory howls of technology by the new cylinders reduces the stress on the workers, who Kafka concludes, 'can work carefree because of the complete absence of risk' (OW 115, 201). The hitherto silent images in the report retrospectively burst into sound: howls of the machines, screams of the workers and the quiet hum of the new cylinders – the images grow noisy.

* * *

Kafka is unjustly famed for his indifference to the outbreak of the First World War, noting in his diary, '2 August. Germany has declared war on Russia – afternoon swimming school' (D 301, 419). Compared to the overheated enthusiasm displayed by most of his contemporaries, the virtues of a cool dip in the Danube should not be underestimated, but nor should the horror that the conflict provoked in Kafka. The autumn of 1914 was one of Kafka's most desperately productive periods, resulting in The Trial, 'In the Penal Colony', the last chapter of America and the soon abandoned 'Building the Kalda Railway'. At the same time, Kafka the insurance official was completing his masterpiece on accident prevention in quarries while beginning an extensive study of the economic and psychic consequences of the war. The results were published in the Annual Reports of 1914 and 1915 and led to his becoming a leading public advocate for the foundation of a psychiatric clinic for the treatment of shell shock and other combat-related traumas. Far from being indifferent to the war and its consequences, Kafka was passionately engaged and became a leading civil servant engaged in managing the economic and human consequences of the conflict.[18]

His extensive study of the economic consequences of the war in the 1914 Annual Report shows another aspect of Kafka's official role; in addition to his juridical and technical knowledge he was adept in critically interpreting statistical data and able to draw appropriately nuanced conclusions from it. Appearing alongside 'Accident Prevention in Quarries', Kafka's statistical contributions to the 1914 Annual Report confront propagandistic rhetoric with detached but devastating statistical analysis. The first of three articles preceding 'Accident Prevention in Quarries' is composed of statistical schedules in which the accident appears not as the event of an individual hand entering an exposed lathe or a rockfall missing workers during their coffee break, but as a statistical population of hands to be injured and workers to be buried alive. The statistical schedules are despatches from the home front, showing the precise, statistical impact of the international conflict on the class war in Bohemia.

The aesthetic of the tables is austere but arresting: in most cases the vertical column lists 106 districts with varying entries on the horizontal column. A synoptic view of the variations allows for a clear picture of the impact of the war on productive activity in northern Bohemia. The first table lists the number of businesses in a district along with newly insured businesses and claims made in 1914. The second table divides the number of enterprises according to their industrial composition, revealing the proportion between industrial and agricultural sectors of production. The fourth and fifth tables present aggregate figures from 1913 and 1914 for the number of shifts worked in each district (3,599,713 for the district of Asch in 1913; 3,297,059 in 1914), the amount of wages paid (10,713,610 Kronen in 1913; 9,682,974 in 1914) and insurance contributions (115,856 Kronen in 1913; 96,114 in 1914). Thus it is possible to see which regions were gaining and which losing from the economic consequences of the war. The remaining two tables compare the number of newly reported accidents according to month for 1913 and 1914, an overall reduction from 26,206 to 20,750 that Kafka then breaks down according to the five-month period from August (outbreak of war in 1914) to December – registering a reduction from 10,990 accidents to 6,703. Kafka does not believe this reduction is due to enhanced safety at work, but rather to a shrinking of insured economic enterprise as well as delays in reporting from the districts due to the diversion of administrative resources to the war effort. He also notes that the threshold for reporting an accident had changed with the war, not only for employers but also for the workers who understand that 'such injuries are in no proportion to the wounds struck by the war' (AS 338). Kafka's subtle interpretation of the accident statistics, reading them against the grain of their immediate sense, is followed by a similar comparative analysis of wage payments between 1913 and 1914.

The analysis of wage payments allows insight into the relative well-being or otherwise of the working class. Kafka's analysis is once again subtle and counter-intuitive. He replaces the list of named districts with a number, and the amount and percentage of wage variation noted for each district: in aggregate wages fell by 90,617,089 Kronen over the year, a fall of 14.49%, thus registering the cost of the war to the working class as a whole in reduced wages. Kafka then gives an analysis of selected districts according to the degree of variation in wages beginning with the highest reduction – 32.40% for Chotebor – and proceeding downwards with reference to the industrial composition of the district. In district number 31 for example – Karlsbad – wages fell by 23.58%, which Kafka explains by the precipitate decline of the porcelain and hotel industries along with a trend-typical reduction in building activity. At the end of this chronicle of the economic catastrophe of the war for the Bohemian working class, Kafka notes that exceptions to the trend where wages increased are 'few and uncharacteristic' (AS 355). Kafka then produces a composite table that correlates wages with shifts worked and deduces that the wage per shift remained largely stable (between 3.20 and 3.23 Kronen in 1913 and 1914); however, he notes that this stability represents a break with the trend of rising daily wage rates evident from 1911. Stability indeed was a mark of regression and may be linked to other wartime restrictions reducing the number of hours worked. Kafka then links this situation to the contributions paid to the Institute and administrative delays by the districts in reporting accidents to portray an image of economic, political and administrative confusion parallel to the confused conduct of the war at the front. What is striking in these analyses – which immediately precede 'Accident Prevention in Quarries' – is their attention to movements within a statistical population, individualized only with respect to district and the economic and political constitution of the districts. The columns give a sense of the war as a destructive avalanche sweeping its way through the more or less fragile industrial and politico-administrative structures that stood in its path.

In these analyses of the accident returns for the districts of Bohemia, Kafka surveys the impact of the 'great accident' that was the war on the constitution of productive industry and the economic condition of the Bohemian working class. Kafka returned to this theme in his last contributions to the series of Annual Reports in the 1915 texts on 'Risk Classification in Wartime', 'The Insurance of Barrack Construction' and 'Accident Prevention'. The first is a short report without statistical armature of the (minimal) changes in risk assignment provoked by the war, and the second a call for the insurance of civilian workers involved in Ministry of War construction work such as building barracks. The third more extensive contribution reports on the difficulties of sustaining the Institute's Accident Prevention Agenda under conditions of wartime production. This report – Kafka's last contribution to the series of Annual Reports – ends with a peculiar detail that is extremely difficult to interpret. It relates a specific accident, the last to be publicly discussed by Kafka in an insurance and accident prevention setting, and in many ways is Kafka's last word on the industrial accident, but one which casts all the previous ones in a strangely defiant light.

The last marginal subheading of the report advises 'Caution in Using Prisoners of War' and offers a breathtakingly sardonic perspective on industrial accident prevention. In it Kafka describes 'a special problem of accident prevention related to the war' recorded 'last year' in Germany but not yet encountered within the Institute's territory. It is the case of a POW under forced labour deliberately provoking an accident: 'A prisoner of war was employed as operator of a large overhead crane. One day, for no good reason, he set the crane's hoist motor at full power. When the hoisting cable broke, the pulley block shot into the air and flew into the workspace behind, without, by chance, hitting anyone' (*OW* 333, 493). Noting that 'There was no doubt that the prisoner of war's principal intention had been to disable the crane and to disrupt the progress of work' (*OW* 333, 493), Kafka passed on to his readers the German authority's advice not to employ POW labour in sensitive areas without comment. Yet what does it mean for him to conclude his report on accident prevention in this way?

The account has a number of salient features: the first is the use of forced labour and the second the ironic description of the event as an accident – 'for no good reason' – an industrial accident; this is followed by a parodic reflection by the accident prevention theorist on how to prevent this kind of accident. But does the POW's act satisfy Kafka's definition of an accident? It is the rare case of an explicit act of sabotage – a defiant accident, a forced labourer using industrial technology as a weapon against itself and its owners. How can this be prevented, and what place does the prevention of industrial sabotage have in a report on accident prevention in general? It represents a little act of sabotage on Kafka's own part, throwing the usual productive activity of producing a report into reverse but without harming any fellow workers. The observation can be connected to Kafka's broader sense of class war where accidents are usually caused by employers sabotaging their workers' lives for profit and the place of the Institute occupying the front line in a class war where accidents serve as a visible sign of a strategy of attrition.

It is striking that Kafka ends his public career of reporting on accident statistics with a case of sabotage, or a defiant accident in which the victim is the machine and the militarized productive process to which it contributes. In this last case, hidden in the reports for over a century, Kafka ironically deploys rhetorical deference to German experience in accident prevention in a sardonic deflation of his own work in accident prevention. It should be read alongside Kafka's comment on his work reported by Brod: 'How modest these people are. They come begging to us. Instead of storming into the Institute and smashing everything to bits, they come begging' (Stach 20, 464). However, Kafka's biographer mentions a previous case of violent defiance at the Institute that became part of its institutional folklore and was undoubtedly known to Kafka: on 29 December 1899 an unemployed labourer on hearing that his demand for compensation had been turned down by the Institute began to scream and vandalize the office; he even pulled a knife on a member of staff before being forcibly restrained by the police. His name was Josef Kafka ...[19]

Accident reports

The little car story ended with Kafka's testimony to the interminable writing of the accident in the policeman's notebook. As an unenthusiastic pioneer in the emergent discourse of automobile accident insurance, Kafka knew the story would continue to unfold until arriving at the desk of one of his French accident insurance colleagues. The accident would provoke consequences and narratives far removed from the immediate testimonies to the event. The story 'Metamorphosis', written towards the end of 1912, and the decription of the death of Therese's mother in *America* (1911–12) may be understood as extended accident reports from the realms of circulation and production, one involving a travelling salesman, the other a construction worker – spheres in which Kafka had expert knowledge. Both narrate the *consequences* of an accident, its immediate impact and the damage it bequeathed to those left to live on and make sense of it.

No story has provoked such a range of incompatible interpretations as the 'Metamorphosis' that became Kafka's signature narrative of the transformation of a commercial traveller into a verminous insect. Aptly described in the title of Stanley Corngold's early book as the *commentator's despair*, the story has provoked some far-fetched interpretative feats ranging from victim Gregor Samsa metamorphosing into the Christian messiah to dark suspicions of incest in the Samsa family worthy of *120 Days of Sodom*. 'Symbolic' readings of the story abound; even the three obnoxious lodgers who join the Samsa family in the third chapter of the story have found themselves cast as a 'symbol' of the male genitalia.[20] But it has only recently been understood as an accident narrative and its many allusions to Sacher-Masoch's *Venus in Furs* (another story that begins with an 'uneasy dream') given their proper weight. It can also be understood as a parable of defiance and sabotage – its protagonist is a forced labourer, a debt slave, and his strike against his conditions of life and work are diverted, like the defiant insistence of the man from the country in the later parable 'Before the Law', into masochistic self-destruction.

The accidental character of the metamorphosis is announced at the very beginning of the story: 'As Gregor Samsa one morning awoke from uneasy dreams he found himself transformed in his bed into a monstruous vermin' (*S* 89, 96). The story begins with an accident, as Stanley Corngold explains in his illuminating commentary: 'There are no empirical events leading up to it, no attempts on Kafka's part to explain precisely why it has occurred, in what sense the change is deserved or otherwise intelligible' (Corngold 2004b, 61). The event that breaks with everything that went before nevertheless has its own necessity, for it emerges in the telling that Samsa is a debt slave, sold to his boss in order to pay off the debts of his father's failed business and supporting his exploitative and parasitic family. The accident of his transformation may somehow be related to his profession and to his masochistic way of defying it by becoming 'vermin', like his masochistic namesake in *Venus in Furs*.

At the risk of adding another strange beast to the menagerie of 'Metamorphosis' interpretations, it might be suggested that this strange story combines an account of masochistic defiance with a report on the impact of an industrial injury. The air of defiance that suffuses the story is repeatedly diverted into resentful compromise. Gregor, who shares the slave name adopted by the obsessed Severin in *Venus in Furs*, defies his repressive family by displaying an image of the dominatrix Wanda on his wall, mounted in a frame he lovingly constructed with his fretsaw during his free evenings.[21] His refusal to get up and go to work, cursing his job – 'The devil take it all!' (*S* 90, 97) – quickly yields to the worry, 'Let me try that with the boss; I'd fly out of my job on wings' (*S* 90, 97). If it wasn't for his parents debts 'I'd have long gone to the boss and told him exactly what I think of him', but 'For the moment, though, I'd better get up since my train goes at five' (*S* 90, 97–8). The same movement of eruption and acquiescence occurs later in the story when his anger at his family clearing the furniture out of his room led him to protect the image of Venus in Furs with his body: 'He sat on his picture and would not give it up. He would rather fly in Grete's face' (*S* 119, 135), but this defiance is hardly engaged than it collapses with him trying to 'propitiate his father' (*S* 120, 136). Similarly, his surge of defiance at the lodgers' indifference towards his sister's violin playing rapidly abates, leaving him to crawl back to his room, disingenuously protesting to himself that his 'good intentions' had been mistaken.

These half-executed, half-swallowed acts of defiance and sabotage lead Gregor into the utter darkness of his room and the decision, prompted by his sister, to 'disappear'. Having defied his job by disappearing from work, he now defies his family by disappearing from their midst. His last breath coincides with the gloaming of the day that will find him thrown out with the rest of the rubbish piled up in his room after his change. This inverted, masochistic defiance sits consistently with the recent reading of the story as an industrial accident report. John Zilcosky's groundbreaking article, '"Samsa war

Reisender": Trains, Trauma, and the Unreadable Body', convincingly situates 'Metamorphosis' within the context of the forgotten medical discourse of train trauma and identifies Samsa as a trauma victim. He is an industrial accident statistic, a professional traveller who on the fateful day suffered from Traveller's Occupational Illness (*Berufskrankheit der Reisender*). Zilcosky shows how train trauma or injury to the nervous system thought to be provoked by the shaking of the body through rail travel along with co-morbid disruptions of perception from travel at speed and anxieties around time and punctuality (pathologies Kafka portrayed in 'Wedding Preparations in the Country')[22] were exacerbated by the rail system having its own time out of phase with public time. It was considered to be an intangible injury prefiguring shell shock or the controversial psychic injury for which Kafka subsequently became an authority.[23] The recognition of such trauma as a medical condition was important for the emergence of the late nineteenth-century insurance industry since state accident insurance schemes were modelled on railway accident liability.[24]

But like shell shock, this injury, the result of a modern industrial accident, lacked physical aetiology and was open to suspicion, especially by the medical profession. It was a technogenic illness, with the train's vibrations leaving imperceptible injuries to mind and body.[25] As with shell shock, the existence of the illness had to be proven, with the burden of proof falling on the victim, making credence essential to diagnosis. The accident narrative of 'Metamorphosis' had then to convince the family, the firm and also in the end the 'insurance doctor' that what happened was strange but true: Samsa's complaint was in the avant-garde of trauma aetiologies.[26] From the outset of the story Samsa's illness, his *metamorphosis*, was considered feigned, a masochistic act of defiance anticipating later diagnoses of shell shock during the First World War. It was variously interpreted as an attempt to force his father to go out to work or to defraud his employer and insurance company. The latter possibility is explicitly addressed early in the story when Gregor worries, 'The boss himself would be sure to come with the sick-insurance doctor, would reproach his parents with their son's laziness, and would cut all excuses short by referring to the insurance doctor for whom there existed only perfectly healthy but workshy people. And would he be completely wrong in this case?' (*S* 91, 98–9). The question concerns the truth or fiction of Gregor's illness/transformation: has he really been injured in the pursuit of his profession or is he dissembling? The once reliable and obedient Gregor has metamorphosed not so much into an insect as into a question mark.

Gregor then has to prove the veracity of his illness to himself and his family and establish its aetiology in an industrial accident for his boss and insurance doctor. Is everybody so sure that this accident is not in reality an act of masochistic defiance? The story describes an experiment in establishing what is required to prove the truth of this illness and its aetiology in an industrial accident to a sceptical family, employer and insurance doctor. The story remains – as has long been recognized – arrested at the event with which it opens. Unlike the country doctor, and unlike Freud in the case of shell shock, medicine is never summoned to decide upon this malaise. Although the hospital across the road looms in and out of vision throughout the story, there is no appeal to a medical decision on the *truth* of the accident or *metamorphosis*, nor is there any hint that the *Krankenkasse* is paying medical insurance to the family for Gregor's time off for an injury at work. In the story he remains confined to familial logic and the doctor is never summoned to adjudicate on the truth of the illness/metamorphosis in the name of medical power as he will later in the eponymous story of *A Country Doctor*.

'Metamorphosis' is located at an intersection of a traditional and oppressive familial logic and the emergent logic of industrial accidents and insurance compensation and capital. It turns out that the father's debt Gregor was working to discharge had already been paid off even though he had been given the impression that it had still five or six years to run. (S 90, 98) This logic of sacrifice continues to unfold in the story, arriving at the revelation that the subject of metamorphosis was less Gregor than the Samsa family.[27] After his departure his family seem to succeed in achieving what Gregor failed to realize even at the cost of sacrificing his human identity: taking the day off their recently resumed jobs they leave their apartment to go for a tram ride in the country.

Zilcosky perceptively describes the Samsa family outing in terms of a distinction between the pathogenetic high-speed train travel that brought on Gregor's illness and the transformative, leisurely tram-ride that takes his family in the first draft to the park, but in the second to the more indefinite 'country' (*ins Freie*). This departure – the family allowing the cleaning lady to throw out the husk of Gregor with the rubbish (powerful evidence for Adorno's case for Kafka's 'refusal' or passage from the human to waste) and then themselves taking flight – differs completely from the accelerated deportation that closes *America* with Karl Rossman rushed by express train into the void. It appears almost emancipatory as the daughter strikes her parents for the first time as voluptuous and sexually mature, making them realize 'the time was coming to look for a suitable man for her too' (S 139, 161). Even thought the family metamorphosis is almost complete there remains a certain ambivalence – the moment of freedom brought by Gregor's sacrifice releases the sister's sexuality, but it also threatens to be immediately brought under control again by the parents deciding to find her a man, to choose her partner and dictate her satisfactions. Just as Gregor was set to work off the family's debt and permitted the compensation of pornography – the picture of Venus in furs on the wall – so too the sister is about to be assigned her place in the family's social and sexual economy.

The broader accident narrative in 'Metamorphosis' ends ambivalently with the momentary liberation of the survivors before the reassertion of the familial domination that was Gregor's undoing. *America* is less ambivalent: the consequences of accidents in the novel are always melancholy for victims and their survivors. Itself a peculiarly accident prone novel, *America* drew on Kafka's work in the 'Accident Section' of the Institute, and a specialist knowledge of accidents in the building trade clearly informs Therese's narration of the death of her mother on a building site.[28] It serves as one of the examples of what Wagenbach has described as the superimposition of 'official and literary languages' – the others being the commentary on the hazardous quarries and the scene of the execution of Josef K. in *The Trial* (Koch and Wagenbach, 37).

Therese's telling the story of her mother's death to Karl Rossmann is a key instance of an accident narrative nested within the larger accident report that is *America*. It is often regarded as an 'embedded narrative' whose structural significance is to serve as a moment in which to 'mirror and condense fundamental aspects of the novel as a whole';[29] its function is analogous with that of the parable 'Before the Law' in *The Trial* and Olga's story in *The Castle*. In the case of *America* it is the story of an accident destined to happen, one taking place under the sign of necessity. It was originally written in the first person, suggesting that it had a special place in a novel largely written in the third person and was subsequently revised to adapt it to a third-person narrative.[30] It exemplifies the genre of accident narrative right down to its subtle framing in terms of the figural conjuncture of landslide and fall.

The ambiguity surrounding Therese's mother's death has been noted, but not correctly identified. It is less a question of whether she fell accidentally or committed suicide than one of the peculiar modality of the accident.[31] From the standpoint of insurance, a relatively stable number of a population of immigrant workers had to die accidentally and in this case it was the turn of Therese's mother. Hence the description of a certain fatality taking its course in her accident, one which should not too quickly be ascribed to suicidal intent on her part.[32] Indeed in the description of her mother's last hours searching for shelter in a New York winter's night, the theme of intractable winds is prominent, from which it can inferred that the huntress or figure of the necessary accident is getting closer.[33]

Therese (Karl Rossmann's colleague at the Grand Occidental Hotel) had 'no secrets' from Karl and one day, while they were both watching the traffic go by from her window, she told the story of how her mother died in a narrative combining descriptions of extreme weather conditions and the fall from a scaffolding. Therese remembers hurrying after her mother during a blizzard, searching for a place to sleep, and how all possible routes forward began to close down except the one leading to the accident. When admitted to a building, they just ranged its icy corridors, balconies and staircases where no door opened and looming figures discouraged entry. In retrospect Therese recalled a point when her mother gave up searching for shelter and concentrated on just keeping moving through the crowded corridors: 'Naturally they were not running in a way to move quickly forward, but only with the most extreme exertion of which they were capable which could have been in reality just as much a mere crawl' (A 321, 155). There is a sense of the architecture itself closing in on the condemned in order to ensure their prompt arrival at the accident:

Therese didn't know whether between midnight and five o'clock they had been in twenty buildings, in two, or only one. The corridors of these tenements were cunningly planned to save space but without consideration of easy orientation; how often did they come down the same corridor. Therese had surely the obscure recollection that they went again out of the door of a house they had been eternally seeking but it also seemed to her that on reaching the street they plunged back into the house again.

(A 321–2, 155)

She could be describing the experience of Rossmann himself, or later Josef K. on whom the world slowly closed in, leaving open no avenues of escape.

Therese describes how her mother went to her fall; with a heavy fatality she picked up a hod, and made her way up the scaffolding, described in terms of a harsh verticality that intimates the *Apparat* in 'On the Penal Colony'. She inconspicuously negotiated her way past the bricklayers working on the top of the wall until she came to a pile of bricks carelessly left at the end of the railing. Whether out of fatigue, fatality or with intent, the mother 'walked into the heap of bricks, and there her skill seemed to have left her, for she overturned the heap of bricks and fell over them into the deep' (A 323, 157). Her fall was succeeded by a landslide: 'Many bricks rolled after her and then after a while a heavy plank loosened itself from somewhere and crashed down on her' (*A* 323, 157). She died of the injuries from her fall and debris that buried her after it; yet the bricks and plank were but a token of the larger, inconspicuous landslide that had been approaching her, compressing and distorting the time and space surrounding her until she fell to her death. Therese's last vision of her mother offers a macabre image of the consummation of her marriage with chance: 'Therese's last memory of her mother was of her lying there with wide opened legs in her checked skirt from Pomerania, and of how the rough plank lying on top of her almost covered her ...' (*A* 323, 157). This mother now lost to her daughter was momentarily found by the world – 'people came running from all directions' – while the soundscape of 'a man shouting angrily from the top of the building' completes the horror of the recollection.

At the end of the reported speech of Therese's story, the narrator, who is clearly no longer Karl Rossmann, reflects on its character as an accident narrative. The shock of the witness reverberates in the details preceding and accompanying the accident, details that are literally scoured for meaning:

> It had grown late when Therese finished her story, She had thoroughly narrated, as was otherwise not her custom, even such insignificant details as the description of the scaffolding poles that separately soared into heaven, until forced to break off with tears in her eyes. She still knew every detail of what happened then even after ten years, and because that sight of her mother up there on the half-finished ground floor was her last memory of the life of her mother and she could never portray it for her friend clearly enough, she wanted to come back to it again at the end of her story, but blocked, she put her face in her hands and said not another word.
>
> (*A* 324, 157)

In the search for some meaning to the accident – an event that defies meaning – no detail can afford to be overlooked. Each has to be scrutinized again and again, for even the slightest and seemingly irrelevant detail may prove to be the key to unlocking the fugitive meaning denied by the accident. In this case, the bricks and plank that followed the fall testify to the avalanche of circumstances that had already conspired to leave no other exit open for the desperate migrant worker than just this fall. She like her fellow immigrant Karl Rossmann did not just fall but was not so gently and literally 'pushed aside'.

Accident warnings

After heavy rains on 1 April 1911 a rockfall at a quarry in northern Bohemia cost the life of a worker and left two others seriously injured. The accident was the direct result of unsafe working practices on the site. Instead of extracting with stepped terraces, the workers were quarrying beneath an overhanging rock which duly collapsed. The accident had reverberations that extended as far as the Ministry of the Interior in Vienna. For it was also an administrative accident waiting to happen, one which involved the Institute and in particular its Appeals Department where, it may be recalled, the responsible official was Dr Franz Kafka. In the 1910 reclassification exercise, this very quarry had been favourably reclassified under the median risk category of 59% on the strength of a favourable report by an official Trades Inspector. The quarry owner appealed and his case was reviewed by Kafka's Appeals Department who agreed on 23 December 1910 a further reduction of the risk classification to 57%, a proportion that was further reduced on appeal to the Office of the Governor to 55% on 6 January 1911. Barely four months later all this was revealed to be a sham and the Institute and its responsible official – Kafka – shown to be dupes of an unscrupulous businessman adept at playing the classification game. The insurance penalties paid by the Institute for this single accident exceeded 10,000 Kronen and opened it to charges of incompetence and public ridicule.

The disaster of 1 April 1911 was in many ways an accident waiting to happen. It was a disaster not only for the workers at the quarry but also for the officials at the Institute. The inadequate working practices at the quarry not only enhanced the risks of an accident taking place there, but also exposed some hazardous administrative practices at the Institute that was insuring them. It was in short a double accident, the slippage of the rocks in the quarry leading to administrative subsidence in the Institute. The structural flaw in the Institute's procedures for risk assessment lay in the source and thus the quality of the information available to its officials to assign risk classifications and set insurance premiums. The 1887 Workers Accident Law expressly forbade independent inspections by the Institute, sabotaging in advance the ability of its officials to make independent judgements by making them reliant on the reports of Trade Inspectors. During the 1905 reclassification exercise the Institute complained to the Ministry of the Interior about the reliability of these reports, suggesting collusion between inspectors and employers to mislead the Institute and lower risk classifications. In an attempt to make its classifications more robust, the Institute supplemented this source of information with questionnaires sent to employers, the scrutiny of wage lists and the audit of accident insurance claims from individual firms. The entry of quarries and quarrying into the compulsory insurance scheme exacerbated these problems by presenting the Institute with constantly changing worksites with informal employment cultures that would evade all but the most constant scrutiny. The legal limits within which the Institute was required to work meant that an accident such as that of 1 April 1911 was inevitable but it was one that would this time, under Kafka's leadership, provoke a series of preventative measures to ensure that it would not happen again.

The decision to reduce the risk classification on what turned out to be an extremely dangerous quarry exposed all the inadequacies of the Institute's sources of information and the procedures that it was bound to follow with respect to them. It was made on the basis of the owner's dishonest response to the Institute's main independent source of information – the questionnaire – corroborated by a Trade Inspector's favourable report. Kafka's erroneous decision expressed a structural fault – an overhanging crag – in the institutional architecture of Austro-Hungarian social insurance by showing neither the integrity of the employer's response to questionnaires nor the Trade Inspector's report could be relied upon. But it also pointed to an administrative failure in the procedures of his own Appeals Department, since it emerged subsequently that insurance payments relating to this quarry during the previous five years amounted to the enormous sum of 33,000 Kronen – a payment that would have required a reclassification of risk to 144%. This information, a clear warning sign of impending disaster, was available to the Institute but the audit did not reach the official (Kafka) responsible for appeals to risk classification.

Kafka's response was vigorous and administratively radical. In an administrative guerrilla campaign of memoranda submitted under the signature of the Director he questioned the impartiality of the Trade Inspectors' reports. It seems that even the employer's responses to the questionnaires often proved more honest than the inspectors' reports:

> In their efforts to obtain the lowest possible classification for certain firms, many trade inspectors go even further. The information in their reports contradicts in these cases the information provided by the owners in the questionnaires. In most of these cases, the disparity between the reports and the questionnaires can of course be explained by the fact that a single inspection conducted on a chance date that happened to be especially unfavourable for determining the true facts (particularly in quarries, brickyards, and the construction industries)

cannot provide as complete and true a picture of a firm as a properly completed questionnaire.

(OW 129, 668)

And in those cases when the Institute was able legally to control the reports, 'in every case where an inspection was conducted, it had the expected result and contradicted the main points of the responsible trade inspector's assessment' (*OW* 138, 680). This was tragically the case with quarry stone works M. no. 443/92 cited at length by Kafka and the site of the fatal 1 April accident.[34]

Kafka's approach to this problem – radical and almost certainly *ultra vires* with respect to the 1887 law – was described in the section of his 1914 report on 'Accident Prevention in Quarries' entitled 'Reasons for Demanding Constant and Overall Inspection for All Quarries'.[35] The background to this revolutionary contribution to administrative accident prevention was the campaign Kafka pursued after the 1911 quarry accident to extend the Institute's powers if not rights of inspection. This accounts for the otherwise unexpected role played in it by the 'criminal case against Josef Renelt' (which features in Kafka's correspondence with Felice as the 'Aussig Trial'). This concerned the Institute's legal action – led by Kafka – against an employer who tried to minimize if not evade paying insurance premiums by underestimating his wage returns *and* dishonestly claiming in reply to the Institute's questionnaire that his quarry workers were mainly occupied in 'orchard work'. It was in the context of a new and aggressive policy of extending wherever possible its powers of inspection in the case of quarries that the Institute decided to use legal action against such an obvious rogue employer, less to compel payment of his insurance premiums than for the opportunity it offered to extend but most importantly legalize the precedent of the Institute's powers of inspection.

As the architect of this new policy, Kafka assumed responsibility for the case which he pursued with his Enforcer, the courageous Institute Engineer Julius Schönfeld. The case quickly focused less on Renelt's negligence than on the legality of the information concerning his practices extracted by Schönfeld during his unannounced visit to the orchard/quarry. In a document dated 25 June 1913 and addressed to the Office of the Governor in Prague, Kafka led the Institute's appeal against Renelt's first-level acquittal, by referring to a 'sworn deposition' of the outcome of an Institute inspection but carefully qualifying it as 'not in any way an inspection of the business' (*OW* 230, 598). Kafka and the defence knew that such an inspection was *ultra vires* with respect to the 1887 Act, and so he sought to describe it in a way that at least verbally remained within the Act. He maintained that the visit was only 'an investigation of the wage situation "on site" which the Institute is legally entitled to carry out according to §23 of the Accident-Insurance Act' (OW 230, 598). Continuing to insulate the evidence against charges of the Institute exceeding its powers of inspection, Kafka tries to make a case for the Institute's new surveillance practices, claiming it was sometimes 'necessary to begin the investigation, not at the main office of the business – in this case with Renelt in Pömmerle – but at the employees nearest work site – in this case with the foreman at the quarry' (OW 230, 598). Kafka justifies the questionable legality of this procedure by referring first to the 'practical reason' of avoiding the employer exercising undue influence on his employees during the visit, second to the fact that the records are kept on site, and finally with a subtle judicial appeal to the spirit if not the letter of the law: '§23 offers no provision whatever to the effect that such on-site investigations must be conducted in the presence of the employer himself or that the employer must be informed or even that his consent must be obtained' (OW 230, 598). This is a reading or rather extension of the law supported by citing an Administrative Court precedent. Kafka on behalf of the Institute is clearly using this case against an employer of almost pantomime villain proportions as a pretext to justify new covert surveillance techniques and thus extending the power of inspection permitted under §23 to cases where it was forbidden under §17.

The Institute's 28 June 1913 Statement on the Renelt case – which continued to focus on the record books for wage payments – gives a further glimpse of the dangers attending such investigations. The Institute's inspector, Schönfeld, who was on the frontline of the Institute's new aggressive inspection policy (he appears in Kafka's postcard to Felice from Aussig as 'sitting opposite me' and reading to him while Kafka writes the postcard) (F 246), insisted on inspecting the wage book. He claimed powers 'as a sworn representative of the Institute' and 'Though the employer acceded to my wish, he was so agitated that he was shaking, and he held the book by its covers with both hands, so I could only leaf through it hurriedly. Since I feared that his agitation, as well as that of the quarry foreman (we were alone in the wooden shack at the quarry), might degenerate into something worse and that they might not be able to control themselves towards me, I gave up for the moment using the book for the purpose of establishing wages' (OW 235, 605; underlining in original: see also the account of a physical attack upon Schönfeld by an agitated employer at an earlier inspection, pp. 245–6:). Renelt's lawyer pressed the issue of the Institute exceeding its powers of inspection in his reply of 14 August 1913 in which he questions 'the difference between "on site-inspections" and "inspection" … in spite of the careful wording in the Workmen Accident

Insurance Institute's statement' (*OW* 238, 610) and insists that the employer's consent is legally required. His defence very cleverly took the offensive by calling on the Institute to initiate disciplinary proceedings against Engineer Schönfeld for exceeding his powers of inspection and thus to disassociate itself from his actions. The larger issues at stake ensured that the case remained blocked, and indeed a settlement with Renelt was not reached until 1922 when Kafka had retired from the Institute and the underlying legal issues were no longer relevant under the new regime of the Republic of Czechoslovakia.

Kafka's report on 'Accident Prevention in Quarries' was his considered response to the double accident of 1911. It attempted to implement accident prevention measures not only for the workers in the quarries but also for the officials in the Institute. It is a text of remarkable complexity and even beauty of which he was justly proud and that he distributed among his friends. The report is divided into three sections. The first reviews the current state of accident prevention in quarries using statistical evidence and describes the possibilities and limits of intervention, concluding with a call for reform: 'Reasons for Demanding Constant and Overall Inspections for All Quarries'. This manifesto for administrative accident prevention serves as a bridge between the statistical analysis of quarry accidents and the second part of the report that presents the results of a questionably legal campaign of photo-surveillance. This section comprises a sequence of 14+1 photographs of dangerous quarries accompanied by a commentary, and is discussed in detail below in Chapter 3 ('Surveillance'). After reviewing this calamitous sequence of accidents waiting to happen, Kafka returns in the third section to 'Means for Remedying These Poor Conditions', all of which point to the necessity of enhancing the Institute's rights and powers of inspection and incorporating a commentary on a 15th photograph *hors series*.

Kafka's reform agenda is explicit from the outset: the article begins with a critique of 'The means available to the Institute and the possibilities and rights the law provides for its work in the field of safety' (*OW* 273, 378). These do not allow it, unlike the comparable case of the German Trade Associations, 'to address the entire field of accident prevention', but mean that it must intervene tactically in a field 'where there is an urgent need from both a social and a statistical standpoint' (*OW* 273, 378). The article that follows is one such targeted intervention, focusing on the dangers of quarry work. Kafka cites the Institute's successes with agricultural and wood-planing machinery before moving to the campaign to clean up the quarries, or in Kafka's words 'the Institute's endeavours to restructure in its territory the quarries whose safety regulations have been neglected in order to install rational operating procedures' (*OW* 274, 379). Kafka is thus clear that the neglect of industrial safety is not restricted to rogue employers like Renalt but was fully consistent with the technical rationalisation of the extraction industry. The implementation of a rationalization agenda by employers at the expense of workers' safety required the Institute to have the authority to collect precise information on operating conditions in the industry and the power to enforce safety measures. As it stood in 1914 the Institute possessed *de jure* authority for neither of these tasks.

Kafka tactically opens his case for implementing a regime of capillary power with budgetary considerations, or the enormous losses borne by all the participants in the Accident Insurance scheme due to bad practice in some firms active in the extraction industry. He then deduces (somewhat mysteriously) from the statistics that 'The issue here is not unforeseen chance occurrences during the operation of machinery but primarily the correct application and management of human labour' (*OW* 274, 379). He is clearly pursuing a tactic of divide and rule in which informing the readers of the report that they were subsidizing avoidable accidents would contribute to ensuring their tacit support for the measures that followed.

In the second part of the first section, Kafka describes the kind of laws required to protect workers, but speaks of them as if they were already in existence. This is one of the many strange temporal effects Kafka employs throughout the article, describing as if it were real the fiction of a future well-regulated extraction industry. The key to arriving at this future is constant oversight and inspection of changing worksites, a step that seemed unavoidable after the 1911 accident when 'The institute therefore took it as its mission to arrange for the implementation of the safety regulations' (*OW* 276, 383). The mission required regular Institute inspections, but since these are illegal and permitted only *after* an accident has occurred, Kafka reserves 'The details of how to conduct the inspections ... for a later time' (*OW* 276, 383) – that is to say, to a time when they have been legalized. He nevertheless appeals in the section on 'Call for the Supervision of Agricultural Quarries' for 'permanent supervision of the quarries' by 'those state agencies that have to assure the public safety' (*OW* 277, 385), namely the Institute that was specifically forbidden to carry out such supervision.

This section, 'Reasons for Demanding Constant and Overall Inspections for all the Quarries', concludes the first part of the report by describing the 'new impetus [given] to our efforts to establish overall and systematic inspection of all quarries' by the accident of 1911. It traces the administrative accident provoked by the quarry disaster to the Institute's lack of the right of inspection; it could not 'as a rule crucially bring about the discovery of such poor conditions, lacking both the right to inspect the firms as well as lacking the necessary authority' (*OW* 282, 393). When the Institute 'actually did inspect a firm and discovered adverse operating conditions, all we achieved was our words against theirs' (*OW* 282, 393) since the Institute's inspections had no legal force and could not be taken into account even in its own risk classification procedures. But the mortal accident of 1911 permitted the Institute to make a retrospective inspection of the industrial accident. Kafka used this opportunity in an innovative, politically astute but questionably legal way to introduce *de facto* systematic inspection and surveillance of quarries.[36] Claiming that after the accident of 1911, 'The Institute could no longer stand idly by. It therefore decided not only to have its own authorities conduct an inspection but also to have the results of the inspection documented photographically and to do the same in other quarries' (*OW* 284, 394-5) Kafka openly defied the letter and the spirit of the law. To extend the Institute's retrospective right to document the 1911 accident for the purposes of its internal inquiry to encompass other potentially dangerous quarries was an audacious step.[37] The decision to use photography to document this and potential future accidents was provoked by Kafka's evident outrage that the owner of the 1911 quarry included an entirely fictional drawing in his response to the Institute's questionnaire showing that all excavation was terraced. Kafka here decided to privilege the veracity of documentary photography over the duplicity of a drawing. His 1914 article on 'Accident Prevention in Quarries' takes a technology used in reports on accidents to point to, and to form an archive of, potential accidents waiting to happen.

The sequence of 14 commented photographs (discussed below) is followed by the third and concluding section of the report devoted to 'Means for Remedying These Poor Conditions'. This section begins with a frank avowal that in spite of the dreadful conditions in the extraction industry and in spite of the view expressed by the Trade Inspector cited at the end of the second section that dangerous practices in the industry 'cannot be eradicated, in spite of all official efforts' (*OW* 294, 409), improvement is possible. Yet, Kafka adds, speaking in the name of the Institute, 'very different means must be applied than any used before' (*OW* 294, 409). The first of these is predictably 'systematic inspection' – the failure of the current inspection regime is underlined again by reference to the 1911 accident and the call issued for 'a different arrangement for inspections' (*OW*, 295, 409). The second reform measure involves the inspection of blasting procedures, with Kafka commenting on German practice and referring to the 15th photograph of a model quarry taken at the permanent exhibition on industrial safety in Charlottenburg, Berlin, as a model of good practice.

The appeal to superior German practice continues in the next measure which advocates 'Photographic Documentation of the Situation after Accidents'. Kafka calls for photographic surveillance less to document 'operating conditions in general' – which will be the task of the annual inspections – but in order to constitute an archive for the purposes of the Institute. Photographic documentation is directed less to preventing accidents in quarries than future administrative accidents in the Institute. Appealing to German practice, Kafka sees the purpose of these photographs as 'retrospectively to document the characteristic situation that led to an accident' (*OW* 297, 412). His main justification for the existence of this archive – which the second section of the report had already implemented – is cognitive; it will 'significantly increase our understanding of the factors giving rise to accidents in individual quarries and in general' (*OW* 297, 413). The archive will constitute a resource for understanding the accident and promoting rational accident prevention in the quarries, but it will also serve as an accident prevention measure for the administrators at work in the Institute. They will be able to show, retrospectively, the dangerous practices that led to accidents and unofficially use the photographic documents in assigning risk evaluations for accident insurance.

The contribution ends with some considerations on the issue of risk evaluations and insurance premiums, of most interest to the employers reading the Annual Reports. In it, Kafka extends his politics of divide and rule in which co-operative employers – the opposite of the distinctively uncooperative Renelt – will be rewarded with favourable risk assessments. Their co-operation will also increase the amount of information available to the Institute, allowing it to understand the character of the accident – in quarries and more generally – and to be able better to heed the warnings and ensure prevention. However, there will always remain the irreducible accident, the unavoidable one that is on its way in spite of all the knowledge gained and all the measures taken to prevent it.

The accidental messiah

In mid-October 1914, Kafka interrupted work on *The Trial* in order to write the story 'In the Penal Colony' and the last chapter of *America*. After reading the story to his friends on 2 December 1914 he let it languish for two years before reading it again at the Goltz art gallery bookshop in Munich on Friday evening, 10 November 1916. One of a series of 'Evenings for Modern Literature', Kafka's story was advertised as a 'Tropical Münchhausiade' and 'a previously unpublished novella'.[38] The evening was memorable for three women in his rapidly shrinking audience allegedly fainting and Kafka finding himself described in the press, not inaccurately, as a 'sensualist of terror'.[39] In spite of the response, the reading proved catalytic, provoking the rapid composition between 16 November 1916 and 17 February 1917 of the stories making up *A Country Doctor* collection[40] and then, in August 1917, Kafka's return to settle unfinished business in the penal colony.

'In the Penal Colony' is dominated by an elaborate machine of execution – the *Apparat* – but its glaring prominence distracts attention from other more understated features of the narrative. It is a consummate contribution to the genre of the accident report, unsurpassed for its technical description of the industrial accident in which a presiding 'Officer' is spiked by his own *Apparat*. This description of the boss's death at work on his own deadly machinery clearly benefits from Kafka's reflections on industrial injury due to hazardous machinery presented in his 1909 report, but it is important not to be too dazzled by the *Apparat*. The story also draws on Kafka's own work as an *ultra vires* travelling investigator visiting dangerous quarries and inquiring into the safety of their owners' machinery and practices. The Travelling Investigator (*Forchungsreisender*) in the novella visits a place of execution on an island at the colonial frontier whose dilapidated topography combines amphitheatre and quarry.[41] The purely cognitive mission of the 'Traveller' – as he is called thereafter in homage perhaps to the metamorphosed traveller Gregor – is undermined from the outset as he finds himself implicated in his object of inquiry in ways he neither foresaw nor ever fully understood. For he and subsequent generations of readers were too blinded by the radiant *Apparat* to heed the clues that pointed to other understandings of what was happening that day in the penal colony.

'In the Penal Colony' *seems* to be a straightforward narrative, but is of course no such thing. A Traveller listens to the description (in French) of the workings of a peculiar machine for capital punishment delivered by its current presiding Officer. The arrival of a new 'humane' Commandant of the penal colony has led to the deliberate neglect of the machine and the reform of the 'Old Commandant's' legal and political regime of festive public executions. During these spectacles the name of a crime was inscribed on the victim's back by the pre-programmed vibrating needles of the *Apparat*, becoming legible to them only at the moment of their ecstatic death. The Officer faithful to the Old Commandant's memory proposes to demonstrate the machine to the Traveller with a Soldier 'guilty' of insubordination. In the course of the conversation the Soldier or victim of the day is unaccountably substituted by the Officer who dies a gruesome death as the *Apparat* self-destructs on his back. Unnerved, the Traveller flees the Island … But is this really the story, or just a masking device designed to distract attention from another, less obtrusive and perhaps even more macabre tale? Might not the glare that surrounds the *Apparat* serve only to distract the attention of its characters and readers from the perverse *messianic* scenario enveloping the Traveller and secretly motivating events on the surface? For accepting the centrality of the *Apparat* is to collude with the Officer's not entirely trustworthy fascination with the machine of death and tacitly to endorse his obsession with maintaining archaic conditions of domination.[42]

Why does the Officer immolate *himself* on the *Apparat*? And why does the story continue after the suicide/execution of the Officer and the destruction of the *Apparat*, to the apparent dissatisfaction of its author?[43] Such questions assume that the *Apparat* is the focus of the story and overlook the tale of messianic mis-recognition nested within it. Events after the Officer's death in the collapsing *Apparat* confirm that the Officer took the Traveller to be the awaited messiah and literally executed what he took to be his order.[44] To appreciate this we need to attend to their dialogue as not only the Traveller's bored and disinterested attendance at a demonstration of the ramshackle *Apparat* but also the Officer's test of his unwitting guest's messianic vocation (which he finds confirmed). In this light the story appears as a perverse comedy of messianic mis-recognition in which the Officer thinks the messiah has arrived and fulfils a prophesy by sacrificing his life in both ending and confirming the old order while the Traveller – undergoing a messianic metamorphosis into an accidental messiah – remains nigh oblivious to this scenario while unwittingly confirming it at almost every step.

Sitting on a cane chair at the edge of the pit in the deserted auditorium, the Traveller listens distractedly to the Officer's description of the 'remarkable *Apparat*' before him and its place in the history of the penal colony. The Officer begins by praising the former Commandant of the colony and reveals the existence of a group of 'his friends' who survive him as well as 'a prophesy' according to which they now live : 'We, his friends, knew even on his death that the organisation of the colony was so locked in on itself that his successor, even with a thousand new plans in his head, would not be able to change any of the old things, at least not for many years. Our prophesy thus came to pass and the new Commandant has had to recognise it' (*S* 141, 166). Yet the prophesy involved more than the inviolability of the old law; it also predicted the messianic return of the Old Commandant.

The Traveller – bored, distracted and almost blinded by the sun in the shadeless valley – fails to appreciate that he has just been informed of the existence of a secret society of friends/disciples of the Old Commandant and that he is steadily but unwittingly being drawn into complicity with them. The Officer supports his claim to explain the *Apparat* and its procedure first by virtue of his possession of sacred legal and technical texts/drawings, and then through a form of apostolic succession. The sacred texts are the Old Commandant's hand-drawn designs carried by the Officer in a leather wallet in his breast pocket; they are so holy that he must wash his hands before touching them. Held up for the Traveller to see but not touch, they seem incomprehensible: 'he saw only labyrinthine intersecting lines that covered the paper so thickly that the white spaces could only be discerned with effort' (*S* 148, 175). The drawings programme the *Apparat* to inscribe the transgressed law on the body of the condemned over a period of 12 hours until reaching the point of ecstatic but fatal legibility.

The Officer explains that the execution and the jurisprudence that guided the condemnation of the accused follows a principle and a procedure seemingly distant from the tradition of Western law: 'The principle according to which I decide is: guilt [*Schuld*] is always without doubt. Other courts may not follow this principle since they have many heads and higher courts above them. This is not the case here, or at least it wasn't with previous commandants' (*S* 145, 171). The procedural consequence of this principle is that the condemned are never informed of their accusation, have no opportunity to defend their innocence and suffer a punishment that is continuous with their trial and which always precedes the declaration of their offence and sentence. The latest, 'enlightened' commandant in turning away from the basic principle of absolute guilt deliberately neglects the old law and its procedures. After lamenting this neglect, the Officer turns to a long and loving description of the trial/punishment in which the moment of death – publicly shared and celebrated by the assembled islanders – coincides with the victim's ecstatic recognition in a paroxysm of legibility of their sentence and the transgression of which they are found to be guilty.

In order to understand the story it is important to look beyond the individual, guilty victim towards the systemic guilt produced and managed by the *Apparat*.[45] As the Officer explains, the *Apparat* is a disciplinary technology that selects victims according to a ritual timetable, and the very fact of being selected is enough to confirm the victim's guilt. While the arrest of the specific individual victim was accidental – they were in the wrong place doing the wrong thing at the wrong time – it was a matter of implacable necessity that *someone* be arrested before the ordained day of execution. Today's hapless condemned – whose job was to guard his superior's door like a dog and who seems 'so doggishly submissive that it seemed you could let him run freely on the slopes and would only have to whistle at the start of the execution for him to come' (*S* 140, 164) – is to be executed for insubordination in allegedly biting and threatening to eat his superior officer. However, he has been selected less because of this offence than because the *Apparat* required a victim that day for the purposes of demonstration. He is ultimately spared the fate of dying from the inscription on his body of the phrase 'Honour thy superiors' through the events arising from the conversation between the Officer and Traveller. He will also be revealed at the end to be rather more complicit with the execution than he appeared to be throughout the Officer's narration.

The Officer, who continues speaking while preparing the *Apparat*, suddenly approaches the Traveller who 'sensing something took a step back' (*S* 152, 180), only to find himself cornered. In spite of speaking French before the victim and the guard who could not understand them, the Officer feels it necessary to take his hand and to lead him aside for 'some words in confidence' (*S* 152, 180). The Traveller accepts the confidence, and learns that the procedure and execution just described 'currently have no more open supporters in our colony. I am their only defender and at the same time the only advocate of the old commandant's legacy' (*S* 153, 180). Yet even if he is the only *open* disciple of the old commandant, there remain, he confides, many clandestine 'followers' who have gone 'into hiding'. The officer then adds, 'If you were to go today, that is on an execution day, to the teahouse and eavesdrop, you will perhaps hear only ambiguous utterances. All of them are loyal followers, but under the current commandant with his current intuitions they are totally useless to me' (*S* 153, 180). It is important to recall this detail since later in the story the voyager will indeed visit the teahouse just revealed as a place of cult where the Old Commandant is buried and his secret followers assemble to await his return in the guise of a new messiah.

The Officer then invites the Traveller to enter a conspiracy to restore the rule of the old commandant and his *Apparat*. The Traveller's protest is stubbornly resisted by the Officer, looking 'not at his face but somewhere on his coat', as if he had expected such dissembled opposition or 'ambiguous utterance' and intoning 'your influence, believe me, cannot be estimated too highly' (*S* 156, 185). The plan is for the Traveller publicly to accuse the New Commandant and for the Officer to then force him to his knees and confess 'Old commandant, I bow down before you' (*S* 159, 188). The ritual genuflection will later be unwittingly performed by the Traveller himself, but for now the objective of the conspiracy is to put the new commandant on trial for neglect of the old law. By this point the Officer is shouting 'That is my plan, will you help me carry it out? But of course you want to, more than that, you must' (*S* 159, 188). Whence this certainty, whence the necessity that the Traveller *must* and will want to help? The Officer clearly regards the

Traveller as an unquestionable ally, someone who cannot help but join him, one perhaps whose coming had been long expected . . .

There is a striking irony in the Officer's plan to use a public forum to condemn the new commandant, for it defends the old law not by its principle that guilt is certain but in a public trial with speeches for the prosecution and an implied right of defence. His conspiracy to restore the old law obeys the principles and procedures of the new, and whether it succeeds or fails can only confirm them. Predictably the Traveller refuses to enter the conspiracy, explaining that he will condemn the old law in private discussion with the new Commandant, which is to say, without any opportunity for the Officer to offer a public defence. For the guilt of the old law and its surviving judge is *not in question for the Traveller*. Kafka presents the paradox of the Officer defending the old law through the principles of the new and the Traveller justifying the new by the principle of indubitable guilt axiomatic for the old law. The intense if unwitting play of paradox in the conspiratorial conversation leaves the *Officer* in the position of betraying the old law by attempting its public vindication and the *Traveller* remaining true to its principle by condemning it without trial.

The judge-officer's consignment of himself to execution by the *Apparat* following this discussion should be understood in the light of these paradoxes. Kafka observes that 'It did not seem as if the officer had been listening' – or that he heard something else behind the Traveller's words, smiling to himself and keeping 'his true thoughts to himself behind the smile' (S 160, 189). What is more, the attendant soldier victim and guard gesture excitedly to each other and themselves whisper conspiratorially as if what they expected had been confirmed. The loyal defender of the law has betrayed it and the apostate messiah revealed himself as his true successor. The Officer too can read the signs and is ready: 'Then it is the time [*Dann ist es also Zeit*] – he said conclusively, and suddenly looked the traveller with shining eyes that held a kind of summons, some call to participate' (S 160, 189). The Traveller, growing uneasy, asks 'The time for what?' dimly sensing he is somehow implicated in the events now unfolding. The Officer liberates the prisoner undergoing execution and forces the Traveller to read out the condemnation 'be just' inscribed in the diagram that will be inscribed on the body of the Officer in breach of all established procedure. The Officer self-condemned for unjustly betraying the old law will not proceed with the execution until the Traveller has reluctantly assented to what is written. His earlier betrayal of the old law is now compounded by his criminal subversion of its procedure. The Officer betrayed the old law by trying publically to defend it, thus making way for the messiah who remains faithful to the law by apparently betraying it. Yet the climax of the Officer's betrayal is still to come, for he forces the Traveller to read out the sentence 'be just' *before* the execution. By doing so he puts both the messiah and the *Apparat* on trial. If, as he hopes, he has been condemned by the true messiah then the *Apparat* will reveal the true nature of his crime, the true nature of the justice he has betrayed; if he has judged himself then the prior knowledge of his crime will make him entirely indigestible to the *Apparat* and will entail either his acquittal or both his and its destruction. Paradoxically both outcomes serve to confirm the sentence and the messianic metamorphosis of the Traveller.

The Traveller does not intervene; the reason given in the story is that *he had no right*: 'If the legal procedure to which the officer was devoted was really so near to being eliminated – possibly following the traveller's intervention, to which for his part he felt obliged – then the officer was acting quite correctly; the traveller would not have acted any differently in his place' (*S* 183, 192). The Officer's industrial accident unfolds before the Traveller's eyes as the *Apparat* self-destructs on the body of the Officer. Yet the Officer has been redeemed since he has died not by the inscription of his own judgement but by the self-destruction of the *Apparat* under the gaze and with the messianic assent of the Traveller. In either case his death seems to confirm the latter's messianic vocation; his words and actions are consistent with the messianic expectations and he confirms the old law by seeming to overthrow it. By unwittingly condemning and executing the Officer, the Traveller assumes first the role of the prophetic judge and then that of a witless messiah.

The macabre death of the Officer underlines that the *Apparat* is a machine that generates accidents – its victims cannot knowingly choose to become accidents. The very fidelity of the Officer perverts the procedure of the *Apparat*; it exists only to transform accidents into necessity by bringing its unknowing *innocent* victims to consciousness of their mortal guilt. The Officer by condemning himself also condemns the *Apparat* by abolishing its very reason to exist: his will takes the place of its necessity. Volunteering himself for execution for a crime known in advance is at best a spectacular betrayal of the old law but perhaps more deeply it is its self-condemnation. With the inscription of the phrase 'be just' on his body, the Judge/Officer is confident that the law will show him where he was unjust and where he failed it, thus vindicating the law under the new messianic dispensation. His faith in the old law is so firm that he is able to judge himself – in the light of the Traveller's unwitting demonstration of fidelity to its procedure – as guilty of injustice with respect to it; he cannot conceive the possibility that it is the law and not he that is guilty of injustice and that the entire legal order of the *Apparat* has been condemned in his person. Here there is indeed a *question* of guilt, but it asks whether guilt lies with the individual or the law itself. If guilt lies with the Officer for unjustly applying the law, then the *Apparat* will duly execute and enlighten him; if guilt is vested in the law, then it will execute both the Officer and itself. The result is mutual destruction as the accident fell on the *Apparat's* own back – 'the machine was obviously going to ruin' (*S* 164, 195) – as well as that of the Officer. In the manner of a meticulous accident report, Kafka describes the machine's descent to scribble: 'The harrow didn't write, it just stabbed, and the bed didn't rotate the body but lifted it trembling into the needles. The Traveller wanted to intervene, in some way to bring the whole thing to a standstill, that was surely not the torture sought by the Officer, that was just direct murder' (*S* 165, 195). The *Apparat* destroyed itself and took the Officer with it, and while the narrator explains moralistically that 'no sign of the promised redemption was to be found' (*S* 186, 196), he also reports that the eyes of the corpse were open, 'calm and convinced', that is to say, just as redeemed in the consciousness of his guilt as all the previous victims of the *Apparat*.

The attempt by the Officer to redeem the *Apparat* by sacrificing himself to it as a guilty individual rather than as an accidental victim of its performance of systemic guilt condemned both him and the *Apparat*. The accident that ensued was the outcome of the messianic complications surrounding the Old Commandant and the hapless Traveller. The latter is mis-recognized by the Officer and the other secret followers of the Old Commandant as a messianic figure whose vocation is to restore the old law. The Officer's self-immolation after what he hoped to be his condemnation by the Messiah/Traveller was intended to redeem the justice of the machine, with the Officer literally trying to take on his own back the systemic guilt of the *Apparat*. The mutual destruction of Officer and *Apparat* was possible due to the presence of the Traveller who, however mistakenly, is considered to bear the promise of a new law that is paradoxically the continuation of the old. When read in this perspective, it becomes clear why the story cannot simply end with the mutual destruction of Officer and *Apparat*; this is only the beginning.[46]

In the original, published ending of 'In the Penal Colony', the Traveller, joined by the prisoner and the soldier, returns from the place of execution to the colony. The soldier points to one of the buildings, as if he had been asked to, and says 'Here is the teahouse' (*S* 166, 196). This is the place, according to the Officer, where the clandestine followers of the old law gather on days of execution like the followers of Sabbatai Zevi at the eastern gate of Salonica to await the arrival of the Messiah. The tables outside are empty, and the place gave the Investigator 'the impression of an historical memory, and he felt the power of past times' (*S* 166, 197). On entering the teahouse he is told by the soldier that 'The Old Man's buried here' because 'the priest wouldn't let him lie in the churchyard. Nobody knew where to bury him for a while, but in the end they buried him here. The officer never told you about that for sure, because of course that's what he was most ashamed of. He even tried several times to dig the old man up by night, but was always chased away' (S 166, 197). The Traveller asks to see the grave, and both condemned man and soldier (who now turn out to be extremely well informed about the Old Commandant) take him to see the grave, moving aside the table that covers it. The Traveller, who has still not fully appreciated what has happened and is happening, describes the 'customers' as 'probably dockworkers, strong men with short, full, shiny black beards. All were without jackets, their shirts were torn, they were a poor and humiliated people' (S 167, 197). What now takes place in this critically neglected part of the story reads as the nightmare confirmation of an unwittingly fulfilled prophesy.

The followers of the Old Commandant rise from their tables, back themselves against the wall and stare at the Traveller: '"It's a foreigner," the whisper fluttered around the traveller, "he wants to see the grave"' (S 167, 197). The Traveller goes down on his knees, the better to read the inscription on the grave, thus accidentally presenting a figure of homage and worship to the assembled followers, and reads the inscription: 'Here rests the Old Commandant. His followers, who no longer dare to name themselves, dug this grave for him and placed the stone. There is a prophesy that after a certain number of years the commandant will rise again and lead his followers from this house in the reconquest of the colony. Have faith and wait!' (S 167, 198). There follows an episode of exquisite but macabre comedy with the followers believing the time has come for the Traveller to lead them in the reconquest of the island accompanied by the latter's growing disquiet and search for an escape from this increasingly bizarre and incomprehensible predicament. Rising from his knees, the Traveller found the men 'standing around him and smiling' (S 167, 198); he interprets this as an invitation to find the inscription ridiculous and, misunderstanding the reason for the men's happiness, distributes some coins and with polite haste leaves for the harbour.[47]

In the final paragraph the Traveller almost escapes unscathed, but is pursued by soldier and prisoner. They have clearly debated with the other followers their messiah's perplexing behaviour in leaving the teahouse without initiating the prophesied insurrection, and have been sent to bring him back. The Traveller interprets their hesitation as due to 'running into acquaintances who held them back' (S 167, 198) and assumes that far from wanting to keep him on the island, they are intent on escaping with him. Their threatening approach, silent and rapid, is met by the Traveller's resistance; now in the boat he picks up a tow rope and forcibly prevents their leaping onboard. The published story ends on this moment of suspension, with the Traveller neither on nor off the Island.

The problem with the ending consists less in the fact that the apparent action of the story ends with the death of the Officer and the destruction of the *Apparat* than that the Traveller's escape from a prophesy he seems unwittingly to fulfil is by no means assured. The historical fusion of the messianic and exodus narratives characteristic of the Religions of the Book is here set in crisis. The messianic task of liberation or exodus from a state of exile has been diverted or even arrested in Kafka's story.

What David Daube called the 'Exodus pattern'[48] is performed in Kafka's repeated searches for the another, the right ending to 'In the Penal Colony'. The published version ends with the attempt to escape the predicament of prophesy, the chase to the port and the suspended embarkation of the Traveller. The other surviving drafts of the ending preserved in Kafka's diaries of 7–9 August 1917 approach the problem with increasing desperation, echoed in yet other attempts mentioned in the *Letters* but which have not survived. The 7 August ending begins with the Traveller asking 'how's that?' before lingering at the scene of execution in a state of paralytic fatigue interrupted by the arrival of the Commandant's messengers and the metamorphosis of the Traveller into a dog in fulfilment of his own prophesy 'I'll be a damned dog if I allow that to happen' (*D* 380, 636) for what he has already allowed to happen. Escorted away in his delirium he embraces the men crying, 'Why does all this happen to me' (*D* 380, 636), still not realizing that there is no reason for his being chosen, no how or why – he is but today's chosen one, the accidental messiah.

In the ending tried on 8 August, the Traveller assumes his messianic responsibility and the role of leader in exodus, except that this proves an exodus towards an even worse exile. The spike that killed the Officer, and with him the old law, remains, and with a wave of his hand the Traveller sends away the hesitating soldier and condemned man. Suddenly asking again 'how's that?' he is tormented by a sense of having forgotten something, that something has been left awry and needs adjustment, that there has been an accident somewhere. He doesn't know what is happening, there's confusion and he's left his 'power of judgement' somewhere in the north. Kafka then repeats the question, 'how's that?' but this time instead of lamenting his loss of judgement the Traveller describes 'A crude error in the reckoning, a fundamentally perverted grasp, a screaming ink-spurting stroke of the pen runs right through the whole' (*D* 380, 637). Not only is the event described out of joint – the inscription of the *Apparat* was not supposed to produce a 'screaming ink-spurt' – but the narration itself is 'hollowed out', leaving the Traveller asking not 'how' or 'why' but 'who': 'Who will set it right? Where is the man to set it right?' (D 380, 637) and, hoping it is not him, refers again to 'the north' where he had previously left his judgement and the 'good old compatriot miller who could stick those two grinning chaps between the millstones' (D 380, 637). The evocation of the millstones – a millennial figure of exile – initiates an exodus in which the 'pathfinders and stone breakers' set forth in search of the snake, 'the great madam' or devil. For her arrival, everything 'had to be banged and shattered into dust' (D 380–1, 637–8). Exodus has folded itself into exile and the 'business' of the marchers or 'snake fodder' 'is to make dust' by grinding, banging and marching all without interruption. It is a combination of Exodus with the labours of exile – apparently a socialist version of the biblical narrative, redemption through labour, except that here it is the labour of creating the very desert through which they are condemned to march. It is not so much Moses leading the Israelites into the desert as setting them to grind down the stones to create the very desert through which their exodus must pass. The folding of exodus into exile and the expectation of the snake who requires everything to be reduced to dust is accompanied by the Traveller accepting the hopeless messianic vocation and metamorphosing into the promised, cheerful messianic commandant ordering the lights to be lit to lead the others through the darkness: 'Hold the lamps high, you up front! You others quietly behind me! Everyone single file. And be still. That was nothing. Don't be afraid. I take full responsibility. I'll lead you out' (D 381, 638). He assumes the messianic vocation by accepting 'responsibility' – Kafka's working title for the collection of stories eventually published as A Country Doctor.

Having tried the options of renouncing the messianic vocation through madness and assuming it but leading the exiled into a self-generated and even deeper exile, the last surviving attempt to end the story on 9 August 1917 tries the impossible scenario of reversing time. Acknowledging a complicity with the prisoner and guard around the corpse of the Officer even while losing all contact with them, the Traveller resists the feeling that 'a perfect order had been established' (D 381, 639). While the others stare at him 'strangely', the Traveller entertains the conjecture that the Officer's 'contention' had been 'mechanically' self-refuted. Slipping back into his cane chair, the Traveller imagines his ship arriving through the 'pathless sands' (for the arena of execution outside the colony has now become the limitless desert/ocean of Exodus) and taking him back in time before the execution. From the ladder climbing up into the ship and back in time he denounces the Officer for executing the prisoner; but then, as if in a theatre (the nature theatre of Devil's Island?) there is a momentary happy ending: the prisoner has not been executed, he is indeed the Traveller's luggage bearer. "'My compliments" the Traveller would have had to say, and say gladly, "a conjurer's trick?"' The Officer denies this, emphasizing that he had indeed been condemned by Traveller: 'a mistake on your part, I was executed as you commanded' (*D* 382, 639), and reveals to the watching crew 'a spike crookedly protruding from his shattered forehead' (*D* 382, 639). In this last surviving attempt to end the story, the narrative, as in the published version, remains stalled at the point of embarkation and escape.

The drafts for alternate endings to 'In the Penal Colony' differ in many respects from the published version. They differ in the emphasis given to the themes of animality and metamorphosis as well as to spectacle and theatre. All of them remain in some sense suspended between exodus, exile and the messianic calling and all try to evade the unwanted and not fully understood messianic responsibility. This leads to the exodus being stalled, whether at an impossible moment of embarkation, on an eternally deferred work-march that creates the very desert through which it marches, or in madness and the descent to animality. Emrich, in one of the rare attempts to interpret the variant endings to 'In the Penal Colony', very perceptively locates the problem in the choice between two laws: 'The new law is the law of the Devil. The old order, for the sake of redemption, sacrificed man; the new order, for the sake of man, has sacrificed redemption. Both orders are barbarous. Neither one can be played off against the other, for neither can be lived' (Emrich, 275). For him the story told on the threshold of the era following the death of God is replete with paradox: 'Man's earthly self-assertion turns into mankind's self-annihilation in the illimitable progress of "work" and the battle of everyone against everyone' (Emrich 275). But at the core of such paradox can be found the necessary accident – this is the trouble that generates a chain of events incapable of closure: the act of accidental messianic misrecognition initiates the blockage that made this story impossible to end. Kafka described the problem of exiting from an impossible predicament as the 'worm at the core', one whose action was explicitly thematized in this interminable story and suffered in the repeated rewritings of its endings.

Accident terminable and interminable

The Octavo Notebooks and the stories of *A Country Doctor* collection are framed at one end by the Munich public reading of 'In the Penal Colony' and at the other by attempts to rewrite its ending. One of the first results of the writing campaign of 1916–17 not included in *A Country Doctor* collection were the fragments concerning the Hunter Gracchus. The fragments combine the themes of the hunt and the hunter with those of the accident – the Hunter has suffered a double accident which means he cannot die; instead he interminably narrates his misfortune, seeking some meaning to his perpetual voyage along the border between life and death.

The Hunter Gracchus stories are the privileged point of departure for Emrich's philosophical reading of Kafka. He approaches them from the standpoint of the tormented universal occupied by the living-dead Hunter; he 'has dropped out of the classifications of this world as well as out of those of the hereafter; he is universally everywhere and nowhere, can no longer be definitely placed; there is no unequivocal determinability for his existence' (Emrich, 8). Yet Emrich does not give full weight to the detail that the Hunter Gracchus's interminable existence began with a double accident. He perceptively notes that the story of Gracchus, as with many others in Kafka begins with an accident 'with this kind of sudden, incomprehensible loss of any possibility of normal orientation' (Emrich, 9),[49] but does not recognize this event as an 'accident'. He correctly understands Gracchus to be a traumatized survivor, but does not ask what exactly it is that he has survived.

What is especially interesting in this case is the doubling of the accident and the initiation of a potentially interminable sequence. Chance, contingency and accidents throng the two fragments. Set on a hot afternoon in Riva on Lake Como, the first fragment opens with two Heracleitean boys 'sitting on the wall of the wharf playing a game with dice' (*S* 109, 266). The dice throws produce a sequence of accidental impressions that add up to a static tableau in which all events are of equal insignificance, equally accidental. History is evoked in the guise of 'a man reading a newspaper in the shadow of the sword waving hero', but is given no more significance than 'a girl at the fountain' or a fruit seller sprawled beside his stall looking at the lake. They in turn are joined by two men in the shade of a bar, glimpsed through an empty door and window frames with the bar owner dozing in front of it and then by a sail boat arriving at the quay from which emerges a man carried on a bier.

The lethargic tableau of a hot afternoon is traversed first by the bier and its bearers and then by a flock of doves hitherto circling the clock tower, there evoking the stasis of the eternal return that accompanies this parodic great noontide. Disaggregating, the doves flock outside the house where the bier has been carried. However, none of these movements animates the scene; this was the task of the new arrival, a man wearing a top hat and dressed in mourning. He descends to the harbour, bringing consistency to the tableau – he brushes aside the fruit peelings scattered around the monument with his cane – linking monument, fruit seller and newspaper reader. He enters the building whence the bier had been carried and encounters a line of 50 small boys bowing at his arrival. The pair of small boys playing dice have now become 50, but as the man passes them their line too disaggregates and they swarm behind him and around the boatman who has stepped out to greet him.

The Mayor of Riva, Salvatore, thus comes to pay his respects to the honoured guest of the city, the Hunter Gracchus. After some formalities, he asks disconcertingly, 'Are you dead?', to which the Hunter replies by narrating the accident in which he lost his life: 'Many years ago, it must already be very many years ago, I fell off a cliff in the Black Forest – that's in Germany – while hunting a chamois. Since then I've been dead' (S 228, 268). The Hunter, in short, died during an accident at work – it was singular, indeed a literal fall to be ranked alongside the one that killed Theresa's mother in *America*. But the accident did not end there, for as the Mayor observes, 'But you're also alive', and all this because of a doubling of the accident. For not only did he fall to his death, but 'My death barge went off course, a wrong turn of the tiller, the moment of carelessness on the part of the captain, a diversion through my beautiful homeland. I don't know what it was, I know only that I remained on earth and that since then my barge sails on earthly waters' (S 228, 269). He seems to have substituted for the vertical trajectory of living in the mountains the horizontal trajectory of travelling the seas – the Hunter metamorphosed into a butterfly fluttering upwards was dragged down again to drift disoriented 'on this infinitely wide and open stairway' incapable of ever reaching the gleaming gate at its summit. He always awakes on earthly waters, mocked by 'the fundamental error [*Grundfehler*] of my erstwhile death' (S 229, 269). Instead of maintaining a vertical trajectory away from life and the earth, the boat became locked in circumnavigation – moving at varying distance from its goal but never reaching it.[50] It is a fate that resembles the movement of the dreamer in 'Children on A Country Road' whose east–west trajectory means his interminable journey will never terminate at the city of the south. The Hunter interminably orbits death, driven by the winds of a debt or S*chuld* he is unable to pay. He is in suspension but can expect no resolution, neither paying with his death as did Rossmann and Josef K. (he has already spent it) nor in redemption. There is no insurance for the double accident of which he is the victim – the one that took his life and the other that took his death – it cannot be resolved or compensated in any way and so he continues moving, unable to pay.

Confronted with this dreadful 'fate', the Mayor seeks meaning in terms of the Hunter's guilt, but Gracchus remains unconvinced: 'I was a hunter, is that some kind of guilt? I was assigned the post of hunter in the Black Forest, in those days there were still wolves. I lay in wait, shot, killed, removed the pelt, is that guilt? My labours were blessed. I was called the great hunter of the Black Forest. Is that guilt?' (S 229, 269). The Mayor admits he is not competent to answer this question[51] but is compelled to ask again, 'But then whose is the guilt?' (S 229, 269). Maybe the lives the Hunter took outweighed the meagre death that was all he had to pay back? Maybe because he blames the boatman and sees himself as an accident victim while knowing that the mistake at the tiller was not the cause of his interminable accident for 'My barge has no tiller, it goes with the wind that blows in the nethermost regions of death' (S 230, 229). His fall followed by his interminable diversion are driven by a wind already encountered in 'Description of a Struggle' that testifies to a coming landslide; his individual fall is part of larger catastrophe in which the Hunter finds himself hunted.

This is confirmed by the second Gracchus fragment narrated in the first person. The Hunter is now lying in the boat illuminated by an obsolete sacramental candle. It gives enough light to see a small picture on the opposite wall 'apparently of a bushman who is aiming his spear at me while taking cover as best he can behind a gorgeously painted shield' (S 229, 271). The encounter with the image can be read in various ways. It is clearly, as John Zilcosky has emphasized, an intimation of a post-colonial critique – the 'bushman' hunting the European.[52] Here Gracchus is the object of the Hunter's gaze, his hunting accident was a hunted accident. But there is a complementarity, for the image of the Hunter caught in the act of concealing himself is frozen and faces him as an equal. Gracchus too 'covered' himself in order to see but not be seen, but like the 'bushman' was seen to be doing so and held at that moment eternally. He like the 'bushman' is suspended in the interminable shameful state of having been seen trying to conceal himself. After referring to it as a 'stupid image', one of the 'stupidist', but perhaps only because he doesn't understand it, he returns to his accident narrative, talking to the Mayor as if he were his insurance man and he making a claim for compensation: 'Everything went according to order. I gave chase, fell, bled in a ravine, was dead, and this boat was supposed to carry me into the beyond' (S 229, 271). In his words, 'I liked to live and liked to die' (S 229, 271) and came to the boat singing and, throwing aside his hunting kit, 'slipped into my shroud like a girl into her wedding dress' (S 229, 271). The fragment breaks off with 'Then happened ***' (S 229, 271), followed in the manuscript by the three stars Kafka used to interrupt the chapter of accidents making up 'In the Penal Colony'. The accident was interminable, and just as it could not begin – for the pure accident can have no reason for being or coming into existence – not could it end, for there was equally no reason for it passing out of existence.

The accident happened and then happened again; it could not be terminated. John Zilcosky's reading points to a larger change of climate in the move from the terminal to the interminable accident: 'Whereas the pre-"Gracchus" heroes appear to die resolutely if harshly and unjustly, the later 1917 protagonists (A Country Doctor, Odradek, the Coal Scuttle Rider) are unable to die' (Zilcosky 185). Gracchus joins Odradek, the non-living but not dead being that lives with a family in the story 'Cares of a Householder' – like him he pursues an elliptical trajectory in which there is no depth and thus no possibility to to sink or rise. It is as if the moment of suspension when Rossmann enters new York harbour in *America* and Josef K. awaits the thrust of the swords in *The Trial* is held forever, with beings like Gracchus and Odradek orbiting on a special ecliptic across history and its events. As two-dimensional existences frozen in repetition, they approximate less the state of the photographic image than the moment just before it was about to be taken.

3 IMAGES

Scripts

Kafka understood his writing as the expression of a *Schriftstellersein* or writerly mode of being that negotiated absence through the mobilization of inscriptive technologies.[1] Writings produced under *Schriftstellersein* are less the expressions of a subject, whether poet (*Dichter*) or author (*Autor*), than manifestations of the predicament of writing as a mode of being.[2] They do not conform to given canonical forms but emerge from the interference between different modes or *regimes* of writing. As an ontological predicament, *Schriftstellersein* precedes acts of writing and, much to Kafka's discomfort, is constituted as much by acts and periods of not-writing. And finally, Kafka's *Schriftstellersein* was unusually attentive to its technological vehicles, evident in his attention to typefaces as well as his preoccupation with the synaesthetics of writing or the slippage between written characters, image, sound, touch and even smell.

This raises the question of how to read Kafka while attending to the material medium through which one gains access to his texts. From the outset he was very attentive to the typographic presentation of his writing, publishing in luxury magazines such as *Hyperion*, as well as paying unusual attention to the choice of typography in *Meditation*. This dimension of his work – the lighting of his text – is lost when these early stories are translated into the uniform typography of an anthology of Kafka's short stories. Such considerations also hold for the typography and cover art of his later published writings, material elements of his texts that are inseparable from their content. In them the text is treated as an image and the attention paid by Kafka to the pace of reading determined by the typography.

Such considerations are even more significant when considering Kafka's unpublished writings, which of course constitute a large part of his *oeuvre*.

The facsimile edition of his manuscripts is not simply a resource for scholars but also a legitimate, arguably the only legitimate, way of reading Kafka. The novel manuscripts are complex artefacts, at once performative acts of composition and revision, but also scripts for reading aloud. Kafka made a distinction between his typed office work and his handwritten stories, insisting on the singularity of the latter, literally autograph texts. For his *Schriftstellersein*, writing was a singular performative act that could not be reproduced or simply transcribed into a neutral typography. Preparing his manuscripts for publication has proven a thankless task for editors since they must necessarily translate his idiom into typographic conventions, even publishing words, sentences and pages that Kafka deleted and so lending them an air of legitimacy, all leading to inevitably compromised texts. The manuscripts were also performative in the sense of being scripts for oral performance; Kafka seems to have written with an eye and an ear to oral delivery, and his letters and diaries are full of references to him reading his work aloud to family, to individuals or groups of friends and even, as we saw in the case of 'In the Penal Colony', to a formal public. This sense of a script demanding elaboration and enhancement through dramatic oral delivery is lost in most editions of the novels, most painfully in the case of *The Castle*, which seems to have been written in order to be performed and heard. This dramatic dimension of his *Schriftstellersein* is often factored into the narrative technique of his writings, as in 'A Report to an Academy', which purports to be a speech given by a humanized ape to a scholarly audience and that became a staple of dramatic recitals during the Weimar Republic.

Another important dimension lost in most editions of Kafka's work is the centrality of the image. Kafka's *Schriftstellersein* was as much schematic/visual as textual.[3] The range of his surviving visual practice is surveyed in Jacqueline Sudaka-Benazeraf's *Le regard de Franz Kafka: Dessins d'un ecrivan* and shows his enduring fascination with the image. His manuscripts, diaries and letters are peppered with drawings, of which Kafka was diffidently proud and some of which, including the 'Writer at his Desk' and the 'Jockey on his Horse', have become widely reproduced icons of the Kafka tourist industry, appearing on tee shirts and tea-cups. His scenes of torture have been less popular. His drawings range from expressive, dynamic near abstract images to reproductions of photographs and landscape features, such as Goethe's house in Weimar, and infallibly form an integral part of the text in which they were generated. They may illustrate in some cases, but on the whole they are directed expressions of the force of writing, moving between word and image.

Although Kafka's texts are touched by cinema and cinematic narrative, they have a special place for photography. Some of his drawings – such as the portrait of Dora Dymant – may be traced to photographs, but scribbling on and around photographic images was an important part of his *Schriftstellersein*. This practice is exemplified by his 1910 postcards to Brod in which text invades the image (Sudaka-Benazeraf 2001, 67), but is of broader significance. Explicit and encrypted commentary on photographic images recur throughout Kafka's writings;[4] they are thematically central to *America* but also important in *The Trial* and *The Castle*. The encounter of photograph and text marks the intersection between the singularity of the photograph and the apparent universality of the textual supplement.[5] Of course this is complicated by Kafka's handwritten idiom that confronts two expressions of singularity, one in space and time and one of character.

The importance of the intersection of text and image for Kafka's *Schriftstellersein* is most clearly displayed in the article 'Accident Prevention in Quarries'. Apart from the circumstances of its publication already mentioned, the article is also an important example of the intersections of text and photography, oral and written presentation and photographic technology and the accident. A large part of the article comprises written commentaries on published photographs, with the commentaries framed as oral presentations of the alarming features of certain quarries to an audience of accident prevention officials. In his comments on these wintry scenes of industrial danger, Kafka weaves together image, text and the accident in a way exemplary for his *Schriftstellersein*. All the senses are at play in this text, written in the shadow of the coming accident or under the threat of a perpetual and slow-moving landslide accelerating into a dangerous rockfall. Text and image evoke the cold, the damp air and the sound of falling rocks that accompanies the murmur of the narrator; the evidence of subterranean shifts are expertly pointed out, with the whole performance indicating through word and image the dark power of the accident that will fall when it will. Even if it has not happened yet, and especially if all seems calm and quiet, the coming accident haunts Kafka's *Schriftstellersein*, from its beginnings in 'Description of a Struggle' to its end in the sudden breaking off of the desperate monologue of the burrower/ hunter trying to insure his burrow against all threat of the inevitable unforeseen that is on its way.

Surveillance

Quarries and rockfalls abound in Kafka's fiction, with Josef K. executed in a quarry and Karl Rossmann buried alive by America. His fiction is also associated with photography: Josef K.'s execution is photographed to ensure his shame outlives him,[6] while photographed executions haunt *America* and implicitly feature in the deadly quarries making up the photographic sequence that is the centrepiece of 'Accident Prevention in Quarries'. Kafka's pursuit of the right to inspect dangerous quarries following the accidents of 1911 led him beyond the law to covert photo-surveillance. The sequence of 14+1 photographs presented with commentary in the report are defiantly *ultra vires* and openly published in the official annual report of the Institute.

The publication of a sequence of photographs with no right to exist was part of Kafka's effort to introduce surveillance as part of the Institute's routine operation. It complemented the legal strategy of moving against a blatantly criminal employer in order to extend the Institute's right to inspection. But he could not assume that the audience of honest and rogue employers who were sent the Annual Reports would automatically approve of his practice. He thus deployed a number of strategies for framing the sequence that prepared readers for the first ever appearance of incriminating photographs in the Annual Reports and the extension of the Institute's perceptual reach to which they testified.[7] The commentaries emphasize the uncanny temporality of the photographs as at once documentary testimony, premonition and admonition and announce in them the beginnings of an administrative archive dedicated to insuring the insurers against future administrative accidents.

The photographs operate at several functional levels that are announced in the descriptive first and prescriptive third parts of the report that frame them. As seen, the entire enterprise is haunted by the 1911 quarry disaster and the forensic photographs that the Institute were permitted to take of the accident scene. In his report, Kafka effects a temporal fold that presents photographs of quarries where accidents had *not yet* taken place as if they documented past accident scenes. A parallel may be drawn with Walter Benjamin's description of Eugene Atget's images of empty streets as crime scene photographs of crimes yet to be committed. The sequence of quarries is presented as if it were an archive of accomplished accidents, except that they are all yet to happen. The crossing over of past and future – testimony and prophesy – in Kafka's apparently technical commentaries conceals the step from documenting historic to surveying potential accident scenes by framing the images according to the Institute's accident prevention mission.

Kafka aligns his sequence of photographs with the Institute's accident prevention agenda in two ways. The first emphasizes its heuristic value as an archive for investigating the causes of accidents essential to effective accident prevention. The photographs are objects of knowledge, and the commentaries serve as contributions to the scientific investigation and classification of accidents essential to reducing their incidence in the future.

An effective accident prevention programme requires such technical knowledge and so the heuristic agenda complements the didactic mission of giving a public lesson in accident prevention. The commentary thus organizes the dangerous quarries into a didactic sequence familiar from prevention propaganda and sufficiently persuasive to divert attention away from the legality of the procurement and publication of these images. This is underlined by the anomolous status of the fifteenth photograph that vouches a vision of the perfect quarry – a photograph of an artificial construction, a fictional quarry – from the permanent industrial safety exhibition in Charlottenburg, Berlin.[8]

Beyond framing the photographs as an archive of good and bad excavation practices and a lesson in accident prevention, Kafka implicitly used their publication as part of his effort to establish and extend the Institute's right to inspection. The photo archive will aid the Institute in assessing risk and provide an insurance policy in case of disputes following accidents. And at another level, the photographs issue a public warning to quarry owners that their sites have been photographed and archived. Kafka indeed uses all means to convince readers of 'Accident Prevention in Quarries' that he had not only the right to take and publish these photographs but also to use them to discipline negligent employers.

The 14+1 photographs support Kafka's case for the Institute's right to independently survey and inspect sites it was obliged to insure. As Kafka carefully notes in the preamble to his comments on the photographs, 'It was not possible to take nearly as many photographs as the Institute would have liked. But what we seek to show is that only systematic and continuing inspections can help to reduce accidents in quarries, while sporadic inspections often serve to conceal actual conditions rather than clarify them' (OW 284, 395).[9] The attempt to extend the capillary power of the Institute by constituting a photographic archive was a very delicate operation given the absence of any authority to do so. Kafka therefore produces a very subtle document that emphasizes its origins in photographing the site of a disastrous accident and then – with this absent photograph of a past disaster at one end of the sequence – presenting photographs of accidents *about* to happen. The sequence presumes an occluded hidden photograph of an actual accident at its outset (1 April 1911) and then analyses the accidents about to come, ending with the Platonic idea of the (fictional) perfect quarry to which none of the previous photographs have even remotely approximated.

It is important not to underestimate the performative dimension of publishing these photographs in the Annual Report. Under the guise of the investigative and didactic elements of a prevention agenda, the sequence throws down a gage to employers and the Ministry. Behind the subtle cognitive and didactic frames the sequence serves notice that the Institute will no longer be passive with respect to the concealment of dangerous practices. In the Annual Report, Kafka and the Institute openly admit to constituting an archive not only of anonymous dangerous practices, but also of specific sites; and while the photographs are not publically identified they will be clearly recognizable to their owners who are served warning that the Institute has an unofficial record of their quarries to which it might resort in the case of disaster. It also announces that they are now in possession of an independent knowledge base against which to assess the truth of firm-owners' responses to questionnaires and Trade Inspectors' reports. The truth-telling performance of parallel photo-sequence and commentary demonstrate the Institute's knowledge and mastery of otherwise indiscernible signs and of attempts at concealment. It serves notice on employers that following the 1911 debacle the Institute is fully prepared to engage in inspection practices and documentation at and beyond the limits set by law. The display of the photographs also contributed to the Institute's divide and rule policy between responsible and free-riding employers by representing surveillance as a benefit to responsible employers. Imposing realistic premiums on high-risk firms would lower the cost to responsible employers and reward accident prevention initiatives. Finally the report also dares the Ministry to remove the cloak of accident prevention in which the sequence is clothed and to question the Institute's new policy, especially in the light of the manifest shortcomings of the existing inspection regime. With these photographs the Institute presents the Ministry with its own insurance policy taken out against future accidents that are inevitable given the legal framework within which it is obliged to work.

Before proceeding to look at the photographs and listen to Kafka's commentaries on them, it is worth reflecting on their source – who took these photographs, under whose instructions, and why were they taken in this way? In his introduction to the Berlin edition of the *Amtliche Schriften*, Klaus Hermsdorf states, perhaps too quickly, that 'it is simply inconceivable that Kafka crawled with a camera through the quarries of Bohemia in order visually to capture illegal excavations' (*AS* 55). Yet certain features of the sequence do point either to Kafka's close involvement with the photo-surveillance, corroborated by his interest in photography and his passionate personal commitment to extending the Institute's powers of inspection after 1911, or to his wishing to make it appear as if he were present. The case for his visiting the sites in person is supported by the time of year – winter thaw – common to the sequence that corresponds with his presence in northern Bohemia during the winter of 1911. The second feature is the role of the anomalous fifteenth and final photograph in the sequence, 'a model from the social-security organizations permanent exhibition in Charlottenburg' (*OW*, 296) that Kafka can have visited as relief from the complications of his relationship with Felice. There are also details in the commentaries and descriptions of details not easily visible in the photographs that point either to Kafka's presence or to his wishing to create the fictional illusion of being present.

The final photograph, whether taken by Kafka or extracted from a trade journal (unlikely given the quality of the image and other details, such as the commentary's references to colour), is the key to the sequence. Kafka imagines giving a 'highly productive' lecture on blasting before this model of the perfect quarry, and indeed his commentaries follow the model of a lecture on a photograph, paralleling the visual commentary on photographs pioneered by Aby Warburg at the same time. The Berlin photograph also seems to have established the aesthetic of the preceding photo-sequence. It has an elevated horizon with two slivers of sky to the upper left and right seen through industrial roofing; this lends it an aspect of harsh, elevated frontality as if the model were photographed from below and alleviated only in this case by the visitors' gantry. There is no human presence and the image is lit less by the sky than by artificial lighting projected from below – an effect also achieved in the outdoor photographs of the preceding sequence. This cold, technical photo-aesthetic marks a break with the prevailing picturesque aesthetic of quarry photography that emphasized the presence of colourfully dressed human figures and adapted the quarry to the conventions of photographing ruins. Whether the photographs were taken by Kafka himself or the redoubtable Schönfeld, it seems likely that they were taken with the Berlin photograph in mind or sight and that in all probability this photograph at least was taken by Kafka himself.[10] It was not only a model quarry but also a model for photographing quarries. Most of the photographs are taken from low viewpoints with minimal horizons and tending to a dark frontality that approximated the conventions of artificial lighting by means of light reflected upward from the remains of thawing snow.

The 14 photographs with four extreme exceptions (VII, VIII, XI and XII) conform to the frontality and elevated horizon characteristic of the Charlottenburg photograph. The lighting values of the sequence viewed as a whole mimics an avalanche wave that moves from minor to catastrophic variations only to conclude in a provisional equilibrium. Five of the photographs (I, II, III, IV and VI) are lit by a triangular shard of light with its base in the upper left of the image. Photograph VI reverses the orientation of the triangular light, while photographs VII and VIII are exceptional in having the sky encompass the entire upper part of the image, giving them a panoramic and more immediately legible aspect. Photograph IX has a narrow horizontal shaft of sky dramatically interrupted by a column of the quarry, while X has a narrow sinuous band of light stretched across the upper segment of the image. Images XI and XII are the most frontal and claustrophobic, without any sky, while the photographs that close the main sequence have large but irregular sector of light combining the frontal and panoramic perspectives that immediately preceded them in the series.

While in all cases the light casts a uniform and unalleviated grey without a defined source, in most the sun seems to be behind the camera and reflecting off the snow – it does not serve as a neutral backdrop but generates powerful contrasts of light and shadow in the main image. The outcome is a certain artificiality of lighting and image that make the quarries appear as theatres of disaster, literally 'nature theatres' setting the scene for the coming accident. As with Atget's premonitory images, they seem to have been taken in the early morning, exploiting the absence of workers and their criminal employers and using the slanting early morning light reflected off the snow and frosty ground to provide a forensic precision that links these images with the conventions of crime-scene photography. The variation in lighting effects between the photographs also gives the sequence a pronounced rhythmic momentum, with the opening sequence of five images running through small variations of the triangular shards diverted in image VI by an inversion of the sky triangle that opens the sequence to the panoramic photographs (VII and VIII). These are followed by the steady encroachment of the quarries on the sky that announces the brutal closure and absence of sky in XI & XII, before ending with images XIII and XIV that juxtapose frontal and panoramic perspectives of the main sequence in an uneasy, even threatening equilibrium.

From the outset, the images are illegible to the lay eye, providing an occasion for Kafka to perform image mastery and truth-telling in the supplementary words of the commentary. The commentator claims authority, he is a master of truth, adept in reading the physiognomy of breaks (a quarry is a *Bruch* in German) and an augur of signs that intimate the coming accident. His commentary is spoken in the prophetic voice that knows not only the past and present but also the probable future. The commentator reads the photographs under a disenchanted sky, sensing danger and suggesting first-hand knowledge of each site and its history. The commentary, in short, *warns* the employers – and not only the owners of the 14 quarries – that the Institute *knows* what they do and understands the consequences of their deeds better than they. And, consistent with the prophetic note that resounds in both photographs and commentaries, the Institute is also waiting, when the time comes, to aid in delivering retribution.

The first photograph strikes the startled viewer as an illegible cubist mass of light grey fragments with deep shadowy clefts staining the image surface (Fig. 5).[11] The camera seems to be hovering in mid-air, revealing what may be concealed from above or below. A diagonal line of light at the centre of the photograph divides the field into light and darkness and gives a sense of depth to the scene. The paragraph of commentary speaks with knowledge and authority, telling us that this is a granite quarry and drawing our attention to the threatening formation of columns and ledges in the upper right. The site is littered with debris and is described as a 'desolate heap of ruins' (OW 285, 396). The commentary alerts us to paths through the ruin at the same time as telling us they are blocked with debris. Kafka, in the voice of the anonymous, institutional commentator, then imagines a worker endangered by the difficulty of passage and evokes the perilous sublime represented by this image: 'The dangers that arise when blasting is carried out under these circumstances are inconceivable' (OW 285, 396). The fiction of the endangered worker evoked by Kafka is completed with a studiously casual demonstration of detailed local knowledge: 'in this quarry, blasting is done exclusively with loose black powder' (OW 285, 396). Thus the sequence of photographs opens with the revelation that the initially illegible photograph should be read as a hieroglyph, literally a death trap or accident waiting to happen.

The second photograph (Fig. 6) extends the sharp splinter of sky towards the right, with a cyst of darkness forming beneath the point that it punctures the picture plane. The stain spreads across the left of the image and seems to drain towards the dark stretch of road that, like a black river, flows

FIGURE 5 Photograph I from 'Accident Prevention in Quarries', 1914.

FIGURE 6 Photograph II from 'Accident Prevention in Quarries', 1914.

horizontally across the lower third of the image, pushing the eye towards the left. The commentary points first to the uncleared rubble and then deduces from the *taches* of shadow dotted across the surface the presence of deadly overhanging rocks. It is unimpressed by the railing at the top right of the image and shows that this 'safety measure' in fact endangered workers the more by accumulating debris at the top of the quarry. In this case, judgement is lapidary: 'the quarry should be shut down altogether, at least at this site' (*OW* 285, 396). The case for closure is compelling. The walls of the quarry are 10–16 metres high, and rubble is piled up to 1–3 metres on soft soil. What seems static architecture in the photograph is revealed as a landslide at its point of departure, waiting only for the smallest occasion (*geringsten Anlass*), such as the spring thaw, to start moving.

The theme of arrested movement introduced in the second commentary continues to surface throughout the sequence – the accident requires but a small occasion to initiate catastrophic movement. The first two commentaries also intimate the inversion that will become more prominent as the commentaries proceed: accidents happening are not a matter of bad luck; if there is any question of luck it is only the good luck of not being there when they eventually take place. The third photograph (Fig. 7) contrasts the shard of sky with the shards of illuminated rock that litter the middle of the image. As if in a tourist guide book, our attention is drawn to the alarming 'projecting rock wall' and the enormous heap of rubble. The indisputable evidence of undermining is contrasted with the owner's lies about conditions in the quarry – 'The questionnaire this firm returned denies that there is any evidence of undermining' (*OW* 286, 397). The commentary thus gives

FIGURE 7 Photograph III from 'Accident Prevention in Quarries', 1914.

notice that the claims of the questionnaire have been tested against the photographic evidence and that a favourable risk assessment should not to be hoped for in the case of this quarry.

The fourth photograph (Fig. 8) and short commentary on it shows some novel features, beginning with the singularly unpicturesque tree behind the railings at the top of the quarry, and the use of letters applied to the image to aid legibility. The letter B points to a loose block poised on top of a projecting wall, a conjuncture raising the probability of an imminent accident to almost the point of certainty. The letter S designates a worker in danger, four metres up without a line, working on a dangerous position. Once again rubble litters the foreground of the scene; the owners are clearly reluctant to divert labour from extraction in order to clear the site. The lettering may refer to an earlier stage of archivization, where the photographer listed details evident at the site for the attention of the viewer or viewers in the office. It certainly hints at a context of review and discussion in the Institute which suggests that photographic scrutiny is collective, impersonal and thus incorruptible.

The fifth photograph (Fig. 9) and commentary announces the trope of inversion that in the next photograph will reverse the polarity of the wedge of skylight illuminating the coming accident.[12] The commentator is professionally amused at the perversity of this quarry; the regulation wedge formation for extraction has been applied, but upside down. He is 'almost tempted to say that the quarry would meet the safety regulations better if it were stood on its head' (*OW* 286, 399) or more simply by turning the photograph upside down. Then at least the ubiquitous rubble and debris – tell-tale signs of employer greed and indifference about the safety of their workers – would fall away and the 'nearly suspended, projecting stone block' on the point of falling would be

FIGURE 8 Photograph IV from 'Accident Prevention in Quarries', 1914.

FIGURE 9 Photograph V from 'Accident Prevention in Quarries', 1914.

secured. The photograph indeed reveals an upside-down world, and tells the truth about it to the readers of the Annual Report.

In the next image (Fig. 10) the wedge of sky is reversed, moving from right to left and disrupting the habit of reading an image as if a text from left to right. This disquiets the reading of the clean vertical walls of the quarry which the commentator observes with forensic scepticism. While the debris littering previous images (Kafka refers to 'inspecting quarries such as those in the previous illustrations') *seems* absent, it has in reality not been removed but only compacted into a 'solid layer'. Thus in spite of the 'better impression' created in comparison with the other inspected quarries, 'we are initially not conscious of how far this quarry too is from fulfilling the regulations' (*OW288*, 400). The commentary closes by pointing to a worker in the lower right of the image crushing gravel – he is almost indiscernible in the photograph, and the reference to his working without goggles surely points to what the commentator saw at the scene rather than to information derived from the photograph.[13]

The sequence now shifts drastically from the frontal images to two spacious panoramic photographs (Figs. 11 and 12) in which the upper part of the picture surface is occupied by sky. The sharp visual transition is held in the verbal commentary by a reference to the presence of another gravel worker without goggles, thus repeating the trope that closed the previous commentary. Silhouetted at work in the middle of the lower third of the

FIGURE 10 Photograph VI from 'Accident Prevention in Quarries', 1914.

FIGURE 11 Photograph VII from 'Accident Prevention in Quarries', 1914.

photograph, it is again impossible to infer the absence of goggles from the photograph alone: the worker himself is almost indiscernible. After this repetition of the theme of endangered vision, the commentary adds a new recurring motif to the sequence. The dilapidated narrow-gauge railway introduced in this image is a branch of the extensive railway network that traverses Kafka's writing and will return in all its ruined splendour in photograph X. This railway is innocent of safety measures: there is no incline of the rail at the outer edge of the embankment and so no means of preventing carriages falling off the embankment; there are no emergency braking or stopping devices built into the track to prevent carts escaping control. In this photograph it is the railway and not the overhanging rocks and loose debris that concentrates all the danger of the quarry; danger is built into its negligent construction. The panoramic quarry is also the scene of an inevitable accident involving either derailed or runaway carriages full of stone. The silhouette of a man crouched over his work shouts vulnerability in the agoraphobic space of this quarry; he in no sense masters this landscape but just as in the claustrophobic quarries that precede it, the landscape *looms* over him. Crouching in the questionable shelter of the perilous railway embankment, this worker is an inessential part of a larger, threatening landscape. The image resounds against those of trench warfare, with individual soldiers thrown into a threatening (as Benjamin would later describe it, 'lunar') landscape of earthworks and trenches – for is there not a close resemblance between a quarry and the landscape of trench warfare? The quarry-trench as a theatre of death modulates the theme of industrial accidents with the indifference to life of the war.[14]

The eighth photograph (Fig. 12) resembles a dismembered mountain, full of dangerous craters and pits where excavation had been ventured and abandoned. The danger here, again not immediately evident from scrutiny of the photograph, consists in the level of ground water, in some places up

FIGURE 12 Photograph VIII from 'Accident Prevention in Quarries', 1914.

to 5–6 metres deep. The death by burial under a landslide of dirt and debris threatened in the previous photographs is succeeded in this image by death through drowning. The commentary stipulates that the photograph was taken in winter and that 'The snow points out the narrow ledges and the steep walls immediately over the water' (*OW* 290, 402). Here the accent is on cold water, icy paths, sheer walls and of course the possibility or rather probability of a worker slipping off the path to drown in the icy pools. But this quarry not only sets the scene for a lonely death by drowning in passive waters; it is also a landscape in danger of collapsing on itself, with the 'rock wall' between present and past excavations carelessly maintained and 'hollowed out by ground water' (*OW* 290, 402). The water not only waits for its victims, but actively undermines the scene they inhabit. Its malevolence is intensified by the 'carelessness' with which the 'wall' dividing the current and past excavations is maintained. The theme of the absence of care – for the landscape but above all for the workers – is a *leitmotif* of the sequence, which is a call by the Institute's accident prevention officer for employers and workers to take more care in preventing these dangerous conditions.

With the ninth photograph (Fig. 13) the sky begins to recede and indeed a chunk of it is blocked out by the encroachment of the quarry in the upper-right corner. This adds an air of threat to a quarry that the commentator warns is not what it seems. The 'background' shows 'the beginnings of a proper excavation', but one set in a context that is 'less thought through' (*OW* 403, 290). The approaches to the excavation are blocked with volatile piles of debris : 'Especially on the left the loose rubble threatens to come crashing down' (*OW* 209, 403). Kafka's critique of this quarry exposes

FIGURE 13 Photograph IX from 'Accident Prevention in Quarries', 1914.

carelessness and inconsistency, noting that the properly excavated part of the dangerous whole 'counts for nothing at all; it even increases the danger because it gives the workers a sense of safety' (*OW* 209, 403). By lowering vigilance, the photogenic part of the quarry paradoxically opens the site to the arrival of the accident. By this point in the commentaries, the idea that the accident is a malevolent pressure looking for chinks in care and attention to break through is becoming established, as is the contrast with the accident-proof model in Charlottenburg at the end of the sequence.

The tenth commentary (Fig. 14) is of a density and beauty worthy of Kafka's night work. We are led to the coming accident along a buckled narrow-gauge railway that enters the scene on the well-lit right of the image and curves slightly to the left before wavering and becoming indistinct in its approach to the catastrophic rock face. Giving up on the buckled railway, the gaze moves left to follow the parallel curve of a baleful river that floods into the image over the lower left corner and flows towards the centre before turning to exit slightly above its point of entry. The uniform dark surface of the river gives the viewer a deceptively smooth path to the rock face that contrasts with the twisted rails on the right. The river seems to flow out of the image only to return as the sinuous dark pine wood that curves over the top of the quarry and exits to the right under a grey cornice of sky. The dark curves of river and wood set the quarry in relief, allowing Kafka to point to the perilous fissures of the rock face and the imminent and present danger of a rockfall. He notes that in March, 'when the ground thawed', the road was covered in rubble and adds that 'The life-threatening danger implicit in this quarry must be obvious to any layman' (*OW* 290, 404). This particular

FIGURE 14 Photograph X from 'Accident Prevention in Quarries', 1914.

quarry does not even require expert knowledge for its danger to become legible, and in any case the viewer of the sequence has by this point been educated in reading the physiognomy of these perilous earthworks.

Kafka modulates the description of visual threat into an aural soundscape of danger, unambiguously placing himself on-site; he has been there and has seen, but what is worse, heard: 'Shards of stone never stop rolling downward, and the echo of stones crashing against one another is a constant background noise' (*OW* 291, 404). This noise, of course, is not available from the photograph, but is immediately switched on by the comment. The falling stone that signals a landslide already in course appears in very different contexts in Kafka's writing but always as the intimation of a coming accident. Here the ambient noise is an alarm announcing the arrival of disaster. At the centre of it, and strangely immobilized, is the figure of a worker later marked with an M. This 'worker at the centre of the picture' is a peculiarly manikin figure with head inclined to the right and hands spread out as if on a work surface; this time he is visibly without goggles and, as if in a *Vexierbild*, is camouflaged against the debris of the rock face and seems already merged into the debris that threatens to crush him.

The scant sky that remained from the short panoramic sequence in photograph X is violently extinguished in the stark frontality of images XI and XII (Figs. 15 and 16). The commentator's expert detachment falters before the enormity of the spectacle: 'The sight of this quarry is terrifying [*erschreckend*]. Debris, rubble and refuse overflow everything' (*OW* 293, 405). Mark 'a' in the dead centre of the image is a dusty worker with his back to the camera working on the rock face and standing on a heap of debris.[15] The commentary then performs an act of archival cross-referencing by informing readers that the 1,000 cubic metres of debris on which he is standing collapsed in the thaw of March 1914. Kafka draws from the Institute's new practice of supplementing its accident archives with dated photographic surveillance of working sites. From the accident report submitted by the owners of the quarry he knew that 'Fortunately, the workers were having their afternoon coffee break at the time of the rock fall, or all of them would have been buried alive' (*OW* 291, 405). Aligning (illegal) photographic evidence of a dangerous site with the facts of the accident allowed Kafka to underline, once again, that the accident was not a matter of chance or luck – it was inevitable; the luck consisted in the workers being on their coffee break when the landslide finally arrived. The dusty human figure at point 'a' is effectively a dead man working. Kafka adds that the employer planned to exploit the rockfall by installing 'motorised gravel production to process this pile of stone, which he had obtained quite without cost' (*OW* 291, 405) and, in a subtext for the insurance-paying

FIGURE 15 Photograph XI from 'Accident Prevention in Quarries', 1914.

FIGURE 16 Photograph XII from 'Accident Prevention in Quarries', 1914.

responsible employers reading the reports, thus hoped to profit both from selling the stone and making an accident insurance claim.

Kafka's twelfth image (Fig. 16) is a close-up of an avalanche of debris that 'crashed down during the thaw' and is included to show 'how rock masses can be set in motion during a thaw' (*OW* 291, 406). The comment is again lapidary, but links the thaw with ice, water and a combined avalanche/ landslide. The rocks are only held from falling by ice, and as this melts the rock begins its descent. The cycle of water freezing and melting is joined to that of stone arrested and in motion. The avalanche of rock assembled by careless work during the winter months – excavation 'performed without regard to the regulations' – is held back by the ice, and when it melts with the coming of spring, the rocks fall. The cold delayed the avalanche, and with the loosening grip of the ice with the thaw, pieces of gravel began to fall, announcing the coming accident.

Photographs XIII and XIV combine the panoramic perspective of photographs VII and VIII with the stark frontality of XI and XII, juxtaposing the two perspectives. Photograph XIII (Fig. 17) is a plausible candidate for the execution site of *The Trial*, with a path skirting a foreground heap of debris held back with a tree trunk. In mid-frame is a chalet complex – a shed and smithy underneath a looming hill – and in front of it a clearing with the remains of snow offering an inviting space were it not for the heap of stones tumbling into it. Kafka draws our attention to the trees, roots exposed and slipping slowly and silently down the hill with the rubble. The roots 'hold fast to the debris' and are the only form of precaution taken in this quarry. Loading is carried out at the foot of the mound, a practice Kafka notes 'all the more dangerous in that the entire slope is in a permanent state of sliding' (*OW* 293, 407). This permanent landslide, perceptible only by such traces as the overturned loading platform, would become visible if the site was regularly photographed. The slightly abstract quality of the commentary suggests that Kafka's knowledge of this site is confined to the photograph: he notes, for example that the buildings '*appear* [*scheint*] to lie in the area of rolling debris' (*OW* 293, 407), a description of the state of things more tentative than the other commentaries. The photograph has a delta of sky carefully cropped to touch the upper-right corner and to spread to a quarter of the left side. The right to left movement from a point to a line of sky has the effect of disrupting the legibility of the image, forcing the eye to move from right

FIGURE 17 Photograph XIII from 'Accident Prevention in Quarries', 1914.

to left against the grain of reading a text, a movement also encouraged by the visual invitation to enter the perilous loading area and move towards the chalets.

The final desolate snowscape of photograph XIV (Fig. 18) intimates a backdrop for the avalanche of non-events that will make up *The Castle* by combining panorama with a threatening heap of debris. There is no obvious visual point of entry to the image and the area of sky to the left is balanced against the large block of rock to the right. An obscure line of posts to the lower left invites us to leave the image as soon as possible. The commentary explains that this is a new quarry and the posts are supposed to separate it from the local railway line. Instead the rubble here 'threatens the nearby railroad with its great piles of trash' (*OW* 293, 408). The last commentary is interrupted by more general considerations on the context and the value of the collection of photographs. After pointing to the danger to the travelling public represented by the fourteenth quarry, Kafka digresses to reflect on the cognitive gain of his photo exercise, noting that 'All these quarries share certain characteristics in spite of their individual differences' (*OW* 293, 408). He means two things by this claim. The first is contextual: none of these hazardous quarries sufficiently respects safety ordinances and yet they continue in existence; they were never penalized by Trade Inspectors nor shut down on the grounds of risk to their workers or the public. And yet they also qualify as claimants for accident insurance, a feature probably determining Kafka's choice of specific quarries to visit. This feature points to the second common characteristic, which is that all the quarries are theatres of industrial accidents, sites of class war in which workers are

FIGURE 18 Photograph XIV from 'Accident Prevention in Quarries', 1914.

maimed and killed for enhanced profits in conditions similar to soldiers at the front. Not only do 'The accident statistics for these quarries show very costly accidents, even mass accidents' (OW 293, 408), but they continue in operation as accidents waiting to happen: 'where accidents have not yet occurred, there exists a strong likelihood [*Wahrscheinlichkeit*] that they will happen any given working day' (OW 293, 408). The accident is inevitable, only *when* it will occur is a question of probability and this is at its height in spring with the thaw – April is the cruellest month for Bohemian quarry workers. And Kafka adds, before moving out of his photo-sequence and into the third and final section of his report, 'we must always keep in mind that these are only examples, whose number can be multiplied at will' (OW 294, 409). The accident is legion, and prevention consists in deferring its onset rather than hoping to abolish its conditions of possibility.

Kafka then returns to the final image of the fictional quarry in Charlottenburg that assembles 'four ideal quarries in full operation' (OW 296, 411) primed for safe blasting. The image presents a model of practice that the Bohemian quarries cannot even hope to approximate. It also serves as a sure pedagogical aid for giving lessons in safe blasting, much needed in Prague where Kafka cites a report on a blasting accident : 'The victim of the accident was gently heating 4 dynamite cartridges on a shovel at a small fire, because the dynamite just having been taken from cold storage had solidified. The cartridges exploded (in a manner not yet explained!).' (OW 295, 410) Kafka's explanation mark in the parenthesis says all that is necessary.

As we have seen, 'Accident Prevention in Quarries' appeared alongside reports on the impact of the war in the 1914 Annual Report. Although presenting the results of the Institute's work in this field following the 1911 accident, it nevertheless complements the focus on the effects of the war in the rest of the Annual Report. It parallels the exercise in reality by numbers performed by Kafka for the wartime political economy of Bohemia with its individuation of a catastrophic tendency according to district with the accident wave sweeping the Bohemian quarries individuated according to visual examples. The visual logic deployed across the quarry sequence and commentaries describes a single accident taking its course through the individual quarries, identifying the accident as a tendency realizing itself over time and contrasted with the timeless ideal quarry that closes the sequence. Just as Kafka's statistical analyses are individuated into commentaries on individual districts, so the individual commentaries on the photographs individuate the statistical population of potential accidents, emphasizing not only what has happened but also what is to come. The photographs punctuate the accident wave or avalanche carrying away the quarries of Bohemia and with them their workers and even unwitting

Nezáleží tu právě na dodatečném jednotlivém poučení, nýbrž na předchozí výchově.

Tak jako říšskoněmeckými odborovými společenstvy pořádány jsou přednášky pro střelmistry (Schiessmeister), budou nutna podobná zařízení i u nás. Právě, pokud se trhacích prací týče, jsou ode dávna zakořeněné předsudky zavedení lepších zařízení na úkor. Zde pak nepomůže pouhé poučování, nýbrž zpravidla jen příklad na místě samém. V mnoha případech bude na př. lze odstraniti pochybnosti o upotřebitelnosti dřevěných nabíječů jen tím, ukáže-li odborník v lomě samém, že i při skrovnější hloubce vyvrtané díry dřevěné nabíječe úplně postačí.

Jaká naivnost jeví se namnoze při trhacích pracích i na místech, o nichž by bylo lze souditi, že jsou dokonale poučena, dokazuje tento popis úrazu, podaný lesní správou o smrtelném úrazu. Zněl: „Úrazem postižený hřál 4 dynamitové patrony, jež byly mu z chladného skladiště právě vydány, u malého ohně, drže je na lopatě, při čemž patrony nevysvětlitelným způsobem (!) vybuchly."

Vyobrazení XV. Obrázek tento nám znázorňuje, jak příkladně německé lomařské družstvo provádí příkazy o odstřelování. Toto zde jest snímek modelu stálé výstavy pro blaho dělnictva v Charlottenburku. Rozumí se samo sebou, že fotografie modelu nemůže znázorniti to, co by snad skutečnost ukázala. Na všechen způsob nabudeme názoru o tom, jak mnoho zbývá ještě na tomto poli vykonati.

Přednáška o trhacích pracích, konaná před tímto modelem, nemůže zůstati bez vydatného účinku.

Model představuje v přirozené velikosti, v přirozeném složení a způsobu dobývání, jakož i v přírodních barvách 4 ideální kamenné lomy v plné práci se všemi jednotlivostmi trhacího zařízení.

81

FIGURE 19 Photograph XV from 'Accident Prevention in Quarries', 1914.

travellers passing by in trains. Just as Durkheim's individual suicides individuate the suicidogenic waves sweeping late nineteenth-century Europe, so these quarries manifest an underlying wave or current. The accident is brought to light as much by its individuation in a single image as by its place in an orchestrated sequence of images that point beyond the flotsam and jetsam of individual quarries to the underlying movement. The photographic sequence documents the coming landslide, sketching the catastrophic accident that will take all in its path, intimated in the dissolving world of the fat man in 'Description of a Struggle'.

The missing photograph

America opens as *The Trial* will end – in a flash of light. Just as the flash from a window exposes a naked Josef K. spreadeagled over a rock awaiting execution, so the mutation of the torch of liberty into a photographic flash gun captures Karl Rossmann upon entry to *America*.[16] He was expelled from home for accidentally impregnating the family maid and, as his ship slowly enters New York Harbour, he bobs between a past slipping behind him and the future promised by the Statue of Liberty. His revery is shattered as the torch of liberty ignites like a crime-scene photographer's flash gun bathing the Statue and Rossmann 'in a new light'. Liberty's enlightened welcome on this sunny morning ignites into something altogether darker and troubling. Under intense illumination, Liberty shape-changes into an allegorical figure of justice, no longer holding the flaming torch of enlightenment and liberty but a sword to execute the law that is also a photographic flash gun to record that justice has been done: 'Her arm with the sword towered up anew and the free winds blew around her figure' (*A* 201, 9). The sword/flash gun captures Rossman's arrival; before even setting foot ashore, his appearance has been recorded and archived by the Statue watching him looking at it.[17] The perceiver is transformed into an object of perception, photographed in the act of looking and recoiling with shame, a movement figured in the retributive sword that Rossman sees looming over him and captured in the last words of Josef. K. – 'it was as if the shame would outlive him'. And this is but the first of a series of uncanny photographs that will accompany and direct Rossmann's fatal free-fall into America. Justice condemns young Rossmann at the threshold of novel and continent, and the dazed movements and miscalculations that follow bring him ever closer to executing its sentence.

Kafka retrospectively confirmed the affinity between the two abandoned novels from the autumns of 1912 and 1914[18] in a diary entry of 30 September

1915: 'Rossman and K., the innocent [*Schuldlose*] and the guilty [*Schuldige*] both punitively executed without distinction, the innocent with a lighter hand, more pushed aside than struck down' (*D* 343–4, 585).[19] Both are novels of procrastination that relate the futile evasive manoeuvres of the already condemned, and the pornographic image of a naked man being ritually executed complements the immigration photograph taken on Rossmann's entering *America*. The shape-changes of Liberty presage Karl's experience of America as less the promised land of freedom and the pursuit of happiness than an elaborate theatre for the execution of an implacable justice.[20] In a flash, Liberty becomes first Justice, then a photographically recording angel and finally a Goddess of the hunt whose deadly pursuit is presaged by 'unrestrained winds' that indeed 'play around her figure' and will torment Karl until the landslide that is America finally arrives to gently but inexorably push him aside. The 'missing person' or 'lost one' of Kafka's title (*Der Verschollene*) is prey introduced into the hunting reserve that is America: sexual prey for the family maid and for Klara Pollunder, economic prey for Delamarche and Robinson and eventually mortal prey for the 'nature theatre of Oklahama'.

The hunting down of Karl Rossman leaves a trail of loss: loss of memory and concentration but also of umbrellas, suitcases, hats and, driving it all, the loss and fateful recovery of a photograph. The quest for the lost photograph traverses an historical and geographical landscape haunted by the photo-reportage of Arthur Holitscher's *Amerika: Heute und Morgen* (*America: Today and Tomorrow*) (1912) that Kafka owned and esteemed, using it as visual inspiration for his novel. The novel equates the modality of the accident with that of the photograph later described by Benjamin, in *A Small History of Photography*, as the transformation of the contingent accident – the missing, the fugitive, the lost or stolen – into necessity. *America* works through such modal transformations, showing how Karl's contingent losses pile up until finally and ineluctably burying him.[21]

The opening flash enhances the darkness that accompanies much of the subsequent action. This is a book of the night, written during the autumn and winter nights of 1912–13 and betraying intense sensitivity to the quality of perception under artificial light and the uncanny menace of nocturnal sound. Yet the opening chapter, 'The Stoker', and the fragmentary last chapter, 'Nature Theatre of Oklahama', from the autumn of 1914 seem bathed in light, but it is the harsh corona of the opening flash accompanying the jagged sights and sounds accompanying Karl's road to perdition. For the opening flash of light is sustained throughout the slow eclipse of the superfluous Rossmann, lighting the story of his extended execution through a slow and irreversible brushing aside.[22]

His revery of arrival rudely interrupted, young Rossmann is jolted back to size; from the guilty centre of the world he reverts to being a young man in the crowd bustling to disembark. His first words 'So high' not only positions him as 'so low' but also contrasts the reality of the Statue of Liberty with his photographic expectations of it. There follows a remorseless sequence of accidents and losses that initiate Rossmann's fated metamorphosis into a lost cause. The glimpse of the swinging stick of his friend carried away by the crowd reminds him of his forgotten umbrella. He 'surveys the situation' and returns into the ship, moving against the current of the crowd until diverted into the labyrinthine world of below-deck where he is immediately lost. In a compressed preview of the disoriented continental wanderings that await him, Rossman 'had to find his way painfully through numerous small rooms, winding corridors, short recurring staircases and a empty room with an abandoned writing table ... until he was completely lost' (A 201–2, 10). Although he can hear the distant sounds of the disembarking crowd and the shutting down of the ship's engines, he meets no one who can tell him the way, not even the author, who has abandoned his writing table. So he knocks on a door he accidentally ran into during his confused rush along the ship's corridors ...

Carried along by a cascade of accidents, Rossmann approaches his fateful encounter with 'The Stoker'. Were it not for the swinging walking stick, the forgotten umbrella and his disorientation below deck, Rossmann would have disappeared into the crowd, the disembarkation concluded and the novel terminated. Instead, he is literally arrested, drawn into the the Stoker's cramped cabin and then stretched out on his bed. The Stoker loathes being looked at and wants to close the door even though Rossman insists the corridor is empty: '"Yes, Now it is" the man said. "But then it's now we are talking about," thought Karl, "talking to this man is tough"' (A 202, 11). Rossman's sense of the present contrasts starkly with the time of the Stoker who seems condemned to live in a future where there might *always be* passers-by, but even Rossmann's grasp on the present is shaken on catching sight of the Stoker's partially packed suitcase. Thrown back by a memory he recalls, 'Oh God, I've completely forgotten my suitcase!' (A 203, 11) and abandons his grasp of the present for the memory of potential loss.[23]

The ensuing conversation with the Stoker places the loss and recovery of the suitcase within a peculiar modal temporality. Karl evokes the sequence of accidents initiated by his forgotten umbrella and his entrusting the suitcase to a certain Butterbaum, only to be brought up short by the Stoker's abrupt return to 'the now' *Jetzt*. Previously the Stoker appealed to *Jetzt* in order to insist on counterfactual possibility – the corridor is empty *now*, but might not always be so – but now he pronounces *Jetzt* as a mark of conclusive necessity: 'And now you have lost your suitcase too. I will say nothing of the umbrella' (*A* 203, 11). The umbrella will indeed return once more before being definitively lost to the novel; but for *now* it remains only to be forgotten. Its absence will be marked by his uncle's authoritative and all-too-present bamboo cane, tapping the floor in the Captain's cabin where he is waiting for him at this moment, but along with the suitcase it is lost for *now* and, according to the Stoker's temporality, may well remain so for all future time.

Rossman attempts to restore possibility to the *now* against the Stoker's *now and probably for all time* by appealing to faith – 'But I believe the suitcase is still not lost' (*A* 203, 11). But this only provokes the Stoker to adopt the hybrid persona of ethnographer and insurance man in assessing the *probability* of the young man's loss. The risk of loss depends on the customs of the port for while in Hamburg Butterbaum would probably wait and watch the case, in New York it is highly probable (*hochstwahrscheinlich*) that both he and the suitcase will have disappeared. Rossman's panic is restrained by the Stoker who adds that the probability of retrieving the suitcase depends on a series of accidents beyond Karl's control and thus concern. In any case they should wait for the ship to empty and then go see if, as is probable, the suitcase has been stolen, leaving Karl to lament its loss for the rest of his days or, less probable but not to be excluded for now, to find Butterbaum improbably waiting or having left word that he had put the case aside for him to collect.

Rossmann slips out of consciousness, distractedly ruminating on the contents of his suitcase: the clean clothes, his second-best suit (fortunately), a salami which he had only sampled but could have used to bribe the Stoker in the same way his father bribed lowly officials with cigarettes. This somnolent inventory is recalled later, when, suspended on another threshold between sleep and waking, Karl remembers what was so precious in the contents of the suitcase, more precious than the case itself: a photograph of his parents. The second inventory takes place at night in a squalid boarding house after a series of improbable adventures involving his rich and powerful uncle and his sinister friends. Expelled again, this time by his uncle and alone on the road, Karl is reunited with his umbrella and suitcase, but also with the cares of protecting them from danger – for him they are objects he can potentially lose. The interval between the first inventory of the lost and the second inventory of the recovered suitcase is filled by Karl being united and then separated from his capitalist uncle and sampling the life of a privileged dependent, one that begins with his involuntary sacrifice of his newly found and just as quickly lost friend, the Stoker.

Now all that's over, he is found surveying the contents of his 'newly won' suitcase by candlelight in a squalid Inn. Karl's second inventory is haunted by the anxiety that he might not remember its contents and that the 'most valuable' items have already been lost or stolen. Although nothing seems to be missing from the case, Karl is dismayed by the disorder of its contents. He spent hours packing and repacking the case during his voyage, and indeed will now repeat this action by candlelight, spreading his property across the table. He is satisfied that his pass and money are still there, along with the washed and neatly ironed clothes that he was wearing on arrival. Slamming his suitcase shut, Rossmann inadvertently awakens his disreputable roommates – Robinson and Delamarche – who after a brief conversation go back to sleep leaving Karl to sink in revery on the sofa. He leafs through the Bible and then contemplates his most precious possession, the photograph of his parents.

The attention Rossmann lends to the photograph is consistent with Kafka's own strikingly intense practice of looking at photographs attested by his letters. His and Karl's hermeneutics of photography has three striking characteristics: close attention to contingent detail (anticipating Benjamin's 'spark of contingency' and Barthes' *punctum*), a view of the individual photograph as a point of intersection between actual and virtual photographic sequences, and third, an attention to the physicality of the photographic print. His fatigued contemplation of the image focuses initially on the detail of the hands of his father, one resting on the back of the sofa in which the mother seemed to be almost submerged and the other clenched into a fist resting on an illustrated book. Karl's looking is immediately modulated by the oblique memory of another photograph, this time of his parents sharply contemplating him while he concentrated on obeying the photographer's demand that he look at the camera. The photograph was of him, but he recalls the spectacle of his parents' disapproving gaze while it was being taken as if were itself a photograph. The existing photograph is thus situated within a virtual sequence or album of other, now absent or even never existent photographs that provide at once a portal for entry into a virtual photographic memory, but also and more importantly situate the given photograph within that archive of surviving, missing and imagined photographs.

The initial contemplation of the photograph and the excursus into its virtual archive of recollected and imaginary neighbours is succeeded by a forensic investigation of the gaze of his father. The hunt for the gaze, one of a series of such efforts to dissolve the separation of the subject and object of the gaze executed in the novel, is facilitated by means of moving the photograph around with respect to the candlelight. Yet the funerary scenario of viewing by candlelight could not lend life to the father, and the photograph is judged unsuccessful with respect to his actuality (*Wirklichkeit*) that now yields but the memory of his father. Karl's gaze moves over to his mother, where his attention falls not so much on her gaze as on her mouth, which was tightly drawn in a way that suggests both suffering and a forced smile. Meditating on the possibility of inferring feelings from an image, Karl looks away for a little while (*ein weilchen lang weg*). Returning from this revery he brings the photograph close to his body, almost kissing the hand of his mother. On the threshold of sleep he enters a time that folds past into present and future: he remembers his mother's announcement of the journey to America 'at the window' (a darkened window because it was 'evening') and revises the vow he made then never to write to his parents (*A* 281, 106). Embracing the photograph he asks himself whether he should write as his parents had asked – his present reality of sharing an attic with a couple of bums surely cancelled any vows made in the proud past. And, moving into divinatory mode, he smiled and scrutinized the photographed faces of his parents to see if they still longed for news of their lost son.

The complex temporality that emerged in Karl's contemplation of the infinite possibilities opened by the door of the photograph – one that permitted entry to other actual and potential galleries of photographs and with them the interpretation and revision of the past and even the divination of a remote future – is oriented around the rueful sense that he is 'really in the right place for him now' (*A* 281, 107). This sense of actuality – *das er hier wirklich an seinem Platze war* – contrasts with the fantasy of where he might have imagined himself being two months before: *then* he could have imagined himself a general in the American army; *now*, however, he is free of such possibilities. Unable to stay awake any longer, the photograph falls from his hands to serve as a pillow on which he lays his face. The coolness of the print against his cheek hot with dashed hopes and disappointment allows him to surrender his previous hopes and possibilities for a consoling surrender to sleep. No longer an object of contemplation, the photograph is now enjoyed physically as a cooling fabric inviting him to slip away. The photographic episode that began with the attempt to infuse light and life into the image, ends with the image drawing the heat and the life out of Karl and bearing him softly and pleasurably into oblivion.

Woken next morning by his ragged roommates, Karl is persuaded to join them on a journey by foot to the nearby city where they say there is work and opportunity. The suitcase is at the centre of their deliberations with the new companions promising to help carry it, but their negotiations are interrupted by the arrival of the *Zimmerfrau* who unceremoniously packs the suitcase by throwing Karl's stuff into it 'with such violence as if they were some animals that she had to bring to heel' (*A* 283, 109). She closed it, pushed it into his hands and threw all three guests out. In the ensuing 'March to Ramses' the weight of the suitcase is a constant issue, with his companions complaining and increasingly reluctant to keep their promise and help carry it. The transit of the suitcase through the suburbs of New York towards Butterford ends at nightfall in a suburban landscape of gardens and a river where the companions resolve to pass the night in the open. Once again Karl abandons his suitcase – at least this time having taken the precaution of locking it – in order to forage for food at the nearby Hotel Occidental.

When Karl returns with provisions he finds his companions asleep and, to his horror, the locked suitcase (the key was in his pocket) lying wide open and half its contents scattered on the grass. The violation of the case provokes a breakdown in the relationship between the three travellers. Robinson and Delamarche do not apologize but pretend Karl is using the excuse of the violated case to escape their company for the superior attractions of his new friends at the hotel. The violent argument escalates over the suitcase, with Karl stepping backwards over the case, Delamarche pushing it aside in order to reach Karl and in doing so making matters worse by putting his foot on one of Karl's white shirt-fronts scattered on the ground. The altercation was interrupted by the arrival of a waiter from the hotel carrying a torch who had come to reclaim the basket Karl borrowed to carry food to his friends; Karl now wishes to return with him, along with his case, once it has been repacked by torchlight.

Bending to pick up the few things (*Sachen*) still scattered on the grass, Karl suddenly straightens with dismay at a dreadful discovery: 'Everything was there, just the photograph was missing' (*A* 301, 131). At this turning point of the narrative, Karl commences his search for the missing photograph. First he asks Delamarche '"I can't find the photograph" ... "what kind of photograph?" asked the latter. "The photograph of my parents" said Karl' (*A* 301, 130). Delamarche responds, '"We didn't see any photograph"', a reply confirmed by Robinson '"There wasn't any photograph in there Herr Rossmann"' (*A* 301, 130). Faced with this testimony to the absent photograph, Karl turns to the waiter-witness with an appeal to necessity: '"But that's quite impossible" said Karl and his beseeching glances drew the waiter closer. "It was lying on the top and now it's gone. If only you hadn't played about with my suitcase"' (*A* 301, 130). The passage from the impossibility of the photograph not being in the case to its actual absence provokes a flurry of interpretation. Karl's first response is to regard the loss as an accident that took place during his companions' search for food. However, Delamarche responds by asserting necessity: '"Any error is excluded" said Delamarche "there was no photograph in the suitcase"' (*A* 301, 130). Maybe he was right: the circumstances of Karl falling asleep on the photograph, his rude awakening and the maid's summary packing of his suitcase all point to the possibility of the photograph being left behind in the guesthouse. Yet Karl cannot conceive this, for his anguish at the loss begins to cloud his judgement. While the waiter continued to search around in the grass, Karl rued '"It was more important to me than all the other things in the suitcase" . . . "it's simply irreplaceable; I will not get a second one"' (A 301, 130). Like Josef K., Karl begins to look for a meaning, some necessity to this loss, unable to accept it as a bare accident. Better malign necessity than none at all.

He is abetted in this by the waiter who, giving up on the search in the grass, suggests frisking the 'gentlemens' pockets'. The insinuation that the photograph has been stolen is immediately endorsed by Karl: '"Yes," said Karl without hesitation, "I must find the photograph"' (A 301, 131). The necessity of restoring the missing photograph and the growing possibility of having to resume life without it begins to corrode Karl's faith in the world, beginning with his erstwhile companions. Yet not entirely, for he begins with an offer, proposing to exchange all his worldly belongings, the whole suitcase, for the missing photograph. His offer is met with silence, interpreted by Karl as stubbornness, and so he proceeds with the search all the while keeping open his offer, even proposing to give his suitcase to the one in whose pockets the photograph is found and so rewarding the thief. Whether proposed as reward or as hecatomb or promised sacrifice, the incentive does not produce the photograph. Indeed, while touching Robinson's 'hot plump chest', 'he became aware' that he was committing an injustice. Yet he smothers this awareness and hurries on with his search.

Not finding the photograph, the demonic waiter gives up for him – 'It's no good' – and Karl promptly surrenders to the scarcely consoling hypothesis: 'They've probably torn up the photograph and thrown the pieces away' (A 302, 131). The suggestion that the photograph had been destroyed makes sense only on the assumption that Robinson and Delamarche had been maliciously disposed to Karl all along and wanted to cause him gratuitous harm. Karl embraces this assumption, declaiming, 'I thought they were my friends, but secretly they only wanted to injure me. Not so much Robinson, he could never have imagined that the photograph was worth so much to me, that's more Delamarche' (A 302, 131). Having arrived at this 'recognition' of the intrinsically evil character of Delamarche, Karl perversely invests the loss of the photograph with the meaning of an evil intent, and situates himself as its victim. At this moment of psychic ruin, Delamarche, Robinson and 'everything else' (alles sonst) sinks into darkness leaving only the waiter with his torchlight to lead the way back to the hotel.

At this moment of the end of a world, the loss of his last link to his family and to Europe – the waiter picks up the suitcase while Karl takes up the basket and both set off. But on reaching the street, Karl is held by an afterthought, and tries to trade once more. He cries into the night, 'Just listen. If one of you really does still have the photograph and will bring it to me at the hotel, he can still have the case and I swear will not be reported' (A 302, 132). In another intimation of the execution in *The Trial*, also by night in a deserted suburb, all that came back was a 'tentative word', an opening akin to the flash of light perceived by Josef K. that here raises Karl's hopes that this was Robinson trying respond only to be silenced by Delamarche ... then silence. Karl waited and then cried again, and then again, 'I am still there' (*Ich bin doch immer da*) – still at his place (in a dangerous quarry it turns out) waiting for a reply.

There was no answering voice, but in the night 'just once a stone rolled down from an overhanging slope, perhaps by chance, perhaps in a bungled throw' (*nur einmal rollte ein Stein den Abhang herab, vielleicht durch Zufall, vielleicht in einem verfehlten wurf*) (A 302, 132). The action has imperceptibly shifted from a garden to a dangerous quarry, with Karl standing beneath the overhang of an unstable excavation. Yet his fate is still not sealed, at least not for now, since with the repeated 'perhaps' (also implied in Josef's K.'s final desperate hopes at the end of *The Trial*) possibility seems to be restored by casting as chance the stark predicament provoked by the irreversible loss of the photograph. The tumbling stone *perhaps* fell by accident or was perhaps thrown by malice aforethought. Yet maybe there is more to it since the metamorphosis of the bucolic suburban landscape into a dangerous quarry – complete with perilous overhanging crag – not only links this scene of traumatic loss with the execution of K. at the end of *The Trial* but also situates both with respect to Kafka's 'Accident Prevention in Quarries'. The latter we saw described photographs of dangerous quarries as accidents waiting to happen, scenes of imminent industrial execution. What is important in the context of Karl's cry into the night is the reply of the falling stone. In the hazardous quarries, dislodged and falling stones point to deeper subterranean shifts moving towards disaster, with the accident understood as the manifestation of literally fundamental necessity. The choice Karl perceives between accident and the bungled throw of a stone is an illusion – for slowly and inexorably an accident/execution is taking its course and he is in its path without insurance and with insufficient accident prevention experience to read the signs and avoid the coming disaster.

As in the case of fellow accident victims Josef K. and the Hunter Gracchus, Karl's error consists not only in searching for someone responsible – a quest that carries him over the borders of paranoia – but also in assuming that the choice between chance accident and malign agency, between *Zufall* and *einem verfehlten wurf*, exhausts all the possibilities of explaining what has befallen him. The statistical tables of the insurance man reveal, after the event, a necessity intrinsic to individual accidents that is neither random nor the outcome of intent. The accident in the quarry is announced, but cannot be predicted – it can be held off by a careful scrutiny of the signs and capable accident prevention work, but once it takes place it will have been inexorable. In the case of Karl, the falling stones have been resounding since the first line of the novel, announcing his inevitable execution. A seismic logic is at work in the escalating series of accidents and coincidences that accompany and increasingly direct the hapless downhill career of Herr Karl Rossman, just ahead of the landslide that will eventually push aside and bury him.

Kafka's fictional writing intensifies the encounter between collective and individual fate, the sense that a quota of accidents must occur but when and to whom remaining unpredictable until after the event. The individual moves through a landscape of risk, traversing fault lines and points of danger, striving to evade or at least defer the onset of the accident. Yet we have seen that writing as accident prevention, as holding off of the inevitable, occupies a strange space and time in which the hope of freedom and the fear of necessity are of little use or relevance. The fictional writings do indeed hand over the life – *habeat vitam* – but unlike *habeas corpus*, this life is not delivered for trial and judgement since the execution of the sentence is already underway. Karl, like Josef K., was condemned on arrival, at the very outset of the novel, by the Statue of Liberty holding aloft a sword. From that moment the sword began slowly to lower itself on Karl, as inexorably as the swords of the executioners were plunged into Josef K. His story though is not a trial – but then neither is Josef K's, whose greatest error is to imagine that it is – but just a long and drawn-out execution. And in both cases it is essentially a photographed execution . . .

The suitcase is once again in transit, but this time towards the hotel, where Karl temporarily suspends his wanderings through the new world to become a lift boy – substituting for the hazardous horizontal movements across New York state the apparently secure and repeated vertical movements of a hotel lift. What will prove but a month's residence at the Hotel Occidental constitutes a parenthesis accompanied by portents. Karl begins his hotel career with a lie by claiming to come from Prague . . . He also keeps open the possibility that the photograph will be returned by his companions, asking the Head Cook: 'It's possible that tomorrow morning, perhaps early, my one-time friends will bring a photograph that I urgently need. Would you be so kind as to telephone the Porter for him to send them to me or have me fetched' (*A* 306, 136). The Head Cook readily agrees but asks if it would suffice to have the photograph left for him, and what kind of a photograph was it? Karl replies truthfully, 'It's a photograph of my parents ... No I must speak to the men myself' (*A* 306, 136). Having arranged for the possible reception of the lost photograph, Karl finds himself sleeping in the Head Cook's reception room, with the reassurance that 'His suitcase was there all right, waiting for him, and certainly had not been so safe for a long time' (*A* 307–8, 138). Yet this reassurance is constantly troubled by the memory of the lost photograph. He finds partial compensation in the Head Cook's photographic gallery, exhibited on a little cupboard in her suite. Framed and under glass, the collection of 'nearly all old photographs' on display was mainly of little girls in uncomfortable traditional dress and a young soldier with a 'proud but repressed smile' (*A* 308, 138).

Sharing his author's attention to the materiality of the photograph, Karl notices that the buttons on the soldier's uniform 'had been subsequently gilded' (*A* 308, 138). This attention to the artifice of the image is extended to the rest of the Head Cook's collection; Karl surmises that all these photographs, like his own missing photograph, stem from Europe and that if he wished he could confirm this by looking at the back of them. But his respect for photographic materiality prevented him from taking them in his hand; instead, surveying the display he imagines a counterfactual world in which he too would 'set up the photograph of his parents in the room he was going to have, just like these photographs here' (*A* 308, 139). The tense in which his wish is framed almost denies the possibility of it ever being realized: he imagines a future in which he has a room of his own and still possesses the photograph of his parents; but the photograph is lost and any future in which it might feature was becoming remote if not unattainably lost, for now.

The lost photograph drags Karl down after it in a series of accidents informed by an increasingly evident but grim necessity. He is expelled from the hotel due to mistaken identity and the hostility of the Hotel Porter whom he offended by asking if a photograph had been left for him. Reunited with Delamarche and Robinson, Karl escapes the hotel in a car which rushed wildly away narrowly avoiding another rendezvous with the accident: 'It looked as if an accident was inevitable, but the all-embracing stream of traffic drew into itself even the sharp path of their vehicle' (*A* 365, 209). A deferred execution, the individual accident absorbed for now by traffic, Rossman finds himself expelled again, but even this is not yet the final sentence. The pattern of deferred sentence that will be central to *The Trial* was described by Kafka in a letter to Felice of 11 November 1912 as '*allerdings ins Endlose angelegt ist*' – the infinitely deferred event of the execution held off by writing.

Karl is liberated to a new captivity by Delamarche and Robinson, this time as a household slave to the singer Brunelda. Just as his arrival in New

York Harbour was accompanied by the music of the ship's band and his entrance to the Nature Theatre of Oklahoma by angelic trumpeters, so is his captivity accompanied by the raucous music of a political rally. A marching band arrives in the street below accompanied by a parodic apparition of Lincoln, anticipating his later manifestation in the Nature Theatre of Oklahama.[24] The enslaved Karl watches the spectacle of a facsimile Liberator working the crowd, ironically asking his captors Delamarche and Brunelda 'what's it about down there?' (*A* 405, 257). Visible to the naked eye amid the musicians and the procession was a 'giant man' who seemed to have on his shoulders another man who was 'waving his top hat to and fro at lightning speed' (*A* 403, 251). The crowds chanted the name of the politician to the rhythm of their clapping hands while the politician gave a speech bathed in car headlights to the growing uproar of a fight between his supporters and opponents. The political breakdown in the street is accompanied by Delamarche and Brunelda's intensifying threats to Karl's liberty that together provoke his first unsuccessful escape attempt.

Kafka's composition of *America* was itself trapped in Brunelda's penthouse, stalled from January 1913 until the summer of 1914 when writing resumed with Karl's exit from the apartment in 'Brunelda's Voyage Out' and then in October with the final chapter, 'Nature Theatre of Oklahama'. The last section was written alongside *The Trial* and 'In the Penal Colony'. This proximity should be warning enough that the Nature Theatre of Oklahoma cannot plausibly be the utopian happy ending to Rossman's adventures in America imagined by Brod, Benjamin and Arendt. It is indeed suspended between the executions of its contemporary novel and novella, proposing an extraordinarily bleak terminus to the American career of Karl Rossmann.

The 1912–13 version leaves Karl in slavery contemplating the fantasmal apparition of the 'Liberator'; and Lincoln returns two years later in the 'Nature Theatre of Oklahoma' where a photograph is restituted and another indirectly evoked. In a further sombre development of the theme of slavery, Karl enrols in the Nature Theatre of Oklahoma with a name that perpetuated the oppression of the abused erstwhile slave population of the United States: 'So as no other name occurred to him at the moment, he gave the nickname he had in his last post: "Negro"' (*A* 306, 429). Adopting the name given him, a name that identifies him with oppressed African Americans, Karl is admitted to the 'Nature Theatre' to the near comic incredulity of its officials. His real name Rossmann, Redman, might have been even more out of place, given Oklahoma's infamous reputation for being the territory that brutally betrayed and expropriated Native Americans not once, but twice.[25]

On admittance, Karl is directed to an abundant welcome feast for all the new staff where he finds a pile of photographic 'views of the theatre of

Oklahoma which lay at a pile at one end of the table and which were supposed to pass from hand to hand' (*A* 435, 313–14). Only one reached Karl at the end of the table, and he contemplated it closely. It effectively replaced the lost photograph of his family and his European past and pointed to his American future:

> This picture showed the box reserved in the theatre for the President of the United States. At first glance one might think it was not a box but the stage itself, for the parapet soared up into the open air. This parapet was made entirely of gold, to the smallest detail. Between its finely carved columns were arrayed medallions of former presidents, one with a strikingly straight nose, curling lips and eyes looking rigidly down beneath vaulted eye-lids. Around the box rays of light fell from above and from all sides, soft and white light that revealed the foreground of the box while its interior behind red curtains falling in changing folds from roof to floor held with cords, appeared like a dark red shimmering void. A duskily glowing empty cavern. One could scarcely imagine human figures in that box, everything looked so majestic.
>
> (*A* 435–6, 314)

Karl's rapture at the photograph is interrupted by the arrival of an old friend who fatally distracts his attention from the interpretation of the photograph. For this view of the 'Nature Theatre' is in a very real sense a 'History Theatre', as it is a widely circulated photograph of the box in the Washington theatre where Abraham Lincoln was assassinated on 14 April 1865. The 'Nature Theatre' is a scene of execution, but specifically the scene of the execution of the President who signed the Emancipation Edict. Kafka thus carefully aligns the 'Nature Theatre' with the doubly literal theatre of an historical event which set back the progress of African Americans for almost a century. The view of the 'Nature Theatre' also has some peculiar formal properties that rehearse a recurrent trope in the novel: the place from which to view, the theatre box, becomes the theatre itself. The spectator – Karl at the outset of the novel and Lincoln on the eve of his assassination – himself becomes the object of a murderous gaze. This view of the 'Nature Theatre' also appears to be a mausoleum, or empty tomb. An ambivalence surrounds whether this box is a tomb whose occupant has been resurrected or whether it is still awaiting an occupant, one compounded by the appearance of a portrait of Lincoln among the presidents commemorated on the front of the box. It is as if this image of the Washington theatre came from a world and a history in which Lincoln was not assassinated and in which he impossibly took his place among the presidents commemorated on the front of the box.

Yet even ambivalence is a rare gesture of alleviation in the 'Nature Theatre's' unremittingly bleak scenario, since the gathering of names connected to the history of racial injustice in the United States – 'Negro', 'Lincoln' – is bound with a third: 'Oklahama'. The misspelling of Oklahoma provides an indirect citation of another photograph, one drawn from the photo-reportage of Arthur Holitscher, *Amerika: Heute und Morgen* (1912). The caption of one of the photographs in this collection in the chapter on racism and lynching, 'The Negroes', reads 'Oklahama Idyll', with a misspelling (in the first and second editions) of Oklahoma that Kafka carefully preserved in his chapter to alert readers to his source. It portrays a racist lynching, with the black victims suspended from the bowing branches of a grove of trees surrounded by an indifferently curious crowd of white spectators posing for the camera. The photographic image that inspired 'The Nature Theatre of Oklahama' was a harvest of 'strange fruit' – one of the genre of images that circulated widely as postcards in the early twentieth century. The 'Nature Theatre of Oklahama' – the 'Oklahama Idyll' – is part of the same 'History Theatre of Washington' and it too is a site of execution: both murderous images from the same history of racial oppression.

Karl is carried to his fate in a fit of distraction similar to the one that accompanied his entry to America. He obeys the instruction of the laughing officials to throw away the precious suitcase that has accompanied him to this point and that he will no longer need where he is going and runs to board the train that will transport him to the Nature Theatre. Yet the photograph restituted for the one he had lost was a clear sign of the impending disaster that he is too dazzled to see coming. The loss of the photograph that situated him within European history was replaced by one which placed him among the dispossessed and oppressed of the history of the United States. His interpretative skills were insufficiently directed to help him read the signs of the catastrophe slowly but ineluctably overwhelming him. The loss of the photograph and its return, a chapter of unfortunate accidents, point to a seismic necessity that was carrying him towards disaster. And it is at the centre of this narrative, as if a condition of its possibility, that Kafka placed the peculiar temporality – that of memory, uncanny presence and intimation – and modality – accident and necessity intertwined – of the photograph.

Pornograph

One of the definitive novels of the twentieth century, *The Trial*, started life as an accident narrative. It begins in the bright light of morning with the being 'captured' (*gefangen*) of Josef K. – changed in the manuscript to 'arrested' (*verhaftet*) (Kafka 1997, 3) – and moves inexorably towards his execution by night. The capture was an accident; there was apparently no reason for it except that 'someone must have denounced Josef K, for without having done anything wrong he was captured one morning' (*T* 1). Although Kafka subsequently juridified the capture, the man who enters K.'s bedroom to 'arrest' him still retains his outdoor, hunting gear. K. was never guilty of acting with criminal intent according to any recognizable juridical definition of guilt – he just happened to get caught, that is to say accused. The *Gericht* that pursues him, like the *Apparat* of 'In the Penal Colony', demands its quota of victims and he is but the latest chosen one. He can miss the point entirely and protest his 'innocence' or he can explore ways of lying low or disappearing and so deferring the execution of his irrevocable sentence.

The accidental character of K.'s death is emphasized by its taking place in a suburban quarry, for while writing *The Trial* by night in his bedroom Kafka was completing 'Accident Prevention in Quarries' by day in the office. Frogmarched away by a pair of music-hall executioners, K. arrives at a liminal point where town 'merged almost without transition into the open fields' (*T* 196, 239). The executioners' destination was 'a small stone quarry, abandoned and bare' (*T* 196, 239) where, after undressing their victim and 'surveying' the site, they chose the most dangerous location 'near the quarry wall where a broken-away rock was lying' (*T* 197, 240). The ominous combination of cliff and a loose boulder ensured that if his executioners took too long they would all be buried under a rockfall and K.'s death classified as another industrial accident. Indeed, Kafka views death whether by order of the court or by the fall of overhanging rocks in a dangerous quarry as equally accidental, which is to say, equally necessary. Yet there was also something very singular about K.'s accident that perhaps accounted for Kafka's move towards a more juridically framed narrative in the final version of the novel.

Josef K. has become the twentieth century's everyman, and most readers take his part against the oppressive court, but who was Josef K.? He is carefully described as a senior investment banker, excelling in a profession that speculates on the debt (*Schuld*) of others; but like Hunter Gracchus, he is an accident prone predator. K. lives off debt, the German term *Schuld* famously acknowledged by Nietzsche and Benjamin as signifying both debt and guilt. Josef K. specializes in financing mainly commercial but also occasionally productive ventures with clients who are traders living dangerously by trying to anticipate the market.[26] He is a key part of a financial circuit that advances credit for businesses to speculate on future markets. He is described as an ambitious, successful even ruthless banker with a taste for personal power that he exercises not only on his clients but also and especially on women. He is by no means an innocent victim of an oppressive court, but a man who thrives on power, who enjoys domination and who meets his nemesis.[27] His preferred technique of domination, applied even to his landlady, is to provoke and exploit debt/guilt: he boasts to his neighbour Frau Bürstner that he can behave as he likes in their landlady's home because she is 'dependent on me, for she has borrowed a large sum of money from me' (T 26, 38). And so it is the manipulator of debt for personal and institutional power who one fine morning finds himself under arrest.

Himself an elite predator, Josef K. abhors the vulgarity of the court's officials, despises its humble locations in tenement blocks in proletarian suburbs and finds unacceptable the idea that it could presume to call *him* to justice. He is outraged by the court's insolence in arresting and calling *a senior official* to account, and defies it with such passion because it has defied him and the power he takes for granted. How then are we to interpret his arrest? It might be viewed as an accident, for in a population of risk-taking bankers a certain number must fail – and this time it is K. who is caught out and called to pay not just for a personal but for a systemic failure. His arrest can also be viewed in terms of class justice, for in this court it is the powerful who are subject to scrutiny and called to justify their lives before the poor, making the trial an exercise in popular justice. It is striking that most of the 'victims' of the court are failed businessmen: Block is a failed 'commercial traveller'/corn dealer and of those K. meets congregated in the gloomy waiting room, 'All were carelessly dressed, in spite of which most of them, by their facial expression, their bearing, the cut of their beards, and many almost imperceptible little details, belonged to the upper classes' (T 55–6, 74). All are business failures, all are guilty of debt'.

Whatever the interpretation, K. after his arrest errs fundamentally both in his understanding of and his approach to the 'court'. He assumes that behind its sordid appearance there is a 'great organisation at work' like his bank, and that it is manned by 'senior officials' like himself who dominate the court as he dominates the bank and to whom he must gain access to strike a deal. He assumes they will grant him credit or even guilt/debt cancellation if only he can get past the barrier of squalid lower judges, those clowns who obstruct his access to real power. He despises the intermediaries he comes to depend such on as the advocate Huld (whose very name Huld 'favour' ironically mutilates *Sc-huld*) for pointlessly dealing with insignificant officials in a currency of minor debt and bribery and wants to move directly to the big deal with the inaccessible main players. He even assumes that this is a court governed by law, one perhaps inaccessible and unknowable but nevertheless the source of all meaning and power; if only he could gain access to this law then he could use or, even better, corrupt it and once again prevail. He continues to act as a hunter and predator even though he has not only become prey but has already been captured and is merely awaiting execution.

K.'s understanding of the court is anything but objective; it is as blinkered as his insight into his own situation. He attributes his increasingly evident failure as a banker to his obsession with the trial, rather than understanding his failure as a potential reason for his trial. An accident victim, he insists on regarding himself as a protagonist. *The Trial*, in short, less obviously but more systematically than its contemporary 'In the Penal Colony', replays Nietzsche's *Genealogy of Morals* as a drama of *ressentiment*, adding the complication of making K. at once the object of a resentful fantasy of popular justice wreaked on the powerful by the powerless and a subject whose own actions are directed by *ressentiment*. The lurid fantasies of domination and subjection that recur throughout *The Trial* – expressed in terms of guilt/debt and shame – lend an insistent pornographic air to the proceedings of the court. For as Nietzsche showed in the *Genealogy of Morals*, the vengeance of the weak must not only be seen to be done, but the gruesome spectacle of punishment has to be enjoyed and be repeatable unto eternity.[28]

A significant but underestimated episode of *The Trial* is the fantasy of revenge entertained by the caretaker of the court. K.'s first defiant speech to the gathered court is comically interrupted by the spectacle of the caretaker's wife having public sex with a student of the law in a corner of the hall. K.'s j'accuse is rudely interrupted by the student's noisy ejaculation – 'his mouth was wide open and he was gazing up to the ceiling' (*T* 41, 57), and K. in spite of himself wants to watch but had to shade his eyes with his hand because the room had filled with glaring steam, a strange white light: 'for the dim daylight whitened the fog and dazzled' (*T* 41, 57). On his next visit to the court out of session he meets the caretaker hurrying back from a vain errand contrived to get him out of the way while his wife was abducted to provide sexual favours. He confides in Josef K. his cherished fantasy of revenge: 'If I wasn't so dependent I would long ago have squashed that student flat right here against the wall. Just beside this announcement. I dream of it all the time. He's squashed flat right here, just above the pavement – arms stretched, fingers spread, his bandy legs writhing in a circle with splashes of blood all round. But so far it's just a dream' (*T* 54, 73). The caretaker imagines the metamorphosis of the student into a swatted mosquito writhing at the point of death – a fantasy he indulges daily and clearly enjoys. Josef K. shares his excitement – 'he had to keep a grip on himself' – and offers to 'take the student in hand', inviting the performative contradiction of the caretaker confidentially whispering to him 'One is always rebellious' (*T* 55, 74). The caretaker's fantasy of revenge is a cameo of the *ressentiment* scenario of the wider novel in which a parasitic, bloodsucking banker is justly swatted and repeatedly watched suffering his protracted death throes.[29]

The pornographic character of the imagined execution of the student corresponds to the lurid fantasies of vengeance Nietzsche describes in *The Genealogy of Morals to be* a hallmark of *ressentiment*. These images invested with desire throng the novel and repeatedly invite interpretation; indeed Josef K.'s quest, described in the interlude between his arrest and execution, is but a series of failed lessons in interpreting visual images such as photographs, paintings and the restricted vistas that open before Josef.K. as well as those in which he is the primary object of scrutiny. It is difficult for him to see or interpret without reference to his own desire, for his view of the world is essentially pornographic.

The elaborate visual scenario of Josef K.'s perdition is prepared in the opening chapter with him lying in bed watching from his pillow 'the old lady who lived opposite observing him with an even for her unusual curiosity' (*T* 3, 9). He is interpreting her interpretation in the light of the breakdown of his habitual breakfast routine. She continues to watch, joined by others as the events of the arrest unfold in K's bedroom. Josef K. transfers his attention to the man who enters his room 'as though one had to accept his appearance' and who did not submit very long to his inquiring look (*T* 3, 9). Forcing his way past the intruder into his landlady's living room, Josef K. encounters the tableau of a man sitting by an open window with a book ensconced in the landlady's room packed with 'furniture, carpets, porcelain and photographs which today had a little more space than usual' (*T* 4, 10). The mention of the photographs precedes the intuition of an imperceptible but uncanny change in the space of the living room. Their presence among the objects of furniture was always anomalous, at once nested within domestic space and its routinization of memory and identity but also testifying to a world beyond it. The narrative moves from the landlady's photographic collection to that of his fellow lodger Fräulein Bürstner, whose room has been commandeered by 'The Inspector' for an initial hearing. An audience of three young men 'were standing looking at Fraulein Bürstner's photographs which were stuck in a mat hanging on the wall. A white blouse dangled from the latch of the open window' (*T* 11, 18). The photos appear in a context of erotic intimacy, their ordering disrupted by being handled by inquisitive strangers. Even as Josef K. contemplates their enjoyment of Frau Burstner's photographs under the sustained scrutiny of his neighbours across the street, his understandably 'distracted gaze' is suddenly focused by the Inspector calling out his name.

During the hearing the Inspector, like a conjuror, contrives a visual tableau 'moving with both hands the few things that lay on the night table, the candle with a box of matches, a book and a pin-cushion as if they were objects which he required for his interrogation' (T 11, 19). The objects, the matches and candle for illumination, the book for the law and the pincushion for the victim, comprise elements of an encrypted communication that K. entirely fails to heed. The Inspector begins by setting the candle in the centre and 'grouping the other things around it' (T 11, 19). He then counts the number of matches left in the box – K.'s chances of enlightenment – before slamming it back on the table in exasperation with K.'s obstinate refusal to concentrate. The individual matches will subsequently flare up in the episodes of failed enlightenment that punctuate the grey light of the novel, but are never successfully applied to the candle to provide the constant light necessary for K. to mount effective defiance.[30] K.'s living in the dark and seeing only what and how he is meant to see undermines his opposition to the court from the outset. His defiance flares, splutters and is extinguished repeatedly throughout the novel, whether framed by the bright morning light of the arrest or by the cool moonlit night of his execution.

The exception to the flickering lighting of *The Trial* is the morbid torchlight that punctuates the growing darkness of the penultimate cathedral episode. This illuminates the last but one of a sequence of meditations on photography and painting that began with the landlady and neighbours' photographic galleries in the first chapter. The uncanny normality of the former is followed by the disruption of the latter, recalling the apparently confused photographic collection of the 'Nature Theatre of Oklahoma'. The disrupted photographic display gives his neighbour evidence of the morning's events when she returns from 'work', corroborating K.'s pretext of apologizing for the intrusion: 'Beside the mat where the photographs were stuck she stopped. "Look," she cried, "my photographs really are all mixed up. That is really horrid. Someone really has been in my room without permission"' (T 23, 34). Yet K.'s apology is motivated by erotic curiosity, and his sympathetic contemplation of her disturbed photographs triggers a sexual attack wholly characteristic of his predatory attitude towards women.

Anthony Perkin's performance of K.'s 'freudian slip' when referring to the phonograph as a pornograph in Orson Welles's film of *The Trial* although absent in Kafka's text is entirely consistent with its intentions. Pornographic imagery plays a central role in K.'s erotic life; we are told that he purchases sexual satisfaction through a habitual weekly visit 'to a girl called Elsa, who worked nights in a bar as a waitress until the early hours and during the day would only receive visits in bed' (T 17, 26). But it is also revealed that he carried an erotic photograph of Elsa as a form of promissory note to tide him over between visits. In a conversation with Advocate Huld's erotically fascinated and fascinating maid Leni, K. facetiously claims Elsa as his fiancée, showing Leni the photograph he carries in his pocket: 'It was a snapshot taken of Elsa as she was finishing a skirt dance, one she liked to perform in the bar, her skirt was still flying around her like a fan, her hands planted on her firm hips, and with her chin thrown up she was laughing over her shoulder at someone who did not appear in the photograph' (T 94, 114). Leni, sitting on his knee, offers a lesson in interpretation: Elsa is tightly laced – displaying her corset – but beneath the rough and clumsy erotic carapace was probably 'soft and friendly' to K. and might even sacrifice herself for him. K. didn't think so, but admits that he 'had not even once looked at the image so precisely' (T 94, 115); he might have been advised to take the time to look at it even more closely. In it Elsa frontally exposes herself to the photographer while taking pleasure in acknowledging the gaze of someone out of view who is watching her being photographed. Representing herself as the pleasured object of multiple gazes, Elsa's distribution of this image to her clients invites them to occupy the position of both photographer and spectator of the photographic scene while adding their gazes to the virtual orgy conducted by the other owners of the image who also gain pleasure through contemplating her in the light of each other's contemplation of her as a shared object of pleasure. K. is a member of Elsa's photographic club, with possession of her image certifying not only entitlement to a regular slot in her bed and pornographic top-ups between sessions, but also the pleasure of imagining her pleasuring and being pleasured by other owners of the same photograph. Leni, however, breaks Elsa's carefully constructed vertiginously pornographic *mis-en-scene* by exposing the complex hetero- and homo-erotic contrivance of the image that the banker K. carries with him as a promissory note or share in the capital of Elsa's sexual favours, and then claiming her own place as a potential rival for K.'s affections.

Leni's interpretation is but one of K.'s many squandered opportunities to see things and their arrangements in a different light. The most important, however, is his encounter with the court painter Titorelli who discreetly warns him to retreat from his position of absolute defiance. Titorelli is working on a portrait of a judge sitting on a chair in front of an allegorical figure – and continues painting while Josef K. watches. He provides a de-accelerated and analytical account of the same flash that dazzled Karl Rossmann on his entry to America: '"It still needs a little more work" replied the painter and, taking a pastel crayon from a table hatched a little at the edge of the figure without making it any clearer for K. "It is justice," said the painter at last. "Now I can recognise it," said K. "here's the blindfold over the eyes, and here are the scales. But aren't there wings on the figure's heels, and isn't it flying?" "Yes," said the painter, "I was instructed to paint it like that; actually it is justice and the goddess of victory both in one." "Not a very good combination, surely," smiled K' (*T* 126, 153). K. thus fatally misunderstands this first warning that victory is the meaning of the pantomime of justice he is pursuing, but it can never be *his* victory. Titorelli allegorically warns K. that he should not behave as if he were in a court of justice, but to take note that he is and has always been engaged in battle with the court. The painter goes even further, as far as he safely can, by silently giving the represented judge a shadow halo – a warning of the demonic – and then altering the background allegorical figure of 'justice': 'But the figure of Justice was left bright except for an almost imperceptible shade, in the brightness the figure seemed to advance, but hardly recalling the Goddess of Justice nor that of Victory she now more completely resembled the Goddess of the Hunt' (*T* 127, 154).

Yet even after this revelation K. still cannot see that behind the unmasking of justice as war and victory there is also hidden the figure of the hunt. If he can't heed the first warning that what appears to be a court of justice is really a battlefield, how can he be expected to see that this battlefield is in its turn really a manhunt in which he is the prey.[31] The artist advises K. to go to ground, to behave like prey and lose his pursuers; he must disappear, merge into the surroundings, walk away and let his scent grow cold – anything but make himself obvious by claiming an acquittal. K., however, is unable to understand the advice and, overcome by the heat of the artist's studio, stumbles out after hastily purchasing three identical landscapes as payment of the debt he feels he has incurred to the artist. The landscapes contrast with the hierarchical productions of Titorelli's portraits – they mark a collapse of transcendence in that they do not participate in a transcendent idea nor represent an object but aspire only to repetition, each attempting to be the same as the others. They form a flat sequence in which minor, accidental differences point to the survival of at least the possibility of transcendence. This possibility will return in the identical dresses of the hostess of the *Herrenhof* at the point where *The Castle* breaks off.

A further missed chance to light the candle and scrutinize the court in its light occurs when K. decides to prepare his own plea. Dissatisfied with Huld's efforts and inspired by his own ruthless business methods, K. fantasizes an escalation of his defiance, producing his own plea and harassing the court officials until gaining his objective: 'One could not relax these efforts, everything had to be organised and supervised, the Court would for once run into an accused who knew how to stick up for his rights' (*T* 110, 133). His concern that in framing a plea he might concede the legitimacy of the court provoked an initial 'feeling of shame', and the eventual rout of his first fantasy of defiance is sealed by the arrival of his rival, the Deputy Manager of the Bank. He was about to seize a blank sheet on his jotter to draft the plea when the Deputy Manager emerged guffawing from a meeting with the Manager, and, taking the pencil from K.'s hand, drew a picture illustrating what seems to have been a dirty joke. The substitution of this image for the plea enhanced K.'s shame, and when he returned to framing the plea a week later he was by now fatally distracted and his force of resistance spent.

K was daunted by the asymptotic character of the plea and the 'interminable labour' accompanying the perceived 'sheer impossibility' of ever completing it. The accidental character of his arrest could be interpreted either in terms of absolute innocence (a possibility raised by both Titorelli and the Priest in the Cathedral), in which case there would be no reason for him to search for or be concerned about its meaning, or the involvement of an *unknown* accusation framed according to an unknown law executed by an inscrutable court. In this case, the submission of a plea entailed an infinite search for meaning, a Sisyphean labour of trying to pre-empt the unknown law 'because to meet an unknown accusation and other possible charges arising from it, ones' whole life down to its pettiest actions and events would have to be recalled and examined from all sides' (*T* 111, 134). Kafka himself had attempted such narrations that emphasized the law of the accident in the sequence of uncompletable diary entries from July 1910, beginning 'When I reflect on it I must say that my education has done me great harm in some respects' (*D* 15, 13). In them even the smallest unrelated, unintentional event or even omission are called to book, performing the impossibility of accounting for the accidents that make up and can devastate a life.

In the penultimate Cathedral scene of *The Trial* – the flaring of K.'s last match – the candlelight is joined by torchlight in a largely deconsecrated space: God has left the building and K. has come not to pray but to show artwork to a visiting Italian business associate. Although he has brought his torch and even though candles seemingly light themselves as he proceeds through the church to the altarpieces looming in the darkness. K. is typically more fascinated by his own torch than the art, illuminating tiny details of the paintings with its greenish light, the 'eternal light' that 'wavered disturbingly before it' (*T* 178, 217). K. guesses from the details that he is contemplating 'a huge armoured knight' looking out of the picture who 'seemed intent to observe an event playing out before him' (*T* 178, 217). Never imagining that he might himself be that observed event, K. stands for a 'good while' before the figure. He then plays his torch over the rest of the image, pockets it and walks away to his final interview with the Priest of the court, the telling of the parable 'Before the Law', and the ensuing debate about its meaning.

The exegesis of the parable by K. and the Priest focuses on perception, misjudgement and delusion. K. argues for the mutually reinforcing delusion of the doorkeeper and the man from the country, while the Priest replies that the law is set beyond human judgement, even beyond truth. His opinion that even truth is subordinated to the necessity of the law and that the doorkeeper is free in being bound to the law meets K.'s naïve objection that this 'makes the lie into world-order' (*T* 192, 235). Putting necessity above truth at once universalizes and abolishes the accident. With this conclusion, the darkness deepens and K. – by now a dead man walking – follows the Priest through the church, the memory of the parable blurring as the candles are successively extinguished, their light yielding to an intimation of the light of his execution: 'the silver image of some saint glimmered before him with its silver sheen and then returned to darkness' (*T* 192, 234). The candlelight gives way to a silvery intimation of the executioner's moonlight as well as an anticipation of the flash that heralds the end of K.'s life and the beginning of his eternal shame. Whether the glint came from the image of a saint or prefigured the executioner's blade is by now governed by the accidental necessity of the law, according to which, in the last words of the Priest, 'The Court wants nothing from you. It takes you when you come and lets you go when you go' (*T* 193, 235).

Josef K.'s execution tableau recalls his photograph of Elsa, but instead of dancing like her he is spreadeagled and tied naked to a fallen rock in a suburban quarry. Like her he looks round for another spectator – 'he turned his still free neck and looked around him' (*T* 198, 241), but unlike Elsa's *mis-en-scene his* sideward gaze fell on a spectator who was also the photographer. The last lines of the novel emphasize its distance from *America* where the light-burst of the initial apparition of the Statue of Liberty is succeeded by strobe-like flashes; by contrast, here the faint flickerings of *The Trial* culminate in a solitary flash: 'His glance fell on the top floor of a house bordering the quarry. With a flicker as of a light going up, the casement of a window there suddenly flew open; a human figure, faint and insubstantial at that distance and height, leaned abruptly far forward and stretched both arms even further out' (*T* 198, 214).[32] The identity of the figure has excited much comment, beginning with K. himself: 'Who was it? A friend? A good man? An accomplice? Someone who wanted to help? Was it one person? Were they all there? Was help at hand?' (*T* 198, 241). But perhaps Josef K. realizes that the outstretched hands are perhaps holding a flash camera and his moment of execution was about to be photographed to become an image circulated for all of them 'all there' – his own photo club – to enjoy at their leisure.

So the executioners were not as he thought nobly waiting for him to grasp the dagger and paradoxically *allow* him in a final act of defiance to put an end to his own life, but merely dragging out the time for the photographer to complete his preparations. His photograph would certify that they had performed their duty while providing a pleasurable spectacle for the judges and a warning to any other accused who might be contemplating defiance. The photograph was essential to the execution, for K. loses not only his life, but becoming a pornograph surrenders any capacity to resist that he still possessed and might have bequeathed to succeeding generations of accused to follow him[33] – his last moment would survive him and circulate as a pornographic image for the pleasure of his enemies and the dread of any potential successors; in short, '"Like a dog!" he said, it was, as if the shame would survive him' (*T* 198, 241). In the manuscript, Kafka deleted a passage between 'he said' and 'it was' that was a protest against dying in this way: 'his last living feeling was shame, to the very point of death he was not to be spared shame' (Kafka 1997, 24–5).

Saints and soldiers

The setting of the penultimate scene of *The Trial* in a Cathedral does not point to any Christian significance attending the end of K.'s progress through the court. For *The Trial* is one of the fables told after the death of God prophesied by Nietzsche's madman. The Cathedral K. visits with his torch and tourist guide book is a deconsecrated space, a mere shell of the sacred now wholly evacuated of divinity. In *The Trial* both Jewish and Christian Gods are dead, and K. approaches the erstwhile sacred space as an aesthete and tourist guide. He does not go to church to worship or to seek consolation or guidance, but to look at the art. His baleful torch transforms religious images into works of art devoid of transcendence. And the inability to heed the voice of the court and understand the parable of the man from the country related to him from the pulpit confirms his full self-condemnation. In the mausoleum of a dead God, all K. can think about is getting back to work, and so – completely disoriented like Nietzsche's murderers of God – he has to be led first to the door and then to his execution.

Nietzsche did not just call for tragic tales of the death of Gods, but also for wicked parodies – and the Pilgrim's parody of *The Trial* would be intensified by the supreme parody of the life and death of transcendence that is *The Castle*. It is also another accident narrative whose very inspiration, Kafka ironically mused in a diary entry of 27 January 1922, came in the accident of being listed among the guests of the Sanitorium in Spindelmühle under the wrong name, that of the hero of *The Trial*: 'Although I had clearly written my name for the hotel, and although they wrote it correctly twice, I am still listed on the board as Josef. K. Should I enlighten them, or should I wait for them to enlighten me?' (*D* 407, 694). The hero K.'s very presence in the novel is just another bureaucratic accident: he has – it seems – been erroneously appointed by Count West West's administration in the Castle as a *Landvermesser* or surveyor/messiah, and the novel relates his attempts to reach the Castle and justify his existence to the official Klamm.[34] As one of Nietzsche's 'superfluous men' (who could be more superfluous than a messiah who arrives after the death of God?), K. sets out to survey what remains of transcendence in a parodically Platonic universe comprising the apparently opposed transcendent and spatio-temporal worlds of *Schloss* and *Dorf* – castle and the village in which participation between the worlds – the condition of possibility of religion and metaphysics – has decayed into sporadic osmosis with the worlds leaking into each other through delayed and distracted messengers, drunken officials, crossed telephone lines, abused women, fire-brigade festivals and belated messiahs like K. Although the bureaucratic hierarchy of the Castle is professedly at the service of the Count West West, he is more removed from this scenario than any Gnostic God. He left behind a divine economy without divinity that Kafka describes in terms of a society of pure obedience. It is also one in which the accident has been made into a principle – anarchy into an *arche* – with hints that transcendence was never anything but ... accidental. Anticipating the suspicion played out in Pasolini's *Salo*, here in the village/castle, as there in the villa, anarchy becomes the law.

The Castle is not just a remorseless parody of the fate of domination after the evacuation of transcendence – the death of God – but it is also the description of what survived as the mad and ragged remnants of such a catastrophic accident. For as Nietzsche's madman said in *The Gay Science*, they knew not what they did when they murdered God; it was an accident and one with increasingly apparent and devastating consequences. As much a work in political philosophy as a novel, *Das Schloss* is an anti-*Republic*, a reflection on life lived after politics in the Corpse rather than City of God. It begins with the onset of darkness and the arrival of K. in the village.[35] Conditions of visibility are difficult with the village 'deep in snow' – submerged in white on white – and our parodic pilgrim stops on a wooden bridge (a humble version of Nietzsche's bridge to the *Übermensch*) that leads from the *Landstrasse* to a village where all the disobedient little boys have long been put to bed. Starting badly, he surveys not what he sees but what he thinks he is meant to see: 'There was nothing to be seen of the castle hill. Fog and darkness surrounded it and not even the weakest glimmer of light indicated a major castle' (*C* 443, 9). In an inaugural error, K. assumes the *Schloss* is there but hidden, even in the absence of any evidence of direct light coming from it (this is a dead star from the outset) and looks *through* the white, misty light mixed with darkness convinced that cosmic emptiness is the illusion, a mere light effect: 'K. stood for a long time on the wooden bridge that led from the Landstrasse to the village and gazed up into the illusory emptiness' (*C* 443, 9). Still convinced something is hidden where he can see only emptiness, K. finally turns his attention to the village and to finding shelter for the night, deferring his quest until the morning.

A travelling investigator would have been intrigued by the ethnography of the *Dorf*. It seems an instance of a tightly governed society ruled literally from above by a legal-rational authority whose sway verged on total domination wielded by a bureaucratic caste of discordantly shabby but charismatic officials. And yet the usual institutions of a state are conspicuously absent from this scenario. The domination of the officials is not underwritten by any claim to the physical or spiritual monopoly of violence – there are hardly any references to military institutions or values nor to organized religion. In the absence of soldiers and priests there remains but one passing reference to the police, and the *Dorf*'s most prominent institutions seem to be the school and the fire brigade, the former housed next to a barn-like redundant church showing that once there was religion here, but now there is no longer. Village society is organized according to cyclopean patriarchal households that pride themselves on their contempt for any ethics of hospitality and pursue a domestic division of labour based on a proto-capitalist putting-out system.[36] While there is some reference to a village council effective in the past, it seems as if politics has retreated, leaving the pubs as the last but highly surveyed public space. A travelling investigator would quickly learn that there are two village pubs – *The Bridge*, just beside the wooden bridge on the road out to the *Landstrasse*; and the *Herrenhof*, on the road up to the Castle. Both are places of lugubrious intoxication, rustic 'entertainments', guarded discussions and listless, prostitution but also, most importantly in the case of the *Herrenhof*, semi-official/semi-illicit contacts between Castle and village. This is is all that seems to be left of life in the village, otherwise numb and frozen under the snow.

K. himself seems to be the unique instance in the village of a relation with the world beyond the *Landstrasse* – the way to the city of fools in Kafka's earlier story; otherwise life in the village is oriented entirely towards the Castle. The latter's dominion is not secured by any transcendent violence or even threat of violence but by osmosis and secretion – politics has become endocrinal with information passing between village and Castle via the deceptively open channels of telephone and messengers and the less calculable but perhaps more reliable openings offered by sexual contact and chance meetings. It is into this already highly surveyed society that K. the land-*surveyor* embarks on his quest, seeking to exploit existing but also to open new channels of communication between village and Castle. His accidental appointment seems to have emerged from past political conflict within the village/Castle dyad catalysed by the subsequently co-opted radical Brunswick. K. is thus a cipher for a disowned political history that from the shreds of surviving evidence seems to have involved a deadly conflict between the Brunswick dynasty and the family of the defiant daughter Amalia.

The fate of the defeated family who strive continually to enter into an alliance with K. casts considerable light on the character of relations between Castle and village. The daughter Amalia's public defiance of a maladroit sexual approach by a Castle official by insulting his messenger leads to the eclipse of her previously economically and socially dominant family. Their ostracism destroys their shoe business – leather-working is the staple of the village economy – and permits its predatory takeover by the Brunswick family. Attempts by Amalia's father to secure 'forgiveness' are met by the Castle's outraged refusal to admit there has been any 'official' fault and its declared view that his misfortunes are the banal outcome of economic failure: 'Sure he was poorer, had lost customers etc., but those were everyday occurrences, matters of business and trade, did the Castle have to concern itself about everything? Of course in reality it did concern itself about everything, but it couldn't just intervene in such things simply to serve the interest of an individual' (*C* 642, 258–9). Like the plaintiffs in *The Trial*, Amalia's father was by this account a chance victim of the vagaries of market forces and could not expect to be insured by the Castle for his misfortune. Of course, from another perspective, the architect of these misfortunes was none other than the Castle itself. In the course of a discussion of bribery – in which Amalia's father and the officials he encounters behave like the man from the country and the doorkeeper in Before the Law – it turns out that the Castle is supported by tax payments from the village, making it directly parasitic on the village economy and not as aloof from its economic life as it pretends to be.

The world of the Castle and the village seems almost an experimental set-up for a society after the death of God in which the structures of transcendence continue to operate but without the earlier transcendent guarantees. The institutions of state and religion have withered away to be replaced by the excrescence of the Castle and its parasitic and corrupt bureaucracy. The extreme degree of obedience shown by the villagers underlines how far the vacated shells of transcendence continue to demand and offer legitimacy to domination. The officials and their servants are themselves near cult objects, already dead but somehow living on, as K. intimated from observing the servant Jerome off duty or in his peep-hole vision of the auto-iconic Klamm. This lack of vitality or of any vivifying distinction characterizes the Castle itself, with the roads leading to it leading away and changing course seemingly at random. Communications whether by messenger or telephone are intermittent, unreliable and unpredictable and, far from displaying an orderly transmission or hierarchical *methexis*, are largely osmotic and occur at unpredictable intervals across a shifting and deteriorating membrane. Distinctions are blurred and relations within the Castle and between Castle and village are governed less by law and procedure than by accident – anarchy paradoxically become law.

K. is vouched one clear and distinct vision of the Castle on the 'brilliant winter morning' of his first day in the village. Leaving the pub where he spent the night, his eidetic intuition of the *Schloss* begins promisingly: 'Now he could see the Castle above him distinctly outlined in the clear air its outline made still more definite by the moulding of ubiquitous snow covering it in a thin layer' (*C* 449, 16). The sharpness of outline contrasts with the indistinctness of the village houses buried in snow drifts and should have satisfied even the most demanding surveyor for 'up on the hill everything soared free and light', were it not for the worrying caveat 'or at least that's how it seemed from down here' (*C* 449, 16). As K. began to survey the distant structure more carefully however, dissonant details emerged in its structure and function. The Castle was neither military not civil, neither fortress nor palace: 'neither an old stronghold nor a new mansion, but an extended structure of a few two storey buildings but mostly low and closely packed huts; if one hadn't known it was a castle one would have taken it for a small town' (*C* 449, 16). His attention focused on the single visible tower of indeterminate function – 'it was impossible to tell whether it belonged to a house or a church' (*C* 449, 16) – except that, in the first of the characteristic avian presences associated with the Castle, 'swarms of crows were circling round it' recalling the swarms of 'Children on a Country Road', but here with far more threatening intent.

With 'eyes fixed on the Castle', K. continued his spiralling approach totally absorbed in contemplation, 'without any distractions' (*C* 449, 17). His eidetic vision of the Castle deteriorates as its object metamorphoses into a crumbling village that K. compares unfavourably to his own *Heimat*. The comparison focuses again on the tower and its distance from K.'s childhood memory of transcendent religious aspiration:

And he compared in his thoughts the church tower at home with the tower up above. That tower, firm in line, soaring up unfalteringly to its tapering point, topped with red tiles and broad in the roof, an earthly building – what can we build otherwise? – but with a loftier goal than the humble dwelling-houses, and a clearer meaning than the muddle of everyday life.

(C 450, 17)

The Castle tower was apparently no such thing. Clearly not part of a church but attached to a house, this tower was not an arrow aimed at transcendence, but 'uniformly round' with grotesque and disquieting features that point to the replacement of religious transcendence by enclosed madness. It was 'pierced by small windows that glittered in the sun, a bit deranged that, and to top it all, what looked like an attic, with irregular, broken, fumbling walls as if designed by the trembling or careless hands of a child, scratched against the blue' (*C* 450, 17). K.'s last words on the Castle before his contemplation was interrupted (and would remain interrupted for the rest of the novel) reveal its pretended legal-rational transcendence to be madness: 'It was as if a melancholy inhabitant who ought to have been locked in the topmost chamber of his house had burst through the roof in order to show himself to the gaze of the world' (*C* 450, 17). The Castle itself is insane, and its tower, far from reaching to God, struck K. as pointing back to the madness confined within it.

A collection of ragged images and photographs are all that remain of former transcendence and they hang in the musty maids' attic room in *The Bridge*, where K. was lodged: 'On the wall a few sacred pictures and photograph of soldiers …' (*C* 464, 34). K. did not even give them a second glance, removing one to pin his letter of appointment from the Official Klamm on its nail. These religious and military images seem to have arrived at the nadir of their descent into insignificance, forgotten in the airless room occupied by women at the very bottom of the village division of labour. K. would soon encounter another photograph, kept under the pillow of the landlady of *The Bridge*, that was by contrast a treasured possession. It showed a young man jumping as part of his training as a messenger and – the gift of Klamm given to her in payment for sex – it depicts the messenger he sent to bring her to him. The photo is a cult image, part of an emergent religion of the angelic messenger shared by even some of the Castle's officials and, on the evidence of the landlady, perhaps by Klamm himself.

The rags and tags of transcendence that flutter in the breeze blowing from a distant catastrophe promise to be reconstituted in a new order near the point where the novel finally breaks off with the never-to-be-spoken words of Gerstäcker's mother. This is the enigmatic conversation about dresses between K. and the landlady of the *Herrenhof*. K. tries to understand the significance of her enormous wardrobe of near identical dresses. Her room, like Titorelli's in *The Trial*, is overheated and devoted to repetition; her carefully curated collection of 'dark, grey, brown, black dresses' (*C* 746, 379), distributed across nearly identical wardrobes, resemble the artist's monochromes that figure repetition as collapsed transcendence. It is entirely appropriate that the dialogue between the landlady and K. should focus on the questions of truth and identity. The hostile landlady asks, 'What actually is it you are?' (*C* 745, 378), to which K. replies that he is a 'land-surveyor'. Both suspect each other of not being what they seem, of not being true: '"You're not telling the truth. Why don't you tell the truth?"' "You don't tell the truth either." "Me? So now you're beginning your impudent remarks again. And if I didn't tell the truth do I have to answer for it to you. And in what way don't I tell the truth then?" "You are not only a landlady as you pretend"' (*C* 745, 379). For K., the landlady is 'aiming at something else' (*C* 746, 379). Both want the truth of the other while no longer believing in the possibility of transcendent truth, but she says 'I aim only at dressing beautifully, and you are either a fool, a child or a very wicked and dangerous person' (*C* 746, 379). But the aim pursued by repetition, as we saw with Tintorelli, is the deflation of hierarchy and the production of an internally referential sequence in which truth consists in minor accidental differences; here, as with Tintorelli's monochromes, there is a sequence but there is no *arche* or *telos*, no origin or end to it.[37] She has ceased to aim for the Castle as a remote seat of transcendence and aims only to dress beautifully in 'oft renovated and worn' (*C* 745, 379) identical dresses. Expelling K. from her presence, she nevertheless opens the possibility of an alliance between them by shouting 'I am getting a new dress tomorrow, perhaps I will permit myself to have you fetched' (*C* 746, 374), emphasizing with the 'new' and the 'perhaps' that this time it will all depend on her – she will call at *her* pleasure and perhaps this might finally initiate a different sequence and a new history.

4 DOMINATIONS

Officials

'A Message from the Emperor', published in *A Country Doctor*, was excerpted from a larger fragment that Brod entitled *The Great Wall of China*. There it appears as a parable of failed communication but in salutary contrast to the structure of domination informing *The Castle*.[1] The dying Emperor entrusts a message to his messenger who like Zeno's hare is unable to traverse the interval between Emperor and his subject in a distant village. A parable of singularity that sets out to explain why no personal message from the Emperor ever arrived even though it was sent from him and meant only for you. It also one in which the structure of transcendence remains at least at the outset largely intact, with the Emperor still sending messages and his messengers still trying to deliver them to his subjects. The intended recipient, 'the tiny shadow that fled to the furthest farthest from the Imperial sun' (S 244, 305), awaits the arrival of the light carried by the indefatigable messenger who 'bears the sign of the sun' but who is unable to break out of the palace let alone arrive at the remote village. The further from the sun the messenger travels, the weaker he becomes and the more insurmountable grow the obstacles confronting him. The message was sent, but the transit of the messenger was blocked by a succession of accidents that fatally de-accelerated his progress.

The contrast with the Castle is salutary, not just because of the distance separating the Chinese Palace and village – on remote sides of the universe and not just the top and bottom of a hill – but also in that the osmotic membrane between *Schloss* and *Dorf* has not yet formed, leaving the messenger to try and fail to make the passage or achieve participation (*methexis*) between transcendence and its shadow. The imperial message testifies to an inoperative Platonic structure while the *Schloss* dresses itself in the parodic guise of a Platonism that has mutated into something else. The key to this metamorphosis is the perversion of the messenger into an official. In the still intact hierarchy of 'A Message from the Emperor' there exist only messengers who literally carry out the orders of the Emperor, but as his power wanes and the impetus of the messengers falters, the latter insensibly congeal into officials who forsake movement in order to occupy place. The parable depicts the metamorphosis of a messenger into an official following the death of the Emperor, for the official is a messenger who despairs of the futility of his mission: 'No one forces his way through here, let alone with a message from a dead man' (*S* 244, 306). From being a bearer of light, the official becomes a dominator, complicit with the obstacles and further compromising the waning energies of transcendence. In place of the messenger's faithful and rapid communication of the imperial message – the implementation of transcendent law – emerge the delay, diversion and ambiguity that make up the Castle's obtuse world of administrative obstacles and accidents.

The Castle is a fascinated meditation on some of the consequences of this reverse metamorphosis from butterfly to chrysalis. Its hero, K., is less interested in gaining access to the Castle than in meeting the official Klamm. He quickly learns the villagers' obsessive interest in the officials and the speculative theology that has emerged to explain them. Although its similarities to Gnostic developments of Platonism have led readers to understand it in terms of archons, lambent traces and the stranger God,[2] it is more comprehensible as a meditation on life after the death of God. While the officials are the ostensible objects of this cult, it is the messengers who are its real figures of salvation and who embody the memory of forsaken transcendence. This is most explicit in the key episode of Amalia's defiance of the sexual advances of the official Sortini. Her crime in tearing up the official's obscene letter consisted not so much in insulting the Castle in the person of its official, but in humiliating the messenger. It was the insult to the messenger that led to the ostracism and ruin of her family as well as the messenger's retreat into the inner arcana of the Castle and the desperate search by Amalia's father and sister to find and placate him. As the messenger was shown incapable of delivering a message, he was condemned to become an *official*. This apparently horrific fate earns the horror of all – villagers, servants and even other Castle officials – and the shunning of the perpetrator and her family. The family, as a last resort to atone for this crime, substitute their own son Barnabas for the insulted messenger,[3] and so he enters the service trying to bear messages between Klamm and K. (even if one of them seems to have been forged by Amalia, placing him in the invidious position of unwittingly delivering a fake message and so setting him on the path to officialdom).

K. learns about the nature of officialdom by researching the specific case of Klamm. He has three principal informants – his steady enemy/ accomplice, the landlady of *The Bridge*, Amalia's sister Olga and Klamm's chief secretary Erlangen – each of whose perception of the official is shaped by their own interests and biases. K. accordingly has a theological dispute with the landlady, a tactical-strategic briefing with Olga and a micro-managerial executive summary from Erlangen. The profile of the official that emerges is complex, made up of shreds of transcendence manifest in his parodic omnipresence, omnipotence and omniscience, all belying the apparent simplicity of K.'s one glimpse of Klamm through the spyhole. Yet his first and only sighting has the virtue of emphasizing the reverse metamorphosis undergone by the butterfly messenger into a chrysalis official. The official is stasis personified, barely awake and immobile compared to the messenger's animated movement; and even when hurtling between *Dorf* and *Schloss*, the officials' enclosed coaches and sleds ensure personal immobility: they are held perpetually behind a desk. The official is protected by a carapace while the messenger is lightly dressed in a uniform[4] (parodied by Barnabas's home-made effort) that maximizes flexibility and free movement, and the official is absolutely forgetful compared to the prodigious trained memories of the messengers. Yet they are not entirely detached from their origins as messengers, for they are consistently described as birds, but now birds of prey and scavengers such as the crows wheeling above the Castle or in K.'s fantasy of Klamm as a predatory eagle.

K.'s first informant in his researches into Klamm and officialdom is the landlady of *The Bridge*, the official's erstwhile lover and maternal substitute for Frieda. She informs on Klamm as a means of forestalling K.'s project of meeting the official to discuss Frieda, who K. has stolen from him. She is a votary in a cult of the messenger/official and has dedicated her life to understanding the official Klamm's inscrutable *actions*, in particular the fact that he only sent for her three times. Nevertheless she possesses treasured relics procured on each of those occasions – the photograph of the messenger sent to fetch her, a wrap and a nightcap. Her entire life has been dedicated to pursuing the meaning of the accident that was her sexual encounter with Klamm twenty years before: 'I was always asking myself one question and even today have not ceased to ask it: why did that happen? Three times Klamm had me called for, but not for a fourth not for and never again for a fourth time!' (*C* 518, 101). The accident of being called three times and then forgotten posed the question that shaped the landlady's entire life, even her marriage: 'What else could I have talked about with my husband, whom I married shortly afterwards? . . . For years our conversations turned on Klamm and the reasons for his change of mind. And if my husband fell asleep during those talks I woke him and we talked on' (C 518, 101). K. tries to establish a link between Klamm's inaction and the fortuitous arrival of the understanding husband Hans, provoking the landlady's weary response to such a childish misunderstanding: 'There is no trace of Klamm in all in these things. Why should he have cared about me, or more precisely, how could he have cared about me? He knew nothing more about me. That he had ceased to have me called was a sign he had forgotten me' (C 520, 103–4). She explained not being sent for in terms of Klamm's radical forgetfulness, a characteristic that is constitutive of being an official.

This forgetfulness is not just absence of memory, but something more terrible with its roots in the despair of the messenger and the substitution of written documents for memory. The landlady is adamant that this is 'not only forgetting, it's more than that. For one can get to know again someone who has been forgotten. With Klamm that is not possible. He has not only completely forgotten the past existence of whoever is no longer called but also the entire future' (C 520, 104). Once engaged, Klamm's amnesia is total and cannot be qualified or subsequently revised; it is for the landlady the only absolute in a system of bureaucratic control in which the documented past is always recallable and subject to revision. Yet there is also something accidental about this forgetting; it just happens and although the landlady has spent her life trying to forget being forgotten, she continues to seek reasons for it. K. is rightly sceptical of absolute forgetfulness as a remnant of transcendence, and his suspicions regarding official forgetting will be confirmed by Erlangen's testimony – the facilitator, even dramaturge of Klamm's memory and amnesia – but for K. the accident of Klamm's sexual attentions initiated a chain of ineluctable consequences that he believes he might be able to exploit in his quest to confront Klamm.

While for K., Klamm is the law informing the accidents of the landlady's life, he is not their legislator and there is no need to postulate intent or intervention. He is the hapless law-maker, the inadvertent and forgetful *occasion* if not *cause* of retrospectively necessary sequences; his omnipresence is not linked to any transcendence and it was through an unavoidable accident that he became the narrative drive of the landlady's life:

Without Klamm you would not have been unhappy, not sitting doing nothing in the garden, without your sadness a shy man like Hans would never have considered talking to you, without Klamm you would have never been found by Hans in tears, without Klamm your good old uncle the publican would not have seen you and Hans calmly sitting there, without Klamm you would not have been indifferent to life and thus would not have married Hans. Now I would say that in all this there is surely enough of Klamm.

(*C* 521, 105)

Without Klamm, none of these events would have taken place, he was their condition of possibility but not their cause; Klamm happened to be, that he happened upon the landlady was an accident, her 'lucky star', and her vaunted fidelity to the event is but subjection to the law of the accident. The landlady is incredulous at this explanation, and shocked by K.'s blasphemous and absurd proposal to confirm it by asking Klamm himself.

Yet when he is weary, as he is during the altercation with Klamm's secretary Momus, K. can suspect Klamm to be omnipresent and omniscient not only by accident but also by malign intent. This is the incarnation of Klamm as eagle or *hunter-angel*: 'he thought of Klamm's remoteness, of his impregnable dwelling, of his silence broken only perhaps by cries the like K. had never ever heard, of his downward pressing gaze that would never let itself be proven or disproven, of his remote wheelings according to incomprehensible laws unperturbed by K.'s depths and only momentarily visible' (*C* 552, 144). The wind of an unknowable law on which Klamm glides as a malign angel of history blows throughout *The Castle*; it made itself felt as K. defied Momus's summons to be examined 'in the name of Klamm'. It made itself felt indoors, in the pub's corridor where 'It was cold and a strong wind was blowing' (*C* 553, 144), but K. has not yet become a weatherman and was perilously misinterpreting the signs, but his discussions with Olga would make him more alert.

As the sister of the defiant Amalia and prudent strategist of her family's resistance, Olga never underestimates the enmity of the officials and in particular the brutality of Klamm: 'he apparently says nothing for hours and then suddenly says something so brutal it makes one shiver' (*C* 627, 239). She set herself to understand their machinery of domination, not as a votary or manager but as an enemy, using all means from sex with servants to infiltrating her brother into the Castle in order to gain intelligence. Hers is a strategic assessment that departs from Klamm's carefully staged intangibility and addresses the problem of resisting an enemy without identity or location.[5] His use of proxies and deputies makes it always uncertain whether Klamm is indeed Klamm; to paraphrase Hegel he is well known but not always recognized:

[O]f course his appearance is well known in the village, some have seen him, everyone has heard of him, and an image of Klamm has been contrived out of glimpses, rumours and indirect sightings, that is correct in its basic characteristics, but only in those. It is otherwise variable and perhaps not even as variable as Klamm's real appearance. It seems that he looks different when he comes to the village than when he leaves, different before than after drinking a beer, different awake, different asleep, different alone, different in conversation and, comprehensibly after all this, completely distinct up there in the castle.

(*C* 608, 216)

Klamm appears to be a role played by several actors; his omnipresence, omniscience and omnipotence are carefully staged as he shows but is never seen. Effective resistance to Klamm and other officials cannot be achieved through frontal assault, as pursued by Amalia and K., since this implicitly accepts the official and the Castle's terms of engagement; instead it must intervene in the gaps or even step out of its spectacle of power. While K. prizes Olga's 'prudence and bravery' he never really appreciates what she has understood and is trying to tell him, that he is engaged in a deadly struggle less with a person than with an implacable role or *mis-en-scene* in which the odds are stacked against him.

Official transcendence is carefully but imperfectly staged. Unlike the angelic messengers who traverse the interval between transcendence and the world of shadows, the official occupies it as a stand-in. Erlangen's testimony is salutary in this respect. As Klamm's accident prevention officer, his job is to prepare the scene for Klamm's appearances in the village and to prevent any unforeseen accidents that might compromise his reputation for inscrutability. K. has been spoiling Klamm's show, first by his unwelcome arrival, then by his unscripted theft of Klamm's mistress and finally by making himself at home in Klamm's carriage and sampling his private cognac. On that occasion Klamm was prevented from performing his role and leaving the Herrenhof even if K. had been got out of the way and all trace of the interruption had been removed – 'the coachman had effaced even his footprints in the snow' (*C* 545, 136) – Klamm's exit had been compromised. As the man responsible for accident prevention in Castle and village, Erlangen had to ensure everyone kept to their script and that his star performer did not keep bumping into walking accidents like K. Erlangen's main problem, though, was that Klamm himself was constitutionally accident prone and hardly able to protect himself from the unforeseen that habitually befell him: 'The bigger a job is, and Klamm's job is, of course, the biggest, the less strength remains to protect oneself from the outside world, and so every petty alteration in the pettiest things can seriously disturb' (*C* 702, 328). Because of this, Erlangen and his colleagues 'are obliged to keep such a watch over Klamm's comfort that we remove even those disturbances that do not bother him – and apparently there are none that bother him – if they strike us as being even possible disturbances' (C 702, 328–9). Erlangen's job is to reduce the incidence not only of actual but also possible accidents; he is the classic accident prevention officer, ensuring that everything runs according to plan or in Klamm's case, according to the official script.

For Klamm and his fellow officials are accidents made into a principle of domination. The parable of the message from the Emperor tells us that their very existence is the outcome of an accident that befell a messenger. Departing in good faith with a message from a dying Emperor, the extinction of the imperial sun upset the momentum of the ambassador who instead of delivering the message de-accelerated and as he approached standstill began reverse metamorphosis into an official. Instead of liberating the man in the village from his patient wait by delivering the message, the messenger's delay became a principle of domination. The man from the country before the gateway to the law like the man by his window in the village *must* wait, perhaps forever; the messenger's accident becoming his law and necessity.

Theatres

In *The Castle* the interval between transcendence and the life of the village is full of carefully staged partial appearances and enigmatic deliveries underlining the importance of spectacle in ensuring domination or, in Weber's terms, 'the probability that a given command (or all commands) will be obeyed by a given group of persons' (Weber, 212). The *Dorf/Schloss* nexus was a *mis-en-scene* evolved to fill the space left by a departed transcendence – the long-gone Count Westwest – by what are effectively a cabaret of sideshows. It was one of the many theatres of domination that had fascinated Kafka from his earliest work and remained central to his scenarios of power, punishment but above all defiance. The amphitheatre of 'In the Penal Colony' and its show execution along with the related quarry of *The Trial* are both sites for the theatre of domination.[6] The descriptions of the presidential box in the Ford's Theatre and the 'Nature Theatre of Oklahoma' are more ambivalent instances, yet they too obey the insight that the theatre of domination is not true, that the transcendence claimed by the official is a masquerade that can be evaded or deflated. The artistry of domination can be met by one of defiance. Kafka's views on how to achieve the latter changed radically, moving from early attempts to adjust the subject/object positions in theatrical domination to the breakout from the theatre of domination to the truth, from theatre to the street. We shall consider these scenarios first from the standpoint of the dominated and then from that of the dominator.

The celebrated diary entry of 23 September 1912 reporting on the night of writing 'The Judgement' is followed by the enigmatic entry 'Ich nur ich bin der Beobachter des Parterres' ('I only I am the observer of the parterre'). The double genitive – the sole observer *in* the parterre and/or *of* the parterre – appears often in Kafka in connection with the theatre. We saw earlier how the deadly implications of the spectated spectator posture was played out in the 'Nature Theatre of Oklahama' through the photo of the history theatre of the assassination of Lincoln – the metamorphosis of a viewer of a comedy into the viewed target and protagonist of an historical tragedy. Yet Kafka did not present this posture just in the light of domination, but also in the light of defiance. This defiance rumbled in the background of 'The Judgement', which departed from the spectacle of an insurrection that returned in the story as the 1905 Russian Revolution. But the implications of viewing this double genitive in the light of defiance – or *as* the light of defiance – had been anticipated in a dream of revolution in Prague recorded almost a year before.

In a diary entry dated 1 XI 11, following one of the longest sequences of entries dedicated to the Yiddish theatre, Kafka describes an unsuccessful effort to become a protagonist in the dramas, as a spectator. The actress Mrs Klug was leaving Prague by train, but was inhibited in her farewells to Kafka since 'She was completely dominated by my presence, but more in her imagination than really' (*D* 99, 165). He reminisces how seldom she invited him to sing with her and yet came to respect him as a spectator and eventually made him her most ardent admirer: 'I beamed when she sang, I laughed and looked at her all the time while she was on stage' (*D* 99, 165). Now from the train she looked at him for a last time and everything became theatre. Kafka as viewed on the platform/stage from the train was the protagonist who removed his hat as the train left while Mrs Klug waved her handkerchief. But, he remembered later, the train didn't really leave but was 'only moving the short length of the railway station in order to put on a play for us, and then was swallowed up' (*D* 101, 165). Kafka, however, was the protagonist, and Mrs Klug the imperious actress assigned the role of a transient spectator. Once the performance of tearful farewell was over and the train swallowed up, Kafka dreamt that Mrs Krug herself became a member of the audience, seated and foreclosed from the perspective of the player Kafka – 'Half asleep that same evening, Mrs Krug appeared to me unnaturally short, almost without legs' – viewed from the stage seated in the audience that is to say – and dominated by Kafka in his imagination – she 'wrung her hands with her face distorted as if a great misfortune had befallen her' (D 101, 167). The misfortune was to move from being viewed to being a viewed/viewer. The viewed/viewer position is volatile and subject to sudden violent change; as we saw with *The Trial*, it took only the opening of a window and a flash of light for K. to become the spectator of his own execution, the shameful possessor of the cherished photograph of his own execution.

Kafka attempted to repeat the performance of inverting the role of spectator and spectated with another actress – Mrs Tschissik – with whose dominion he also became infatuated. This time, however, the performance was an embarrassing debacle. In a Nietzschean object lesson of the perils of gratitude, Kafka sought to steal one of the Yiddish theatre's shows by presenting a splendid bouquet of flowers to the actress, waiting intently for the moment to intervene and shift the scene from the stage to the 'I only I' of the observer from the parterre, to become the real actor gazed on by both the audience and the would-be actors onstage. But the show started late and the insurrection of the parterre unravelled. The flowers began to wilt so the waiter took them to the kitchen where 'the kitchen help and several dirty regular guests handed them from one to another and smelled them' (D 105, 174). He could only 'look on' and missed the moment when the waiter passed up the flowers to Mrs Tschissik who put them aside. This time the coup failed – 'No one noticed my love and I had intended to show it to all, and so make it valuable in the eyes of Mrs Tschissik; the bouquet was hardly noticed' (D 105, 174). Mrs Tschissik later privately thanked him for the bouquet, having just learnt that it was from Kafka, but this was worse than nothing. Having failed to become a protagonist, Kafka that evening slumped – 'instead of distinguishing myself I sat sunk in my chair' – the observer in the parterre, and when she looked at him 'I looked away' (D 108, 178). It was after this rout that Kafka has one of his great dreams of insurrection, a Parisian uprising set in the streets of Prague.

This entry (9 XI 11) begins with the statement 'dreamt the day before yesterday: pure theatre, now I'm up in the gallery, now I'm on the stage' (D 111, 182) – now the spectator, now the actor. The dream opens with the same sexualized strategy employed against Mrs Klug and Mrs Tschissik – he 'pointed' to an actress he once liked who was playing a man – only to move to something far more extraordinary. From a state of hovering between viewer and viewed, the entire scenario metamorphoses into the history theatre of Prague. The transformation of the theatre begins by an expansion of the set that swallows the entire theatre, leaving no outside from which it can be viewed, and transforming the light into something new: 'In one act, the set was so large that nothing else was to be seen, no stage, no auditorium, no dark, no footlights' (*D* 111, 182). In place of the theatrical *mis-en-scene* Kafka imagines 'great crowds of spectators' moving across a life-size but malleable and mobile Prague cityscape. This pure theatre of cruelty in which there was no outside from which to view its performances, no actors and no audience, possessed in Prague 'the most beautiful set in all the world and of all time' (*D* 112, 182). While the effect of this 4-dimensional set is cinematographic, its performance is not projected but instantiated, not screened as a representation but plastic. The lighting no longer obeyed the direct beams of stage lighting convention, but 'that of dark, autumnal clouds. The light of the dimmed sun glittered dispersed from this or that stained glass window on the south east side of the square' (*D* 112, 183).

The 4-dimensional set hosted an 'imperial fete and a revolution' (*D* 112, 183), a *mis-en-scene* of both domination and defiance: 'The revolution was so huge with giant crowds of people sent back and forth, that the like never really took place in Prague; they had apparently located it in Prague only because of the set, while really it belonged in Paris' (*D* 112, 183). Kafka describes how the revolution had broken out, forcing the fete off the set, and how 'the people had forced their way into the castle, I myself ran out into the open right over the ledges of the fountain in the courtyard, but it was supposed to be impossible for the court to return to the castle' (*D* 112, 183). The overrunning of the Castle by the people – a movement frozen in the icy stasis of castle and village in *The Castle* – was an irreversible act, but Kafka remains intrigued by the exchange of actor/audience positions and looks past the potential destruction of the entire *mis-en-scene* of city/village and Castle: 'Just then many people streamed past me into the square, mostly spectators whom I knew from the street and who had perhaps just arrived' (*D* 113, 184). In the final scene, Kafka sees himself among the actor/ spectator crowd with a girl: 'Among them there was also a familiar girl, but I do not know which; beside her walked a young, elegant man in a yellow-brown ulster with small checks, his right hand deep in his pocket' (*D* 113, 184). He watches the girl and his revolutionary avatar walk towards 'Niklassstrasse' and then 'From this moment [*Augenblick*] on I saw no more' (*D* 113, 184). The blindness with which the vision ends is characteristically ambivalent – does the dreamer see no more because he is now fully an actor and no longer a spectator in the revolutionary theatre of 'Oklahama', Paris or Prague or is it because he and the girl have walked off the set and away towards their own, private story?

The ambivalence is intensified in yet another dream recorded in the diaries ten days later (19. XI 11) when Kafka returns to perverting the theatrical scenario of subject and object of the gaze. The fusion of scene and spectator that was accomplished on the 'most beautiful set in the world' makes way for an uncomfortable twisting of the scene. We are back in the parterre, but this time 'I sit right up at the front, think I am sitting in the first row until it finally appears it is the second' (D 119, 193). Not only this, for in this theatre the rows of seats face away from the stage making the auditorium the spectacle: 'The back of the row is turned towards the stage so that one can see the auditorium comfortably, the stage only by turning' (D 119, 193). Thus the audience contemplates themselves – they are all heavily dressed in their winter clothes, and those behind, in the first row, cannot easily be seen but are certainly heard. The dreamer is excited at the spectacle of the winter-coated backs, a woman dressed as a man, an actor playing his friend Löwy from the Yiddish theatre ('but very unlike the real one'), giving an excited but learned speech, and the box of the Kisch family on the second tier. The play by Schnitzler adapted by Ütitz begins, the curtain is raised and theatre darkens.

As the spectacle of the audience slips into the darkness, the scene of a banquet appears on a stage, which can only be seen by twisting round – 'you look down with your chin on the back of the seat' (D 120, 194) – and trying to see past the mostly blue large flat hats of the ladies in the first row. It is easy to lose confidence in this obtuse theatre, and naturally things start to go wrong. The scene ends, but the curtain doesn't come down, leaving the theatre in darkness. The stage is now occupied by two critics writing their reviews and a leaping stage manager. The dreamer looks away and up into the auditorium. It is lit artificially 'by simple paraffin lamps that are stuck up on simple chandeliers, like those in the streets, and now, of course, burn only very low' (D 121, 196). Then there is an accident that changes the entire scene: 'Suddenly, impure paraffin or a damaged wick is probably the cause, the light spurts out of one of these lanterns and sparks pour down in a broad gush on the crowded audience that forms a mass as black as earth' (D 121, 196). The accidental lighting flash leaves a dark after-image of the audience reduced to a barely visible black mass, but it is not enough to set fire to the theatre and quickly becomes part of the scene, leaving everyone where they were. There follows another event, this time an attempt at enlightenment: a 'gentleman rises out of this mass, and walks on it towards the lamp' (D 121, 196). The audience have become the stage on which an actor walks towards the extinguished lamp. He 'apparently wants to fix the lamp', contemplates it but when nothing happens 'returns quietly to his place in which he is swallowed up' (D 121–2, 196). The dreamer watching this actor emerge and return to the darkness of the audience/stage then exchanges himself with the actor, and takes a bow to the blackness – the familiar movement between the watcher and the watched, but still played out in a twisted theatre. The climate is one of stasis, of accepting the scenario and waiting for something to happen.

It is in one of the later fragments that Kafka overcomes his ambivalence and edges toward the explicit endorsement of the destruction of the *mis-en-scene* of the theatre of domination. Like the earlier diary entries, it departs from the assumption that we are both viewers and viewed but proposes that such a scenario is a machine for producing obedience that can only be escaped by destroying the theatre. He begins by describing 'a life between stage scenery. It is bright, that is a morning in the open air, then it suddenly gets dark and it already evening. This is not a very complicated deception, but one must adapt to it as long as one is standing on the stage' (*WP* 346; *NII* 358). Kafka proposes a radical exit from the scenario, following Plato's advice in the parable of the cave that the philosopher leave the cave but with the proviso now that he destroy it on departure: 'One may only break out, if one has the strength, against the background, cutting through the canvas and then through the tatters of the painted sky, going across some bits of junk and escaping into the really narrow, dark, damp street, which because it is near the theatre is called Theatre Street yet is true and has all the depths of truth itself' (*WP* 346; *NII* 358). Instead of seeking to adjust the scenario, the actor breaks out of the two-dimensional *mis-en-scene* and into the city. The city street is now the scene of truth – the movement from surface to 4-dimensional truth – but a doubt remains, for although part of the city, this is still 'Theatre street'.

Walls

The intensifying defiance Kafka registered in the theatre of domination alerts us to the fragility of domination, especially after the death of God and the ensuing migration of transcendent principles. The return of Plato's philosopher messenger to the cave with news of the truth has been delayed and the lights in the cave extinguished; the shadows cease to move and the audience is confronted with the need to create their own new scenarios. Kafka's stories situate domination as a response to actual and threatened defiance; its *mis-en-scene* is reactive, defensive and essentially lacking in initiative. In this sense Kafka's tales of the death of Gods and Emperors narrate a defiant life provoking increasingly desperate and grotesque expedients of domination. He becomes a surveyor of such expedients, tracking the raising of walls and the preparation of spectacles intent on holding back the looming defiance. Erlangen's carefully constructed *mis-en-scene* for Klamm is such a spectacle intended to protect the official 'from the external world' and ensure that no 'accidents' befall him. It is a theatrical spectacle, a preparation of the scene that Klamm the dominator – a comedian of the absolute – will shuffle across, but such spectacles are essentially protective walls. The insecurity that attends the raising of walls – ever power's declaration of its vulnerability – fascinated Kafka; as immune barriers they enable an illusion of security while at the same time fatally undermining it. They can at best delay defiance, as shown by the man from the country's fatal hesitation before the protective wall of the law. If only he had understood that its mere existence testified to domination's fear and vulnerability and that the gatekeeper was just part of its insurance policy against his potential defiance. But such policies are not entirely reliable since the wall can equally compromise and delay the exercise of domination, as in the case of the imperial messenger exhausted and eventually prevented from executing the imperial will by the obstacles posed by the very walls meant to protect the Emperor. The messenger's mutation into an official is intimately tied to the obstacles to domination raised by the walls meant to sustain and protect it from the defiance gathering force beyond the horizon.

The wall and its vicissitudes are a leitmotif in Kafka, from the Great Wall of China to the earth as a protective wall in 'The Burrow'. But it insensibly modulates into the theme of the city, a clustering of walls and a concentrated site of potential domination and emancipation. The builders of the wall that would serve as the foundations for the tower of Babel – a tangible connection between transcendence and its shadows – are diverted into becoming the founders of warring cities. The extended text of 'The Great Wall of China' from 1917 is one of a series of imperial narratives from this year that meditate on the strategy of protective enclosure. It narrates the researches of a village scholar/engineer into the legends surrounding the building of the Great Wall of China. The first legend to be scrutinized maintains that the wall is complete, erected through a piecemeal system of labour gangs working on small sub-sections, but then 'Of course constructing in this way left many gaps that were only later and slowly filled in, some even after the completion of the wall had been announced. Indeed some gaps must still have been left never to be filled in, and some hold these are much larger than the built sections ...' (S 235, 289). The gaps in the wall and its consequent porosity not only rendered it unfit for defence, it even provoked and concentrated new threats to security: 'the wall was surely conceived, as is widely maintained and recognized, as protection from the Northern peoples. How though can a wall protect if it is not complete?' (S 235, 289–90). If there are gaps in the wall – as there must be given the scale of the project and the piecemeal technique of construction – how can it provide the necessary closure? Worse than this, even if complete, the protective wall becomes a fixed target that in turn needs to be protected; using a double negative the narrator reflects:

> Indeed such a wall does not only not protect [*kann nicht nur nicht Schutzen*], the building itself is in constant danger. The pieces of wall left abandoned in bleak regions can always be easily destroyed by the nomads, given that in those days, wary of the wall building they changed their encampments with incomprehensible speed like locusts and for this reason perhaps had a better overview of the progress of the wall than the builders themselves.
>
> (S 235, 290)

The strategy of enclosure not only provoked defiance but also stimulated the Empire's adversaries to develop guerrilla strategies of extreme mobility and invent new kinds of oppositional knowledge. Consistent with Sun Tzu's very unsocratic preference for knowledge of the enemy over knowledge of the self, Kafka's nomadic knowledge consists in knowing the limits of the imperial adversary better than the Emperor knew them himself.

The narrator then hypothesizes that the main purpose of the wall was not so much to protect against external enemies than to make the *building* of it serve as a means to distract attention from internal tensions and so secure protection against an *internal* enemy. By mobilizing the population in the service of a military-industrial cultural revolution, the high command [*Führerschaft*] dissolved parochial life and its habits into a single, imperial task that aspired to the closure of a protective ring. As the workers left their villages for the wall they were met everywhere

> with greetings, flags, banners, they had never seen how vast, rich, beautiful and loveable their land was, each fellow-countryman was a brother, for whom one was building a protecting wall and who with all he had and for all his life gave thanks for it. Unity! Unity!, shoulder to shoulder, a ring of the people. Blood no longer confined to the paltry circulation of the body but sweetly ebbing and flowing throughout infinite China.
>
> (S 238, 292)

Singular life, the blood of the individual body, is dissolved into the life of the people and the collective life's blood of the Empire. The wall of stone protecting China from without has become a wall of blood (a circle or *Schloss*) intended to protect China from itself. Yet it is striking that the high command has disposed everything to ensure that the people learn only what they are meant to from this experience, unlike the nomads beyond the frontier or the narrator himself and fellow sceptics, the 'best of the people'. The anonymous high command sought to align the revolutionary anticycles of history, the revolution 'of all human thoughts and desires and the counter-revolution of human goals and achievements' (S 239–40, 294), by contemplating them in the borrowed light of transcendence: 'for through the window the reflected glory of divine worlds lit the hands of the high command as they traced their plans' (S 240, 294). Unfortunately for them the plans were never executed, closure – *das Schloss* – never completed and the 'best of people' never deceived.

The narrator compares the building of the Great Wall with the Tower of Babel, noting immediately that only the former earnt 'divine approval'. While both structures arose from energies combined in the pursuit of a single aim, the transcendent scaling of the heavens with a tower contrasted sharply with the people's immanent goal of containing themselves within a wall. Citing an architectural theorist who analysed the Great Wall of China as the foundation for a future Tower of Babel, the narrator shows how the foundational task was already understood as a strategic response to existing and potential defiance: 'Human nature, essentially superficial and like the swirling dust, accepts no bondage, if it fetters itself it will soon begin madly to tear at the fetters and will scatter its wall, chain and itself across all the heavens' (S 239, 294). It is this defiant energy that the high command would contain, but with only limited success. For in spite of their efforts to cloak their work in divine light, the wall's construction generated a new body of profane knowledge – of which the narrator is a subtle representative – issuing from a 'secret principle' held by the people: 'Seek to understand with all your powers the decrees of the high command, but only up to a determinate limit and then cease to reflect' (S 241, 295). The maxim expresses the pointlessness of reflecting on the inevitable, destructive failure of the high command's project of enclosure; it is enough to understand the contrast between transcendent goals and temporal achievements and to recognize that the futile attempt to unite them is the high command's problem and not ours.

The narrator proceeds to his own strategic assessment of the failure of the wall in terms of the vacated transcendent structure of Empire. He begins by questioning the imaginary enemy beyond the wall, moving on to ask why the people accepted the call to mobilization? The object of his analysis is the high command itself, whose dominion is distinguished from that of the imperial officials; there is indeed conflict between them. The former, the Mandarins, are of fickle judgement, toys of the moment while the goal of the high command is fixed and eternal; the Mandarins 'aroused by a pleasant dream quickly call a meeting, decide and the same evening drum the people out of their beds to fulfil the order even if it is just a matter of some lights to honour the God who yesterday showed himself favourable to the masters. Yet the day after, with the lights barely spent, they thrash them in some obscure corner' (S 241–2, 297). The quickly spent flashes of the officials' bids to placate transcendence, their reversible and capricious decisions, are contrasted with the absolute consistency of the high command 'that has been for always along with the decision to build the wall' (S 242, 296). But under the guise of praising the eternity of the high command, the narrator mounts a subtle critique: the high command has existed only so long as the decision to build a wall, and that only for so long as there has been internal and external defiance. The Empire wages war with itself on the battlefield of eternity with the Emperor surrounded by 'the brilliant yet sombre throng of his courtiers' (S 243, 298) opposed to the high command, the people and itself. The eternity of the high command, the transcendent principle or *arche* holds itself to be the truth of Empire even as the figure of transcendence, the Emperor, falls in and out of history: 'The empire is immortal, but the individual emperor falls and plunges; even entire dynasties go under breathing their last in a single death rattle' (S 243, 299). The men from the country hear but distorted and delayed scraps of news about such events, and even if by chance they are present they understand nothing: 'The people will never learn of these struggles and sufferings, like latecomers, like strangers in a city they stand at the end of packed side-streets contentedly nibbling their packed lunches while far ahead in the town centre square the execution of their master is taking its course' (S 243, 299). And even if a madman carrying a lantern runs into their midst or a boatman or official arrives telling them that the God/Emperor is dead, they will retain their equanimity – what, really, is it to them?. It is at this point in his narrative that Kafka arrives at the parable of the imperial messenger that he excerpted and published separately in *A Country Doctor*.

In a sense, the people are already emancipated and happy to leave transcendence to those who need it to dominate them; they reserve their reflection and obedience within a secret limit of their own choosing. The narrator, growing more audacious in voicing such secret knowledge, suggests 'If one wanted to conclude from such appearances that fundamentally we have no Emperor, one would not be so far from the truth' (S 246, 301). His tactic is to consider transcendence as literally transcendent, that is to say, as having nothing to do with us. Kafka's narrator draws the conclusion that 'the consequence of such views is a life to a certain extent free and undominated. It is by no means without ethics, in all my travels I have hardly ever encountered such ethical purity as in my *Heimat*. But it is a life not subject to contemporary law, one obeying only the wisdom and warnings that have been passed down to us from ancient times' (S 247, 302). The people also reserve the right to interpret ancient wisdom as they see fit and to ignore the rule of contemporary law. The narrator, describing a scene of spectacular transcendence opposed to an indifferent life beyond the law traces it to the weakness of both government and people. The government remains at the level of Foucauldian sovereign power; it never developed the capillary power necessary for effective governmentality: 'this most ancient empire on earth has been unable or too distracted by other things to constitute imperial rule with sufficient clarity to extend continuously and reliably to the remotest borders of the Empire' (S 247, 302). The Empire instead pursued a strategy of closure concentrated on fixing the border rather than improving its communications and ability to achieve participation or *methexis* within its borders. The people themselves are complicit, afflicted by 'weak faith and imagination, for which they never succeeded in drawing to their subjected hearts the vitality and objectivity of an Empire submerged in Peking' (S 247, 302). The spirit of the Emperor, dead and buried in Peking, has not been resurrected in the people. Their reserved obedience has rendered it impossible for them to hear any more than scraps of information about imperial power, and they can only view contact with it in terms of being 'consumed'. Indeed, this is what happens when their blood is fused by the high command into a single military-industrial worker; they are all consumed in building a wall to protect their rulers from … them. The narrator ends with the childhood memory of a passing boatman who told his father about the building of the wall, thus looping a narrative that began with the announced completion of the wall only to end with an announcement of its beginning; the story escapes through a gap in itself to tell other stories of the death of gods and the rise and fall of walls and empires.

The babble of voices drowning out the dying fall of the imperial decree in the Great Wall of China may be contrasted with the soliloquy of Kafka's last reflection on the arcanum of domination executed in 'The Burrow'.[7] A first-person animal voice speaks from the insecurity of its protective bunker; at once High Command and labour force this hunted-hunter has created a total defensive environment under the earth, with vaults and tunnels intended to provide total security against any unforeseen accidents or adversaries. And yet gnawing doubt about the security of this enclosed, protected life prevails from the very outset, since 'I have set up my burrow and it *seems* to be successful' (S 325, 465; my emphasis). The creature is haunted by *seems*, or the feeling of having inadvertently forgotten something and so leaving itself unwittingly vulnerable to some dreadful accident. This anxiety is related to its awareness of the role played by accident in its piecemeal and improvised construction: 'Visible from the outside is just what seems to be a big hole that in fact goes nowhere for after a few steps one bumps into natural firm rock. I do not vaunt myself with having planned this ruse deliberately, it was just left over from one of the many false starts, but it then seemed to me a good idea to leave this one hole uncovered' (S 325, 465). The false entrance is not only a diversion, it is also an *aide memoire* for the role played by chance and accident in the construction of the burrow. Indeed, the building history of the burrow is narrated as less the execution of a plan than a chapter of accidents accompanied by the animal's improvised responses to them.

The worry about something having been left to chance – 'even now at the high point of my life I cannot enjoy a complete hour of tranquility' (S 325, 465) – modulates with the hunter's anxiety about himself being hunted. This predator built a lair in which to store his prey away from the attentions of fellow hunters, but the possibility of their coming informs literally every move he makes. He must forever seek the previously unnoticed weak points in his design by surveying the burrow from outside and patrolling its borders. If before life had been a Hobbesian war of each against all, an unsecured life of constant fear and vulnerability, then life in the burrow with its obsessed search for the one overlooked weak point seems to be even less eligible: 'I am not all that far from deciding to go far away, to resume my previous desolate life where there was no security, one full of indiscriminate dangers which made each individual danger difficult to see and fear, as I am constantly taught when comparing my secure burrow with life elsewhere' (S 336, 479). But these moments of despair, the fear that building the burrow itself was the fatal error or deadly accident, undermines the structure and renders it literally uncanny or uninhabitable.

The anxieties of enclosed life proceed from two obsessively worked over fears. The first is the sense of unpredictable but imminent danger – the very accident the defensive work was meant to insure against – and the second the strategic vulnerability of having to defend a defensive wall. The constant strategic vigilance and testing of limits means that the burrow is an infinite source of error and weakness; its fatal flaw is perhaps visible only to the better informed enemy. For this reason the burrower must continually venture out of the burrow in order to ensure all is well and ascertain whether its fixed position is attracting attention, even at the risk of this very manoeuvre prompting the danger it was meant to forestall. The ageing hunter is aware that the very cunning of his structure contributes to the strategic education of his enemy/annihilator who is always a step ahead, contemptuously defying his vain precautions and sleepy vigilance: 'it is I who sleeps while the annihilator watches. Perhaps he is one of those who casually strolls past the entrance, always making sure, no differently from me, that the door is still unharmed and holding back their attack, only passing by because they know that the owner is not indoors, or perhaps because they even already know he is trying to hide nearby in the bushes' (S 335, 478) ashamed to have been seen trying to hide himself. And so he abandons his observation post outside his door, feeling 'I have nothing more to learn here, now nor later' (S 335, 478). His enemy has become wholly abstract – the 'annihilator' – and the creature can no longer test himself against and learn from his attacks but can only contemplate the integrity of his defensive burrow against some *possible* offensive; he knows nevertheless that he has adverted his gaze and has been fatally distracted by a preoccupation with the wall that was meant to be his insurance policy for old age. Indeed, the protective wall is in the end his greatest worry and vulnerability: 'What were all the petty dangers to which I dedicated time thinking over compared with this one? Did I hope as owner of the burrow to have an advantage over all comers? Precisely being the owner of this vast, vulnerable work makes me defenceless against any serious attack; I have grown used to the happiness of ownership and the vulnerability of the burrow has made me vulnerable, its injuries hurt me as if they were mine' (S 355, 502). The protective burrow has itself to be protected; instead of offering security it has become just another source of vulnerability. Building it has been a perverse game, merely playing with imagined dangers which, because conceivable were 'not the dangers that really threaten' (S 355, 503). The latter are the accidents that cannot be predicted or avoided, the unforeseeable offensives of an implacable, absolute enemy or annihilator.

The burrower begins to learn that it is not sovereign even in its own domain. It comes to regret that it has no allies, having eliminated them earlier as sources of possible danger; it regrets that it cannot come to a negotiated peace with its enemy since it gave and can expect no quarter. The dominator is left occupying his crumbling walls and conscious of growing ever older, weaker and more stupid. A life's work of hunting and building has become a beacon announcing his whereabouts to his enemies, that is, if he is lucky enough to still have any since prey is not the enemy of the hunter, it's just prey. For as he returns from his reconnaissance, the hunter is debilitatingly haunted by his own uncanny bunker – he hears a whistling sound that announces the coming of an omnipresent, omnipotent and omniscient annihilator. This divine enemy is everywhere, impossible to escape in the burrow and with 'the monstrous possibilities that its labour power appears to give it' (S 359, 507) it is irresistible and knows not only where he is now but also his every past and future move. If the imperial degree of the Emperor was drowned out by all the voices carrying and interpreting it, here the insecure and haunted voice of the animal is hollowed out by the white noise of the approaching hunter-god. The fragment breaks off with the rout of the animal's strategic intelligence in the face of this threat. Recognizing the futility of both negotiation and resistance, the animal retreats from strategic foresight to the bare, pallid *hope* that the noise is not coming for him and that maybe if he makes himself inconspicuous (sitting in his enormous, well-provisioned bunker!) he might be passed over by it. Instead, huddling in his burrow like prey he can only hope for the security of hearing but not being heard: 'it will be decisive if and what the beast knows about me and how much. The more I think about it, the less probable it seems to me that the beast has heard me; it is possible, but hard to imagine that it has some news of me, it can't have heard of me' (*S* 359, 507). Relying on the not entirely apt precedent of an enemy diverting their approach in the early stages of hollowing out the bunker, the animal waits. The fragment breaks off on the realization that by now the decision no longer rests with him and that whether the beast is coming for him or not is purely a matter of accident, that is to say, the inscrutable strategic calculations of the annihilator. Prey that cannot pray, the creature has surrendered the initiative and waits for the inevitable.

The narrative of the burrow resembles *The Trial* in placing its readers in a position of sympathy with the dominator/predator. It can also be read from the standpoint of the 'small fry' or the animals without voice routinely preyed upon by the burrower or who stumble accidentally into his domain. For these animals, the burrower's most feared adversary – the annihilator – is their redeemer and the noise so feared by the dominator for them announces the coming of a messiah of the dominated. The white noise with the attributes of divinity announces the advent of an avenger, of an enemy that knows what to do to make the dominator give up and surrender his walls without a struggle, precisely as advocated by Sun Tzu and modern manuals of guerrilla warfare. While cunningly invited by Kafka to commiserate with the sorrows of the wall-builder, as we were with those of the banker and sexual predator Josef K., the burrow can also be read as an allegory of the internal limits of domination and a moral lesson in the anxieties of power. But as with many of his later fragments, particularly those featuring the village colonel or commandant, it can also be read as a strategic reflection on how to unnerve domination, a lesson in how fiction can serve to undo the stories domination tries to tell itself about its invulnerability, stories that help it forget for a while the very defiance its defensive walls were built to protect it from.

Cities

The ageing burrower's melancholy realization that his protective wall is futile and his dwelling become a mausoleum points to the fundamental ambivalence of the protective wall. The structure intended to sustain and enhance life also encloses and encrypts it. The protective wall serves both life and death; it realizes and restricts by making life possible but at the same time intolerable. It can enclose a space for life in the city, or for death in the crypt or graveyard. Yet both city and graveyard share the properties of enclosure. In a sense all walls are graveyard walls, the life that built them is already dead even while they continue to stand and be inhabited. The peculiar gravity of the city issues from the ambivalence described in the limit case of the solitary burrower unable to escape his own construction while realizing that it is his grave. He returns to it and is tormented by the whistling wind of the future, of the others who are coming to inhabit the *Bau* to which he dedicated his life and that gave his life meaning. Yet the solitary burrower is bereft of any trust in or hospitality for that future and the others that are bringing it to him; he can only imagine them and it as at best an enemy or at worst a predator dedicated to his annihilation.

The attraction and repulsion of the enclosing wall and its articulation in the streets, dwellings, gates and squares of the city drive Kafka's narratives of city experience, most of which feature the approach to – or departure from – cities. We saw the protagonists of 'Description of a Struggle' make their protracted exit from the city, while the dream boy from the same narrative is drawn irresistibly towards the city of the south, even if he is doomed only to orbit it and never arrive. The ambivalence is clear in the early stories of father–son conflict, 'The Urban World' and 'The Judgement': in the one, exit to the city figures liberation, while in the other it draws the young man to his suicidal auto-execution. The ramifying walls of the enclosed Imperial City prevent the messenger from ever escaping it – with the death of the Emperor he enters into a decaying orbit towards the stasis of officialdom, while the execution of Josef K. in *The Trial* requires he be lifted off his feet by his executioners and – freed from its gravity – forcibly carried out of the city towards the suburban killing fields. Raban's departure from the city towards his fiancée in the country threatens to be perpetually deferred by the distractions of the city, and he is left in that fragment eternally suspended between the poles of a reluctant departure and a deferred arrival.

As a site both of defiance and domination, the city is founded on defiance of an enemy. The enclosure of a wall releases the internal ramifications that make up the complexity and the vulnerability of city life. The city is in a sense an accident, a response to real and anticipated defiance replete with unintended outcomes. One account of the accidental foundation of cities is related in the fragment 'The City Coat of Arms'. While the idea behind the Tower of Babel was to defy God and build a tower 'that will reach to heaven' (S 433, 374), the growing sense of the asymptotic character of the task and the probability that future generations would be better equipped technically to achieve it 'disabled their forces and people concerned themselves less with building the tower than constructing a city for the workmen' (S 433, 375). Differences over the best quarters 'provoked disputes that escalated into bloody conflicts' (S 433, 375) even if 'time was spent not only fighting; in the intervals the city was embellished, which admittedly provoked fresh envy and fresh conflict' (S 433–4, 375). As a result, 'by the time of the second or third generation the meaninglessness of building a tower up to heaven was already recognised, but everybody was far too bound together to leave the city' (S 434, 375). The same force of gravity that ensured the tower would not rise also ensured that no one would leave the city; the only escape was to imagine the destruction of the city from without on 'the prophesied day on which the city would be smashed to pieces by five short, consecutive blows from a gigantic fist' (S 434, 375).[8] Just as the foundation of the city could not be predicted, nor could the date of the messianic fist that would come both to destroy and bring peace to it.

In a group of fragments contemporary with 'The City Coat of Arms' and 'The Great Wall of China', Kafka reflects further on the origin of cities. One traces the founding of the city to the arrival of a messianic explorer and 'land surveyor' – anticipating the figure of K. in *The Castle* – who apportioned property rights: 'This is the area, five meters long, five meters wide, not large then but it is still one's own ground. Who has arranged it thus?' (*WP* 259, *NII* 241). In trying to answer, the narrator recalls the arrival of a 'strange man': 'Once there came a stranger with a lot of leather harness over his garment, belts, shoulder straps, halters and pouches. He took a notebook from one pouch, made a note and then asked: "Where is the petitioner?"' (*WP* 259, *NII* 240). The stranger enters a scenario of division, for only 'Half of the occupants of the house were gathered around him in a great semi-circle' (*WP* 259, *NII* 240) – the other half absent – and fulfils the great task of dividing the property. The authoritative survey by an outsider places responsibility for the plan for the city outside of the control of the inhabitants; it is imposed upon and accepted by some of them, but by no means all.

This account of the intelligible origin of property division in the decision of a stranger who decides inexplicably in the manner of the high command in the case of the Chinese Wall is complemented by another version of the origin of the city, closer to the burrower's account of his *Bau*. In this fragment the city wall is fixed, but building continues frantically within it: 'There is continually building in the city. Not in order to extend it, for it satisfies our needs and its borders have remained unaltered for a long time, yet there seems to be a certain reluctance to contemplate enlarging it ...' (*WP* 260; *NII* 506). Rather than expend the destructive force necessary to expand the city walls – they would first have to be broken – the inhabitants 'prefer to restrict' themselves to'building over squares and gardens, putting new storeys on old houses ...' (*WP* 260; *NII* 506). They are drawn into an involuted effort to safeguard whatever exists by means of 'continual building operations' (*WP* 260; *NII* 506). The inertia or 'lethargic restlessness' (*WP* 261; *NII* 506) that afflicts the inhabitants of the closed cities is compensated by the quality of the building materials available – 'We are after all, in the land of quarries, building almost only in stone; even marble is available, and whatever people neglect in building-work is made up by the permanence and solidity of the material' (*WP* 260; *NII* 506). The city is governed by a necessity that has no particular justification apart from being bequeathed by the dead; the life expressed in building is already mortified. The accident that closed the city walls happened a long time ago and has become the necessity of the present; as Kafka put it in a later fragment, 'It was a city among cities, its past was greater than its present is, but even this present amounts to something quite considerable' (375).

This fragment is also fascinating for its account of a past conflict, for it situates the city within a collapsed bipolar configuration that recalls the *Dorf/Schloss* arrangement of *The Castle*. Except in this case the building on the 'Roman Hill [*Romberg*] outside the town' (*WP* 261, 507) was already in ruins and the subject of legend. The pattern of a building on a hill dominating the settlement below it is precisely the configuration K. enters as a land surveyor in *The Castle*, but in this case it seems as if the slow destruction of the building on the hill is both a condition and consequence of the enclosure of the city below. For the *Dorf* to become a city it is necessary to deny access to the dominators on the hill by erecting a wall and destroying their high places. After centuries of enclosed peace and embalmed life, the inhabitants of the city have forgotten the significance of the ruin that towers above them, and they tell stories that – like the storeys added to their crumbling buildings – sit on an old and forgotten foundation. It seems to some 'that the ruin was the remains of a country villa "built more than a thousand years ago" ... it was built for a rich merchant, who had grown old and solitary' (like the burrowing animal) and that 'it began to decay as soon as he died' for 'you would not find among us anyone who would want to live so far outside the town' (*WP* 261; *NII* 507). The building, it was said, was left to decay, 'and the destructive work of the centuries is usually more thorough than that of its builders' (*WP* 261; *NII* 507). Yet the stories do not add up: the name of the hill – 'Roman Hill' – carries with it a memory of imperial domination by another spatially and temporally distant city, and what remains does not add up to a rich eccentric's country house. Kafka tells us that a solitary walker strolling without the city on a 'quiet Sunday' will find 'foundation walls' enclosing hard ground (usually the sign of a military training ground inside a fortress) but mistaken by the stroller as 'crushed by the pressure of passing time' (*WP* 261, *NII* 507). The site is strewn with 'smashed columns' and what is guessed to be the 'worthless torso of a statue', all of which point not only to an important building but also to its violent end. The site of destruction, like a quarry, has 'piles of rubble' and 'stones sunk into the ground' (*WP* 262, *NII* 507), unusual for the leisure palace or villa claimed by 'tradition'. The ruin still resists entry – 'one can scarcely squeeze through the low-growing but dense briars, scratching oneself on thorns till the blood runs' (*WP* 262, *NII* 507), but this is understood by the complacent narrator not as a memory of the previous fortress but according to the historical legend of a 'beautiful park, with trees and terraces, which is said to have survived long after the house itself was gone' (*WP* 262, *NII* 507). The repeated references to conjecture and rumour in connection with the *Romberg* suggests that the destruction of the building on it has been shrouded with anodyne stories, making it an eccentric extension of the city rather than its implacable adversary.

The separation of dominators and dominated that attends the bipolar configuration of the village and the castle has been cancelled in the story of the city and the 'villa' on the hill. The fragments narrate a possible future for *The Castle* in which the land surveyor and the people of the village form a city by enclosing the village. But this can only be accomplished through the destruction of the enclosed castle that dominates it from above and kept its access to the village open and unpredictable. The city in other words brings domination into itself; its law and necessity may originally have come from without in a revolutionary act or other unpredictable accident, but it is no longer dependent on a bipolar structure: citizens are at the same time dominators and dominated, and the city at once a site of free and emancipated life as well as its burial. The buildings of the living are erected on the crypts of the dead, until they in turn become the foundations for future generations to build upon; what is important, Kafka reminds us, is to maintain the momentum of building.

While this group of fragments describes the historic sources for the ambivalence of the city as a site of life and death, emancipation and domination, a later fragment takes up the theme of the city of the sun described in 'A Message from the Emperor'. In the latter, the Emperor is the 'Imperial Sun' with the messenger bearing his livery and a message sent from the light to the shadow; but on the death of the Emperor the messenger can barely imagine persevering long enough to traverse the stairs, courtyards and palaces of the imperial city and after thousands of years impossibly 'burst through the outermost gate' (S 5, 306). In the later fragment beginning 'The city resembles the sun', urban light is both defiant and dominant. Kafka spells out the simile in a genealogy of the city understood in terms of its spatio-historical phases: 'in a central circle all the light is intensely concentrated, it is dazzling, one loses one's way, one cannot find the streets, the houses, if once one has entered it one simply does not get out of it again' (WP 319, NII 259). It is impossible to escape the first circle because of the sheer intensity of the pure light; this is the centre of the city but also of the violent and indistinguishable act of defiance that founds its law. The first circle, understood spatially and temporally, is succeeded by a second, larger circle of light in which it is possible to discern distinctions and thus move about within it; here 'the light is still very strong, but it is no longer an unbroken radiance, there are little dark alleys, hidden passages, even very small squares where all is twilight and coolness' (WP 319, NII 259). This high-definition lighting fades in the subsequent circle where 'the light is already so diffuse that one has to search for it, here large areas of the city lie only in a cold grey glimmer' (WP 319, NII 260). The radiance of the inner circle here tends to grey as the distinct outline of the city blurs into a suburban fog. The final circle 'is the open country, dull in colour, late-autumnal, barely lit by a sort of sheet lightning' (WP 319, NII 260), the type of landscape preferred by Titorelli in his repetitive monochromes. It is the borderland between city and open country traversed by Karl Rossmann and Josef K. on their way to their executions; here the light of the distant city flashes intermittently, visible only at night, like the 'city of the south' in an insomniac shimmer beyond the horizon.

Kafka locates his parable of urban disorientation, 'A Comment',[9] in a city of permanent grey where the radiating light of the imperial centre is long extinguished. He had described it earlier as a city of twilight; in a fragment related to the parable he wrote, 'In this city it is perpetual early morning with the sky an even smooth grey that scarcely grows any lighter at all, the streets are deserted, clean and silent . . .' (WP 319, NII, 260). This is the city of Nietzsche's last man; it does not have the bright core of the divine centre nor the attendant harsh relief of the second circle, but is a perpetual suburban grey. No one is about, but the streets are clean and animated by an ominous wind: 'somewhere a loose window blind moves slowly to- and fro-, somewhere the ends of a towel that has been hung over the balcony railing of a top storey fly up in the air, somewhere a curtain flutters faintly at an open window, otherwise nothing stirs' (*WP* 319; *NII* 260). It is a city of fluttering rags, unconnected except for the auguring wind traversing them from who knows what distant meteorological disturbance. It is also the setting for 'A Comment' – early morning, clean and deserted streets traversed by a wind that brings both spatial and temporal disruption: 'It was very early in the morning, the streets clean and deserted. I was going to the station. As I compared the clock on a tower with my watch I saw that it was much later than I had believed' (*S* 456; *NII* 530). It is as if the wind of the early morning has ripped into the consistency of time; the discrepancy between subjective and objective time together with the difficulty of navigating the streets makes the narrator unsure of the way, that is to say, the way to the station and out of this city. He makes the mistake of asking a figure of authority for guidance: 'luckily there was a policeman at hand, I ran up to him and breathlessly asked him the way. He smiled and said: "Do you expect to discover the way from me?" "Yes," I said, "since I cannot find it myself"' (*S* 456; *NII* 530). Only the policeman seems aware of the irony of being asked for advice on how to leave the city; how can the traveller think that obedience to authority will help him escape? He has to decide for himself, or surrender to the tutelage of others and remain in the city, blocked like the imperial messenger; nevertheless, the policeman volunteers his advice: '"Give it up, give it up," said he, and turned away with a great flourish like a man who wants to be alone with his laughter' (*S* 456; *NII* 530). Yet at least it can be said that in the grey city there is no longer the blinding light of authority and the clearly illuminated way; it is for the traveller to stay or to go; the city like the court in the *The Trial* is ambivalent: 'it receives you when you come and relinquishes you when you go' (*T* 193, 235).

Laws

Kafka's three great machines of the law – *Apparat*, *Gericht* and *Schloss* – work less to deliver justice than to lend necessity to accidents. While appearing to apply the law to individual cases, they are first and foremost necessity machines, making laws out of accidents. They are also anarchic *arcana* whose secret is not the content of the law – as Kafka misleadingly suggested in 'The Problem of Our Laws' – but the non-existence of law. While appearing to apply a transcendent law to singular cases, these machines of law are fundamentally anarchic and serve to make binding what are essentially accidental choices and outcomes.[10] In the case of the *Apparat* and the *Gericht*, this is achieved through capital punishment; by killing the accused – who can be anybody – death lends the selection of a victim the character of ineluctable necessity. The machines create necessity by producing death: the *Apparat* through the terminal inscription of a transgressed imperative on the bodies of its victims, and the *Gericht* through its death sentences and ritualistic executions.

The *Schloss* differs in not being a punitive institution; but while there is no death penalty in *The Castle*, this makes the legitimacy produced by its legal machinery even more uncanny. The necessity of the laws of the *Schloss* are not underwritten by the power to take life, by any monopoly of violence but by the acknowledged absence of law. While it may appear legal-rational, the *Schloss* is fundamentally anarchic and its open secret is that accident is the rule, or as the inn keeper explains to K, 'chances are always on the side of the masters' (*C* 474, 45). This is explained in K.'s dialogue with the village Superintendent or local representative of the Castle who claims K.'s appointment was an accident, the 'merest detail' (*C* 498, 76), but that such accidents are the rule of this institution. Appearances to the contrary, the Castle is not an imperial or Leninist structure in which hierarchical bureaucratic organization provides a transmission belt for the orders of a transcendent legislator, but one in which channels of communication are intermittent and inconsistent, blocked and distorted in ways that maximize the possibility of accidents and makes their incidence curiously necessary. This is the mystery of K.'s appointment that he finds so difficult to grasp; he has been appointed by accident, but this accident has somehow become absolutely necessary. The Superintendent explains, 'It is a working principle of the Authorities that the general possibility of error cannot be reckoned with. This principle is justified by the consummate organisation of the whole, and it is necessary if the maximum speed of settling business is to be attained' (*C* 503, 82). It is less that errors do not happen than that they immediately become necessary and true. The Castle's 'consummate organisation' maximizes the possibility of error, deviation and delay while at the same time lending them the character of necessity. K. has difficulty grasping this, since he mistakenly approaches the Castle as a legal-rational institution that sometimes made mistakes in applying the rules, and so the Superintendent patiently spells it out again for the 'outsider'. It is not the function of the 'control authorities' in the Castle 'to hunt out errors in the vulgar sense, for errors don't happen, and even when uniquely an error does happen, as in your case, who can definitively say that it is an error' (*C* 503, 82). Errors are to be understood mystically as necessary accidents whose reason is not apparent either to those below in the village, or even to the 'authorities' above in the Castle, but that nevertheless possess their own necessity.

Indeed, the Superintendent goes on to explain that the Castle's decisions are never made by reasoning according to principles, but always happen by accident, a property he describes as a 'peculiar characteristic of our administrative apparatus [*Apparates*]' (*C* 506, 86). In the entropic disorder that is Castle procedure – exemplified by the Superintendent's own hopeless archive – decisions emerge obscurely and leave few traces. While his wife and K.'s assistants ransack his *arcana* of castle documents in search of a key document, the Superintendent calmly explains the accidental origins of the law: 'When a case has been deliberated for a very long time, it may happen that it is settled without deliberations being completed, suddenly, in a flash, in an unpredictable and untraceable place but also in most cases correctly if arbitrarily' (*C* 506, 86). The decision is not reached rationally but flashes out of the saturated facts with all the unpredictability of lightning; but once it has happened it is 'in most cases' arbitrarily correct. It is 'correct' not because it approximates to the truth of the case, but because it is a decision that institutes necessity and makes what has happened 'true'.

It comes as no surprise to learn that such decisions are rarely made by officials – who as personified stasis, messenger butterflies who regressed to the chrysalis, are constitutionally incapable of delivering definitive actions – but are indeed accidents, generated by systemic pressures within the Castle. The enclosed character of the apparatus combined with the constant circulation of files creates a pressure that causes the apparatus first to overheat and then discharge like a meteorological phenomenon; the result is a lightning flash decision followed by sudden decompression and deferred rumbles of thunder as the remote consequences of the event unfold. The Castle, the Superintendent explains, behaves more like a weather system than a legal-rational institution: 'It's as if the administrative apparatus were unable any longer to bear the tension, the year-long irritation provoked by the same probably trivial case and had reached the decision by itself, without the assistance of the officials' (*C* 507, 86). The ostensibly legal-rational procedure followed by the Castle acts as a pressure cooker, escalating until returning to normal levels of operation by means of a violent discharge. The entire process, in other words, depends on the accident of a forced opening in the *Schloss*, the release of pressure at a weak point that serves as a safety valve for the apparatus as a whole. And yet such accident/decisions assume necessity in retrospect; they claim legal necessity as judgements made according to an arcane law. The force of law breaking through weak points in the closure of the *Schloss* is quickly demystified by the Superintendent: 'Of course no miracle took place and for sure some official or other hit upon a written or unwritten solution, but exactly which official decided and according to what grounds couldn't be established, at least by us, from here, or even by the office itself' (*C* 507, 86). This points to another peculiar character of such decisions, namely that they are not communicated and become *de facto* if not *de jure* secrets: 'The only annoying thing about them – it's usually the case with such things – is that one hears about it too late and continues to go on passionately about something that was decided ages ago' (*C* 507, 87). There is no messenger to bring news of these decisions issuing not from the glare of the imperial sun but from the obscurity of the apparatus, and they remain uncommunicated while reverberating like thunder following a flash of lightning. They become laws that assume necessity and universality but at the same time remain completely inscrutable arcana beyond appeal.

K. himself is a distant clap of thunder following a precipitate decision of this order. Yet he reasonably continues to regard the Castle as if it were the kind of institution that decided cases according to recognized laws. This leads him to the same 'melancholy conclusion' drawn by Josef K. after the exegesis of 'Before the Law' in the Cathedral: not only is truth subordinate to the necessity of the law, but there is also an extra-legal necessity shadowing the necessity of the law itself. K. must come to terms with the predicament that not only legal necessity but also its universality is accidental, that 'lying' and not the truth is its 'universal principle'.

Yet fatally, like his namesake, K. is unable to relinquish fond Platonic nostalgia for a transcendent law communicated and applied to individual cases. He responds to the Superintendent's exposition of Castle procedures with an indignation that echoes Josef K.'s reaction to the *Gericht*, vainly protesting that 'a serious abuse of my person and probably of the law is being carried on' (*C* 508, 88), forgetting his earlier and more appropriate amused and empowering insight into 'the ludicrous bungling which in certain circumstances can decide the life of a human being' (*C* 502, 80). But the Superintendent warns him that both responses are superficial. K. must understand that accidents such as his very existence are not unfortunate deviations from the law, but the law itself. His is the Nietzschean lesson that life is an accident, that there is no longer any transcendentally secured law, justice or truth that might govern and make sense of it but only chance events that 'always favour the masters'.

But not always – there are also some accidental deviations even from this rule. Kafka makes this clear in the episode with the official Bürgel that Brod added to the second edition of *The Castle*. K., after separating from Frieda, is called by the official Erlangen to his room in the Herrenhof – ironically to request his separation from Frieda in order to minimize any ambient disturbance for Klamm. K. blunders by accident into the wrong room where he wakes up an official, Bürgel, who relates the extraordinary coincidence that sometimes ensures that a petitioner happens by accident upon the room of an official who, unknown to him, has taken an interest in his case. Such as official is disarmed and reveals and promises to do much for the petitioner; yet it is an impossibly rare and extraordinary accident. Indeed, Bürgel is relating precisely the event that has befallen K. by stumbling into his room – the utterly improbable accident – but unfortunately K. falls asleep and does not gain any advantage from this gift of chance.

To be an official does not entail applying a rule, issuing an order or even making a decision, but in finding a way to make what happens appear necessary. This cannot be done by reference to a transcendent law, but only by tirelessly researching the sequence of random events and inventing plausible stories to lend them necessity. These stories should not be understood as *aggadah*, stories commenting on the law, as Benjamin believed in his classic essay on Kafka that uses the distinction between *halachic* and *aggadic* legal commentary, for they are stories provoked by the *absence* of law. These stories of dominion are intended to lend necessity to *a* chain of events and make it appear as *the* chain of events that expresses the unfolding of a law. *The Castle* itself is such a story, with the difference that in this unique case the accident – K. – not only insists on having his own say but also in seeing the comedy in the stories of the accidental birth of necessity.

5 LIGHTS

Philosophical light

The lighting of philosophical scenarios has always played an important if unobtrusive role in narratives of truth and certainty from Plato's cave through Descartes' inner light to Nietzsche's bright noons and dark midnights. These scenes of illumination share a fixed and central source of light, for philosophy was always Copernican in its metaphorical and literal helio-centrism. The subjects and objects of philosophy were always ultimately oriented with respect to a single light source, even when they were troubled by memories of the 'starry heavens above' and the possibility of as many lights of truth as there are stars or in Nietzsche's case, dancing stars. With Kafka, the centrality of the light source is fundamentally questioned not only by his attention to how the *mis-en-scene* of his narratives are lit, but also by the dispersal of the sources of light and their qualities. The lighting of his scenes ranges from twilight to candles, from moonlight to electric light, all accompanied by close attention to the different qualities of illumination, its hue, colour, brightness as well the ways in which illuminated subjects and objects respond to lights. This sensitivity opens different possibilities of visibility, obscurity, illumination and enlightened domination and defiance. Kafka abandons the philosophical pursuit of a reliable and neutral light source – as in the solar model – along with the deceptively objective lighting of its objects and the predictable gazes and views it makes possible. His work departs from the possibility that light is accidental, intermittent and unpredictable – with incalculable consequences for the objects that flicker in and out of vision and the blinking glances that cannot fix on them. His writings explore the consequences of Nietzsche's question of what can be seen and what kinds of subject can see in the light of a dancing star?

A remarkable diary entry from 4 October 1911 could almost have been written against the prevailing philosophical discourse of light and enlightenment inaugurated by Plato in *The Republic* and still alive in the inner light of Descartes' *Discourse on the Method* and after. In it Kafka muses on the implications for perception of the surrender of a single light source – the projecting light in Plato's cave or Descartes 'inner light'. The entry shows the extent to which Kafka remained Nietzschean in refusing to follow the death of God with the birth of a substitute subject: he will have no Copernican turn or replacement suns. For him the heliocentric scenario is inseparable from monotheism, monarchy and hierarchy and entails a single source of light, divinity or political power diffusing itself across the world. Instead, his is a profound reflection on the death of God and the absence of a ruling centre announced by Nietzsche in T*he Gay Science*. This absence is played through in terms of artificial light or the appeal to many different light sources each creating their own transient world of objects. It is an autumn evening, and the sun has already set . . .

Evoking Descartes' oneiric chamber beside the fire in the *Discourse on the Method*, Kafka lies half-awake reclining on his sofa watching coloured light play across his room. Supine and daydreaming, he in no way qualifies as the conscious, centred upright Cartesian subject ready to step forward and take the place of the deposed God or sun. His first reflection breaks with any notion of an orderly and reliable process of perception – it questions the intermittency of perception or 'why does one need more time to know a colour, but once after the decisive turn of the understanding one is suddenly ever more convinced of the colour' (*D* 63, 42). It is not only discrete chromatic perceptions that lack a fixed quality but the medium of perception itself that here is shifting and uncertain. This is not the neutral white light that apparently allows the faithful representation of the objects perceived in it, but a shifting coloured light that bathes its objects in different chromatic hues. In his horizontal, relaxed and nigh suspended state, Kafka solicits an *epoché* in which the medium of perception becomes his object of perception. He focuses attention on the light that allows him to see rather than the objects it illuminates. In his room, unlike in the Platonic cave, it is not shadows lit by a single, invisible light source that flit across the walls but mobile, coloured lights. In this kaleidoscopic scenario, Kafka watches and describes the random mixtures of colour that light his walls, floor and ceiling and that on this singular autumn evening – this one night only – constitute his medium of perception.

Kafka attempts in vain to fix the shifting colours that make his perception possible by describing their qualities and their sources. He begins by trying to fix the impression (*Eindruck*) of greenish light coming through the engraved matt glass of his bedroom door into a conviction that it is green light. This green glare is but the effect of the hall and kitchen lights meeting simultaneously on the glass door of his room, and pouring itself down the glass (*so giesst sich*), appearing first as 'greenish' and then only after reflection as green light. As opposed to the simplicity of the Platonic scenario, the immediate source of light here is an illuminated surface – the glass door – with more remote light sources in the hall and the kitchen lamps.[1] But no sooner is the source of the medium of light located than it changes, for here the medium of perception is as inconstant as perception itself, open to unpredictable change and mutation. The steady white light required for clear and distinct perception is no longer available.

Still manning the couch, Kafka watches the light-stained door change colour as someone switches off the hall light. The stained green surface turns to blue, a blue comprised of different hues depending on proximity to the light source: the surface of the glass door nearest the kitchen is lit with a dark blue light that changes to light blue as it approaches white. This near-white light has the property of dissolving the outlines of the vegetal and geometric figures that we now learn are engraved on the glass of the door – 'Stylised poppies, tendrils, various triangles and leaves' (*D* 63 43) – and vein the light with their shadowy outlines. His observations have discovered that light is not only differentiated according to colour, but also according to hue, understood not only in terms of degrees of whiteness but also the presence of shadow; moreover, a shadow not uniformly distributed but veined. But once again, before this impression can solidify into a conviction and the medium of perception settle into a relative if flawed stability, Kafka's gaze is distracted by other sources of light flooding his room – the lights and shadows cast through his window by the electric lights of the street and those on the bridge opposite. The light and shadows are confused, the medium of perception itself 'in part corrupted, overlapping, and hard to examine' (*D* 63, 43). In this case the impression does not solidify into a conviction and perception is left as uncertain as its shifting medium.

Kafka explains this unstable medium of perception in terms of the accidental conjuncture of different lights: 'For in the installation of the electric street lamps below and the furnishing of this room no domestic consideration was taken as to how this room would look at this moment from this sofa without its own light on' (*D* 63, 43). There is an effect, but without any design: the event of tonight's light show was random, accidental. There is no governing intelligence overseeing the world viewed from Kafka's bedroom, no pre-established harmony between the placing of the sources of light and the objects they illuminate. But what kind of attention would be required to foresee all the circumstances of this moment in time (early evening, 4 October 1911) and place (a sofa, in a room, in an apartment on a street by the river in Prague)? And yet all these accidental circumstances are somehow *necessary* and not only as circumstance but also as the medium in which they are perceived.

As if to emphasize this, Kafka allows the constant light of the street lamps to be disturbed by the flickering glare of the lights of a passing tram that shudder across the wall and ceiling, leaving the impression of a 'whitish, wraithlike mechanical juddering' (*D* 63, 43) light that is broken as it passes over the corner of the room. This juddering light is, nevertheless, part of the medium of perception through which Kafka perceives and in which the objects in his room are perceived. There is no necessity to this transit, no necessity to the light that makes perception and objects of perception possible. The conditions of possibility of experience are here neither universal nor necessary but singular and accidental – they yield no deduction, but only shifting patterns that cannot secure perception but do invite daydreams and fictions.

That all this has been a philosophical parable in the tradition of Plato's cave and Descartes' chamber is emphasized by Kafka's sole description of the effect of this shifting medium of perception on the perception of an object. This object is a globe, and with this, suddenly, Kafka's room becomes a cosmos which contains the earth floating in space and bathed in light. Except that this world is not basking in the divine light of sun, but sits on the greenly lit laundry basket in the 'first fresh and complete reflection of the streetlights' with a glare on its roundness (the polar regions) and a sense that the light is too strong for it. The glare has the paradoxical effect of muddying the colours of the globe – the blue of the sea and colours of human political divisions are left 'rather brownish like a autumn apple' (*D* 64, 43). The vision of cosmic accident afflicting the world and reducing the colours of its lands and seas to a uniform matt brown is a devastating reduction of the colours of the world. In this parable, Kafka reclines outside the world contemplating first the inconstant and impure light in which it is bathed and then contemplating the world in miniature in the form of a globe – a contemplation that of course includes his contemplation – and then reducing it and all its colours to that of a withered apple. The world after the death of God viewed by the madman, but this time not declaiming in the town square but lying on his sofa somewhere in the remote cosmos of his bedroom. But then the revery is disrupted by a sudden illumination – someone has switched on the hall light – but the effect only compounds the deadly reduction of the bright world to a russet *lederapfel*. The burst of light – reminiscent of those at the beginning of *America* and the end of *The Trial* – transforms Kafka's bed into a catafalque: it lights the wall behind the bed 'apparently pressing the bed down', widening 'the dark bedposts' (*D* 64, 43) and raising the ceiling over the bed. The bed is thus left in a mortuary state corresponding to the overripe apple of the globe, pressed by the light into the earth under a remote and distant ceiling. The accident is transformed into a mortified necessity.

Drawing back from this scenario, it is possible to see in it an exploration of a predicament in which there is no longer a fixed source of light. It asks what happens to perception when the light is shifting and answers that it illuminates objects in different ways, making them into different objects. It is light that governs perception, not a subject opposed to an object but a shifting and unpredictable medium. The colour of experience is neither fixed nor constant but mobile, changeable at once joyful and mournful; it can appear as a chromatic field, as the juddering repetitions of cinematic light or the russet tones of mellow fruitfulness. In the view from Kafka's couch the world is lit by many lights that may drain it of its vitality, leaving it brown and wrinkled, or revivify it by making all fixity but a moment of arrested kaleidoscopic movement.

Accidental light

The miniature analogue of the cosmic accident contemplated from the couch recurs full-scale in the fragments attending and succeeding the emergence of the *Country Doctor* stories. As we shall see, the eponymous country doctor has to deal with a wound from such an accident, but we should remember that the death of God is as much a cosmic as it is a social or psychological catastrophe. Kafka entertains the conjecture, hinted at in Nietzsche, that God's death was somehow accidental, unintended, and that we are so bedazzled by it as not yet fully able to realize what we have done.[2]

Some idea of Kafka's view of the scale of this catastrophe may be gained from the enigmatic but violent fragment 'With a hard blow':

> With a hard blow the light streamed down, tearing the fabric flying in all directions, mercilessly burning through the remains of the empty, wide-meshed net. Down below, like an animal caught by surprise, the earth twitched and stood still. Mutually spellbound, they gazed at each other. And the third, shunning this encounter, dodged to one side.
>
> (*WP* 276; *NII* 548)

The fragment makes light into a destructive antagonist, that burns through a fabric that reveals a hunter's net under which the earth quivers like a trapped animal. Light and the earth confront one another and a 'third' slips away avoiding the entire scenario. Light is the subject of this equivocal action: but it is the incandescent light *liberating* a captured animal/earth by burning through the fabric and consuming the net that had descended on it or is light the hunter confronting its trapped prey ready for the kill? Light and the earth gaze at each other in a moment of suspended mutual fascination that could equally precede emancipation or annihilation; the moment of suspension in which light contemplates the earth lasts enough for 'a third' to evade this encounter. Is the 'third' the evil hunter disturbed at his work by the eruption of light burning his net or is it God temporarily escaping his own death scene?

The fragment is immediately followed by an apparently very different one to which it is linked through the theme of the accident: 'Once I broke my leg, it was the most beautiful experience of my life' (*WP* 276; *NII* 548). The association between a fatal or emancipatory light and the accident is spelt out in a further fragment from the Third Octavo Notebook, written in Zürau in autumn 1917, which also operates at a cosmic scale but with the absolute, incandescent light of 'With a hard blow' replaced by a barely discernible glimmer: 'Seen with the terrestrial sullied eye, we are in the situation of travellers in a train that has met with an accident in a tunnel, and this at a place where the light at the beginning can no longer be seen, and the light at the end is such a tiny glimmer that the gaze must continually search for it and is always losing it again, and furthermore, both the beginning and the end are not even certainties' (*WP* 73; *NII* 33). Here the confrontation of absolute light and terrestrial existence is succeeded by a transcendental accident. The only certainty in this scenario is the accident, and from its standpoint neither the beginning of the chain of causes that led to it nor the consequences that might follow can be assured; there is but a dim light in the future that may help orient an escape. The mangled railway carriage in the tunnel metamorphoses into a Platonic cave where the light is extinguished and perception governed by the mood and extent of the injury of accident victims scattered around it. In place of the fascinated dreamers in the Platonic theatre, Kafka proposes the victims of a railway accident: 'Round about us, however, in the confusion of our senses, or in the super-sensitiveness of our senses, we have nothing but monstrosities and a kaleidoscopic play of things that is either delightful or exhausting according to the mood or injury of each individual' (*WP* 73; *NII* 33). Plato's citizens living in the shadows projected by the light of transcendence are replaced by accident victims; the moderately benign illusions of the former by the extreme hallucinations of the latter for whom white light is a distant and intangible flicker. This is no place for philosophizing, with Kafka adding in the following fragment, 'What shall I do? Or: Why should I do it are not questions to be asked in such places'

(*WP* 73; *NII* 33). Kant's what do I know, what should I do, and what can I hope for are not appropriate questions for such hopeless victims, but must they be left in the dark, dying bereft of philosophy?

Kafka's perversion of Plato's cave into a railway tunnel accident is followed by three fragments that he later excerpted as the 4th, 5th and 6th Zürau fragments. The first of these finds the dead licking the waves of the river of death that because it flows down from us 'still has the salty taste of our seas' (*WP* 38; *NII* 114). Where there is no light and nothing more to see or hear, there remains taste; and this is enough for salvation, since the river recoils from the dead and carries them back 'into life'. The resurrected 'are happy, and sing songs of thanksgiving' (*WP* 38; *NII* 114), but their joy is short-lived, for the 5th Zürau aphorism declares, 'From a certain point on there is no more return. This point has to be reached' (*WP* 38; *NII* 114). The railway accident seems to have reached this point – there is no chain of causal connections that can be traced back, for although a consequence of what went before, the accident also broke the sequence that preceded it. Once it happened it necessarily happened, but this not a necessity rooted in a discernible chain of preceding causes. The accident, the 6th fragment continues, is everlasting; it does not relate in any straightforward way to the past, but will decisively change what is to come in the future: 'The decisive moment in the development of mankind is perpetual. That is why the revolutionary spiritual movements that consider everything that came before to be negligible are right, because nothing has happened yet' (*WP* 38–9; *NII* 114). The future that follows an accident – such as the inadvertent putting to death of God – is radically other than that prepared by the past that preceded the accident and was interrupted by it. In this scenario, the accident becomes the absolute or fixed point of orientation according to which past, present and future may be measured. Returning to the Octavo Notebook, if 'The history of mankind is the instant between two strides taken by a traveller' (*WP* 73), then the future history of the superman will be that which follows the traveller falling and breaking a leg.

Kafka makes another approach to the absolute accident through the wound that it leaves, a wound that constitutes a direct link between the earlier, incandescent blow of light and the story of the country doctor. Once again the accident is described in extremely violent terms: 'He has leant his head to one side, and where his neck is exposed, there is a wound, boiling in burning blood and flesh struck by a flash of lightning that still continues' (*WP* 337; *NII* 347). Here the absolute character of the accident is described in terms of the flash of lightning but one which is not instantaneous, but perpetual. It is as if time has stopped with this flash and the burn wound kept perpetually open, awaiting the attention of a healer. The character of the light of the accident is hard to determine – it is incandescent, burning away what preceded it and providing a delirious kaleidoscopic light in which to glimpse what is to come. Yet there is also the glimmer of a different light at the end of the tunnel, or something in the burning light that is emancipatory. It is this ambivalent light of the accident that Kafka will pursue in his reflections on the light of evil.

Evil light

Kafka was presciently aware that the way beyond good and evil to love and the *Übermensch* passionately advocated by Nietzsche was difficult and littered with insurmountable obstacles. And yet a way had to be found, for God was dead and the path of good and evil invented by his officials/priests had passed its course, even if its spectral law continued to weigh on the living and even to intensify its dying force. It would not be easy to ignore or forget the commands of the dead Emperor; in the twilight of the officials they might come to weigh even heavier and serve as a maddening and insuperable distraction. They might divert the step beyond good and evil – the way out of the shadow world to the light – towards the intensification of evil. Kafka almost uniquely for his time faced the possibility of a world of pure evil, of domination by priestly/official *ressentiment* unalleviated by any surviving trace of nobility or the divine. It is as if the death of God far from liberating his murderers brought with it the death of the Good. One way beyond good and evil could plausibly lead to the domination of the officials with their spectral laws ruling by a necessity untouched by any hint or hope for the good and the true.

Kafka's reflections on evil and the way that comprise his 109 Zürau aphorisms meditate on such a possibility, and trace the dominion of evil to the uncanny survival of law and its necessity after the death of its legislator. This law is figured as the eternal which persists even after the eclipse of eternal objects. Kafka carefully selected and extracted the aphorisms from the same notebooks of his convalescence with his sister in the village of Zürau in 1917 that formed the matrix of the *Country Doctor* stories; they exist as a prepared typescript from 1918–20 and thus as close as possible to an authorized text. Yet in them the search for a way from the tree of the knowledge of good and evil to the tree of life is continually stalled by the survival of an absolute without content, the inscrutable necessity of law. The force of gravity exerted by such a law is sufficient to restrain all but the most subtle escapes, whether through esoteric fictions or the short bursts of energy emitted by the aphorisms that remaining true to their Hippocratic origin were at once diagnostic, prognostic and therapeutic.[3]

The eternal emerges in the aphorisms as a pharmakon able equally to poison and confine as to enhance and liberate life.

The Zürau aphorisms also register the impact of Kafka's study of Kierkegaard, not only in terms of vocabulary but also for their turn towards theological concerns and expressions. During his stay in the village and shortly thereafter Kafka studied carefully Kierkegaard's *Fear and Trembling*, but its effect on his thinking has to be gauged carefully.[4] It would not be correct to see in it any renunciation of his earlier philosophical passions for phenomenology[5] or for Nietzsche in favour of a Kierkegaardian step out of the aesthetic to the ethical or religious stages. Indeed, his reading of Kierkegaard was refracted by Nietzschean concerns such as the impact on Kierkegaard's reflections on sin and faith of the claim that God is dead. How, for example, would we understand Abraham and the command to sacrifice his son Isaac central to *Fear and Trembling* if we assumed there was no longer any God to command in this way – and yet the command is still heard and holds? Was Abraham simply mad, or does such intent tell us something about the dislocation of reason and madness following the death of God? Is it possible to continue to think and act in terms of sin after the departure of God, and what would it mean to have faith when there is no longer even remotely a God to provide its object? How is it possible to live beyond the laws and maxims of good and evil issued by the departed Commandant, or put even more simply – how is it possible to move from the rotting fruits of the tree of the knowledge of good and evil to those of the tree of life? While well aware of the significance of Kierkegaard's Christological way to renewed faith, it was not one that Kafka was prepared to follow or even embark upon.

The climate of the Zürau aphorisms is exemplified by the limpid meditation on the eternal found in the notebooks between aphorisms 98 and 99. Aphorism 98 sceptically views 'the representation of the infinite expanse and copiousness of the cosmos' as 'the outcome of a mixture pushed to its limit of laborious creation and free self-determination' (*WP* 50; *NII* 135). Any temptation to read this as a Gnostic proposition favourably contrasting eternal freedom with temporal labour is dispelled by aphorism 99 which correlates oppression with 'even the weakest conviction of the coming eternal justification of our temporality' (*WP* 50; *NII* 135). Pursuing the way of eternal justification can poison our lives; seeking to justify ourselves by absolute laws might occasionally elevate, but they usually cast down. The danger is especially clear after the death of God and the crisis of faith that for Kafka was the cause and consequence of this event. Earlier, in aphorism 50, Kafka claimed that 'Man cannot live without a permanent trust in something indestructible in itself, though both the indestructible element and the trust may remain permanently concealed from him'

(*WP* 43; *NII* 124). The enhancement of life through the presence of the eternal or the indestructible is here brought to light through 'faith in a personal god' (*WP* 43; *NII* 124) – but when this faith is lost, the required trust – supported by faith in the divine – falters.

Kafka's aphorisms explore this predicament of securing 'trust' in the absence of the 'indestructible' or eternal, and pointedly even in the face of its enmity. The inner dialogue that Kafka struck out in his notebook manuscript between aphorisms 98 and 99 (see Kafka 2011, 24–31) is notable, even if disowned by its author, for seeking a way to secure such trust once faith in the eternal has passed leaving only its still effective, but malign shells. It begins forensically with a questioning voice: 'I should welcome eternity, and when I do find it I am sad. I should feel myself perfect by virtue of eternity – and feel myself depressed' (*WP* 105; *NII* 86).[6] A second voice enters, troubled by the *obligation* or necessity to welcome a feeling of being uplifted by eternity. Since when has eternity been the friend of we who live in time? 'You say: I should – feel. In saying this do you express a commandment that is within yourself' (*WP* 105; *NII* 86). Is there a law enjoining us to welcome rather than fear or abhor eternity, and if so how is it justified and what is its modality: is it permanent and necessary or occasional and accidental? Lacking a law by which to decide, the first voice is unsure but replies believing 'it is a continual commandment, but I hear it only occasionally' (*WP* 105; *NII* 86). The command to welcome the eternal does not sound directly, for 'it is not audible in itself, it muffles or embitters the voice holding me to do the other thing; that is to say, the voice that makes me ill at ease with eternity' (*WP* 105, NII 86). The voice that motivates action in time is embittered and undone by the voice of the eternal; the eternal command, however, is not so much muffled by the claims of the temporal as made to appear as a dream: 'it is as though I was just letting the dream go on talking at random' (*WP* 106, NII 86). The eternal can blight the temporal, while seeming to have no necessity, just an accidental delirium.

The idea that law or eternal command is a singular mad voice raving in the margins of life, one without universality or necessity, scandalizes the second voice: 'Does it seem senseless as a dream, incoherent, inevitable, unique, making you happy or frightening you equally without cause, not wholly communicable but demanding to be communicated?' (*WP* 106; *NII* 87). The first voice confirms all these properties. It is senseless since it is a law that can only be respected by defiance: 'for only if I do not obey it can I maintain myself here' (*WP* 106; *NII* 87); it is incoherent because 'I don't know whose command it is and what he is aiming at' (*WP* 106; *NII* 87) since there is no longer a faith in God.[7] And it is inevitable because it descends surprisingly but also as predictably as a dream descends on a sleeper, and it is singular or without relation – 'I cannot obey it' – since this would bring it into relation with time which is impossible since 'it does not mingle with reality' and must keep its 'immaculate uniqueness' (*WP* 106; *NII* 87). It is an obstacle in the way, an accidental pharmakon that 'makes me happy or frightens me, both without cause' (*WP* 106; *NII* 86). Finally, unlike a Platonic idea the eternal law cannot be communicated because it is not intelligible and yet 'for the same reason it demands to be communicated' (*WP* 106; *NII* 86). It is a remnant of the law, a mad memory of God that can lift up our lives but more frequently casts it down. The following entry in the notebook – 'Christ, moment' (*WP* 106, *NII* 87) – marks the literal parting of ways between Kafka and Kierkegaard's Christological solution of the tension between the eternal and time. The way of incarnation and the singular manifestation of the eternal in history bringing salvation would not be pursued by Kafka; he began to explore other ways beyond the opposition of time and eternity.

The eternal command begins to assume the physiognomy of evil, raising the possibility that the way beyond good and evil can lead to extinction of the good and the uncontested reign of evil. This possibility is explored from a number of perspectives in the aphorisms. What is the way beyond good and evil that takes us to the reign of pure evil – the mad law – and what are the alternatives to it? The first aphorism takes us back to the tightrope walker or model of the dedicated artist encountered in the early pages of *Also Sprach Zarathrustra*. The place of art and the artist after the death of God is a recurrent figure in the notebooks[8] and explored in Kafka's last collection of stories, *The Hunger Artist*.[9] Nietzsche's Zarathustra honours the artist who died pursuing his art on the tightrope in the face of the hostility and disdain of the audience by burying his body broken after his fall. Kafka's version of the tightrope begins like Nietzsche's, with the rope offering the way for the tightrope walker, but stretched just above the ground: 'The true way is along a rope that is not spanned high in the air, but only just above the ground' (38). It then radically diverges from Nietzsche in that 'It seems intended more to cause stumbling than to be walked along' (*WP* 38; *NII* 113). The gesture of stumbling returns to Kierkegaard and the notion of the scandal – Christ as a scandal or stumbling block – except that here it is the means of art that is scandalous or cause for stumbling. The way in the first aphorism is thus a trap, a hunter's tripwire designed to cause an accident to down its prey; and while Zarathustra's acrobat was accidented by the dwarf, Kafka's low wire is designed to trip whoever stumbles upon it.[10]

The way beyond good and evil as a tripwire intended to cause an accident is considered explicitly in aphorism 55, which begins with the proposition, 'Everything is deception: seeking the minimum of illusion, keeping within the ordinary limitations, seeking the maximum' (*WP* 44; *NII* 125). Kafka analyses the pitfalls of each strategic option in the struggle to get beyond good and evil. In pursuing the way of minimizing illusion, of disavowing anything in appearance that is not the truth, 'One cheats the Good by making it too easy for oneself to get it, and the Evil by imposing all too unfavourable conditions of warfare upon it' (WP 44; NII 125). It runs the danger of the good it attains and the evil it overcomes becoming themselves illusions, too easily gained and thus too easily vanquished. The second path remains on this side of good and evil, not even attempting to go beyond, and ensures 'one cheats the Good by not striving for it even in earthly terms' (WP 44; NII 125), while the third way heads towards the reign of pure evil bereft of the good: 'one cheats the good by staying as aloof from it as possible, and evil by hoping to make it powerless through intensifying it to the utmost' (WP 44; NII 125). This strategy wagers on evil being powerless without the opposition of the good. Of these three ways, Kafka will prefer the second, since it at least does not cheat evil – which retains its power by virtue of its perennial antagonism with the good.

The way is replete with ironies: it returns always to itself and is always already beyond itself; it appears as a way, but is already past its goal. To trip over it is to fall and be suddenly shocked into awareness of all this. The way is a device for provoking accidents, a trip wire or a trap. The way also can be understood abstractly as a figure of the eternal return, serving as point of departure and arrival for the infinite: 'The way is infinitely long, nothing can be subtracted from it, nothing can be added, and yet everyone applies his own childish yardstick to it' (WP 42; NII 122). By making it stretch infinitely and trying to measure or pursue it, the way trips the traveller as they try to cross over it. The goal of the infinite way is its point of departure; by setting off instead of staying at home, the traveller is already stumbling. Another way of expressing this is the realization that it is not necessary to be afflicted by the eternal in this way, as proposed in aphorism 24: 'Grasping the good fortune that the ground on which you are standing cannot be larger than the two feet covering it' (WP 40; NII 118). Standing ground or resistance is to realize that the way is not to be traversed but we are already at its goal; to set off is to stumble and become perplexed about how to move on or go back: 'There is a goal but no way; what we call a way is hesitation' (WP 40; NII 118). The afflicted faith is undone by the eternal, always convincing us that where we are is but a point of departure, never arrival: it negates what is already given, and will never allow us to succeed; or, in the words of aphorism 27, 'Doing the negative thing is imposed on us, an addition; the positive thing is given to us from the start' (WP 41; NII 119). The negative thing – acting under law – is imposed on us while affirming life without law is a point of stasis in both senses of the term, as standstill but also rebellion. In this view we are always already beyond good and evil, but fall back from this position whenever we appeal to law to help us in our perplexity before the infinite. It comes to the point that striving for the infinite becomes the pre- or anti-law that shadows the law itself and that consequently, in the following aphorism 28, 'When one has accepted and absorbed evil, it no longer demands to be believed' (*WP* 41; *NII* 119). Or put in Kierkegaardian and theatrical terms, 'It is as if the back and forth between general and particular were taking place on the real stage, and as if on the other hand life in general were only sketched in on the background scenery' (*NII* 103–4). The history of law and the conflicts of law are on the main stage, while life itself just a detail in the scenery. Art shines its beam on that detail, or as we saw earlier when visiting the theatre with Kafka, life breaks out into the street, leaving the theatre of good and evil to play on behind it for the dead who still want to watch.

The central aphorisms of the Zürau collection replay these themes through an extended meditation on the biblical story of the Fall told in the book of Genesis that consistently contrasts the tree of the knowledge of good and evil with the tree of life. The short series of aphorisms, 82–6, begin by asking, 'Why do we lament about the Fall? It is not why we were expelled from Paradise, but rather because we had not yet eaten of the tree of life. We find ourselves in sin independently of guilt' (*WP* 47; *NII* 131). The Fall is a sin of commission, expulsion from Paradise a consequence of the sin of omission in, after gaining the knowledge of good and evil and submitting ourselves to its law, not going beyond it and partaking of the tree of life. The failure to eat of the tree of life was the main transgression, since 'We were created to live in Paradise and Paradise was meant to serve us. Our vocation has been changed, whether Paradise's vocation has also changed has not been said' (*WP* 47; *NII* 131). An accident took place in Paradise transgressing the law that ordained us to live. It is one that aphorism 85 tells us led to the invention of the light of evil which is but 'a radiation of human consciousness in certain transitional positions. In reality it is not the sensual world that is mere appearance, but its evil that in any case for our eyes constitutes the sensual world' (*WP* 48; *NII* 132). The light of evil attends the way of the law of good and evil, but it is ironic, as is spelt out in the tremendous aphorism 86.

Before approaching the disquisition on the light of evil in aphorism 86, it is necessary to linger with Kafka over two further ironies attending the Fall. The first is that we never left Paradise; we are still there suspended at the point of hesitating before eating of the tree of life, for 'If what is supposed to have been destroyed in Paradise was destructible, then it was not decisive; but if it was indestructible then we are living in a false belief' (aphorism 74, *WP* 46; *NII* 129). If Paradise could be so easily destroyed, then it was not 'essential', but if it was indestructible then of course it has not been destroyed and we are still there and the whole history of good and evil has been but a sideshow. How though is it possible for us to hold to such a catastrophic and tenacious false belief? Kafka in complete consistency finds the answer in the eternal. Aphorism 64/5 already spelt this out: 'Expulsion from Paradise is in its main aspect eternal, that is to say although expulsion from Paradise is final, and life in the world unavoidable, the eternity of the process nevertheless makes it possible not only that we might remain in Paradise permanently, but that we may in fact be there permanently, no matter whether we know it here or not' (WP 45; NII 127). Paradise it seems is surrounded by a tripwire over which we eternally stumble in our impatience for eternity; what we think of as an eternal state of exile is but an illusion; instead of standing on our two feet in Paradise, we are eternally arrested in the act of tripping over the wire apparently separating it from the world. It is from the standpoint of the accident, of falling but with still one foot in Paradise, that the world assumes the physiognomy of evil.

Aphorism 86 explores the implications of these views on the way into and beyond the world of good and evil. Kafka begins by claiming 'Since the Fall we have been essentially equal in our capacity to know Good and Evil' but that 'only beyond (Jenseits) this knowledge do the real differences begin' (WP 48; NII 132). To remain confined within the knowledge of good and evil and thus under the law is to fail the good because since law is infinite and we but finite and thus any striving for it must necessarily fail: 'He has not been given the strength for this, hence he must destroy himself, even at the risk of even then not gaining the necessary strength' (WP 48; NII 132). Kafka explains parenthetically that 'This is also the meaning of the threat of death associated with the ban on eating from the Tree of Knowledge; perhaps this is also the original meaning of natural death' (WP 48; NII 132). Given the risk of death associated with pursuit of the eternal, Kafka's protagonist 'prefers to undo the knowledge of Good and Evil (the term 'The Fall' has its origin in this fear)' (WP 48; NII 132). It is this hesitation that maintains the protagonist on this side of the knowledge of good and evil, that is, of knowledge *in terms* of good and evil rather than the Nietzschean knowledge *of* good and evil, of the truth of good and evil.[11] The inability to step beyond it, the 'wish to rest for a moment' and to accept good and evil, is to stumble past the tree of life. The way beyond good and evil leads past the tree of life, and seeks to prevent the accident of belief in the eternal. For on this side of the law, according to aphorism 96, 'The joys of this life are not *life's*, but *our* fear of ascending into a higher life' (WP 50; NII 135), while to go beyond it is to forget the eternal and to not let this life be judged good or evil in light of a supposed 'higher life' or law. This would be to make the lie a principle of world order, for as Kafka reflected in a note, 'There is only duality – truth and lies. Truth is indivisible, and thus cannot know itself. Whoever wants to know it must be a lie'

(*NII* 69). There are in addition, two truths represented by the trees of the knowledge of good and evil and life – one is a truth of the active, the other of the passive; the first 'separates good from evil' while the second is 'good itself', life that knows nothing of either good or evil. (*NII* 84). The first is given, the second only intimated, the first the truth of the moment, the second of eternity – but not the eternity of good and evil, for the light of this eternal good 'dissolves the first truth' of law and good and evil. Life means 'being in the midst of life' not contemplating it – the latter seeks to hold back 'with the wind' and Kafka notes, 'I do not want to do that' (*NII* 91).

In the end the difference between life and death consists simply in being able to breathe or to suffocate. There are, unfortunately, many ways of suffocating: 'There is no having, only a being, only a state of being that craves the last breath, craves suffocation' (aphorism 35, *WP* 41; *NII* 120). The breath of life beyond good and evil is described in the enigmatic aphorism 17: 'A place I have never been before: breath comes differently, a neighbouring star shining brighter than the sun' (*WP* 40; *NII* 117). The imperial sun of the law and good and evil is eclipsed by a more radiant star; even more radical than Nietzsche, Kafka imagines the great noontide or Zenith is eclipsed by the light of defiance, the dancing star given birth at the end of *Also Sprach Zarathustra*. In the final aphorism of the Zürau sequence we arrive in the light of stasis; no longer distracted by the eternal, the claim and the offer of the imperial sun, no longer dismayed and distracted at the portals of the law, no longer in fascinated captive orbit around the sun or the eternal but just at home: 'It is not necessary for you to leave the house. Stay at your table and listen. Don't even listen, just wait. Don't even wait, be completely quiet and alone. The world will offer itself to you to be unmasked, it can't do otherwise, in raptures it will writhe before you' (*WP* 53; *NII* 140). This is stasis not as arrest or standstill but as a resistance that refuses to participate. In Nietzsche's words, but never spoken by him, Kafka brings us the great noontide of the dancing star.

Healing light

Kafka's fictions recall the ancient *therapon*, or dream, in which Asclepius the God of healing visits the sick with oneiric advice and a healing light. 'Children on a Country Road' was the first of such healing dreams, but as a reader of Nietzsche's forthright critique of Wagner's oneiric soundscapes Kafka's attitude towards any view of art as a *therapon* had to be ambivalent. This was especially the case if the healing was a response to the death of God and its analogues in the passing of the Emperor and the twilight following the extinction of the sun. The ambivalence is not only a question of attitude, but is structural and involves the mutual dependence of light and darkness. Although Kafka can and does imagine devastating moments of pure light, most of his illuminations are nuanced, slanted and involve a matter of degree. They all involve a correlation between the mixture of light and dark experienced in degrees of bedazzlement and illusion through which the world manifests itself.

A reference to pure, destructive light is added as a parenthesis to the 54th aphorism: 'With the strongest light [*stärkstem Licht*] one can dissolve the world' (*WP* 44; *NII*). Yet the reference to *strongest* emphasizes that this is but the maximum intensity of a gradiated illumination. The aphorism continues with three lesser degrees of intensity or mixtures of light and darkness that dazzle the viewer and, Kafka fears, confirm the world. The three variants correspond to the three levels of illusion that would be described in aphorism 55 as the mixtures of good and evil that characterize illusion. In the first, the world solidifies into an object viewed under light – 'For weak eyes the world solidifies' – followed by the second stage in which it becomes an antagonist 'for eyes weaker still it grows fists' until finally 'before those even weaker it becomes shame-faced and smashes anyone who dares to intuit it' (*WP* 44; *NII* 125). The degrees of weak vision permit the recoil of the world, but they remain in contrast with the possibility of the world being wholly dissolved by light. As with the combinations of good and evil in aphorism 55, Kafka seems to settle on the second option as the most appropriate for art – a partially dazzled antagonistic relation to a world with raised fists.

Yet this antagonism comes with a price, since destructive light can also be self-destructive. An entry in the third notebook, just before the extracted aphorisms 87 and 88, imagines art as a cautious but fascinated moth flitting in the Platonic cave attracted by the incandescent light of truth: 'Art flies around truth, but with the definite intention of not getting burnt. Its capacity lies in finding in the dark void a place where the beam of light can be intensely caught, without this having been perceptible before' (*WP* 98; *NII* 77–8). It is searching for a light in the darkness, what Corngold in Gnostic tenor describes as a lambent trace. The view of art as a moth attempting to contain its self-destructive attraction to the light is consistent with the degrees of dazzlement described in aphorism 54 paralleling the degrees of illusion in aphorism 55, except that it is approaching the condition of maximum light in which partially disabled vision or dazzlement becomes blindness. The moth/artist does not seek a smooth mixture of light and dark, but a sudden illumination where before there was none. This can result in dazzlement but also in the partial retreat of the world as its shield of illusion is compromised. This state is succinctly described in the 63rd aphorism: 'Our art consists in being-dazzled by the truth. The light upon the grotesque mask as it shrinks back is true, and nothing else' (*WP* 45; *NII* 127). The light of truth suddenly illuminating the darkness disables vision, but it also causes the world to appear as it is and then retreat in shame.

The light that flashes up in the darkness appears in the nocturnes Kafka wrote after 1917 and is usually carried by a messianic figure cast as a healer, who brings therapeutic light from beyond the world. The parallel with Plato's parable of the cave and the return of the philosopher-saviour bearing the light along with its Gnostic elaborations is patent, except that darkness now has a different quality. The light of the sun has been extinguished and the healer must bring a new light, a predicament expressed in the fragment from the 8th Octavo Notebook: 'The lamp splintered into pieces, a strange man with a fresh light came into the room. I rose, my family with me, we greeted him, no notice was taken' (*WP* 156; *NII* 429). The oblivion of the light-bearer, too dazzled to see, complements that of the illuminated. In one of the short series of dark water fragments dating from 1916–17, Kafka describes the meditations of an off-duty jailor on his way home from a shift guarding prisoners: 'When I come along the water at night, from the direction of the tower, now, every night, the tough dark water is moved, almost like a body, under the light of the lantern. As if I were slowly passing the lantern over a sleeper and, simply from the effect of the light, he were to stretch and turn over without awakening' (*WP* 228; *NII* 17). In this case, the light-bearer/jailor has an effect on the dreamer who responds to the light but without waking or being consciously aware of the light.

At one point in *The Castle*, K. reveals that he too was a healer: 'Now he, K., had some medical knowledge and, more valuably, experience in treating the sick. In some cases he had succeeded where doctors had given up. He had been able to cure. At home they had always called him "The bitter herb" on account of his healing powers' (*C* 580, 178). Part of K.'s messianic vocation involved producing miraculous healing, but the effects of his work were ambivalent, described literally as a *pharmakon* or bitter herb. K. brings light from the memory of a place outside the *Dorf/Schloss* dyad but he is perpetually dazzled, by day by snow, by night by electric light, and his medical judgement is far from infallible. His healing brings catastrophe to many, above all the bedazzled Frieda who in the end makes what seems to be a doomed effort to return to the half-light of the *Herrenhof*. Yet there is never pure light or pure darkness; each remains in symbiosis with the other, prompting the efforts of K. to recalibrate their degree.

The title story of the collection *A Country Doctor* is one of Kafka's most accomplished nocturnes. The world is in darkness compounded by thick driving snow and the country doctor has been called out by a mistaken ring of his bell, but lacks a horse. His maid Rose is trying to borrow one, but returns unsuccessfully from the village 'waving her lantern' (*S* 220, 253). 'Absently' the doctor kicks the door of his pigsty and sees by the light of a 'dim stable lantern swinging from a rope within' (*S* 156, 253) a groom and two mighty horses. While the doctor is carried away into the night, the groom pursues the maid who takes refuge in darkness: 'I can see how she puts out the lights in the hall, and then chasing through the rooms put out all the lights in them as well, so as to escape detection' (*S* 221, 254). The doctor arrives at his patient, a sickly young man, and when examining him by candlelight can find nothing wrong. He is distracted with remorse for the fate of his maid and only on re-examination discovers the boy's wound, which is both like a quarry dug into the side of his body and a flower. Echoing the maid's name, it is 'Rose red, in various shades, dark in the depths, paler towards the edges, finely grained with blood welling unevenly, open like a mine at the surface' (*S* 223, 257). In the depths of the vaginal wound are giant maggots that are 'rose red themselves and blood spattered in addition' and while 'wriggling with their little white heads', scramble with 'their numerous legs towards the light' (*S* 223, 257). The lighting of the scene changes from smoky candlelight to moonlight as the door opens and other villagers enter the room. Moonlight recurs in Kafka as a baleful light, one that lit his description of a struggle as well the execution in *The Trial*, one of the blandest mixtures of reflected light and dark.

At this point the sickroom becomes a stage for the performance of healing after the death of God. The country doctor reflects ruefully, 'People are like that in my district. Always demanding the impossible of their doctor. They have lost their old faith; the priest sits at home and picks his vestment to pieces, one by one; but the doctor is expected to accomplish everything with his sensitive surgical hand' (*S* 214, 257–8). His patient is as ambivalent as the lighting of his sickroom, asking first of all, 'Doctor, let me die' and then 'will you save me', but instead of intensifying the light to draw out the worms, the doctor colludes with village practice and allows himself to be undressed and laid in the shadows beside the sick boy. All lights are extinguished, the door is shut but in any case 'clouds cover the moon' and the doctor is accused by a voice that begins saying, 'I have very little faith in you' and concludes with 'What I'd like best is to scratch your eyes out' (*S* 224–5, 258). The doctor's response identifies the boy's wound as an accident, even though it seems it was one he was born with. For the country doctor's experience allows him to 'see things in the round' – what for the boy is a singular catastrophe is for the doctor a statistic. It is the necessary accident that seeks out its victims, among them this boy: 'I have been in all the sick-rooms, far and wide, and I can tell you this: your wound is not so bad. Made with two slanting blows of the axe. Many there are who proffer their side and can hardly hear the axe in the forest, let alone that it is coming closer' (*S* 225, 259). With this he orders his patient to face necessity and die, little knowing that his own, singular axe-ident was on its way. Bungling his escape in the shadows, the doctor falls like Hunter Gracchus to his own interminable accident:

> Naked, exposed to the frost of this unhappiest of ages, with an earthly carriage, unearthly horses, old man that I am, I go drifting around. My fur coat is hanging from the back of the carriage, but I cannot reach it, and not one of my busy pack of patients lifts a finger. Betrayed! Betrayed! If you once respond to a faulty ring on the night bell – it can never be made good.
>
> (*S* 225, 259–60)

As Josef K. and the Hunter Gracchus learnt to their cost, once it has happened there is little salvation to be expected from the accident.

Yet Kafka does not entirely abandon hope, precisely because of the mutual dependence of light and shadow: 'Nothing of that, slanting through the words come vestiges of light' (*WP* 287). When the shadow is at its bleakest, illuminations are still possible; indeed there are even more occasions than when light and shadow are equally blended. One such case is the Platonic cave now flooded with water: 'I was rowing on a lake. It was in a domed cave without daylight, and yet it was bright with a clear, steady light shining down from the bluish pallid stone' (*WP* 310; *NII* 251). Kafka describes a moment of stasis, rowing around a closed lake, illuminated by ultra-violet radiation emitted by the walls of the cave. There are no shadows and this seems to be an environment completely secured from danger. The cave is the secured world of Nietzsche's last men, the heirs to the murderers of God. The lighting is constant and unremitting, but without a focus and 'Although there was no trace of wind the waves were high, but not so much as to pose a danger to my small but strongly made boat' (*WP* 311; *NII* 251). The rower is absorbed in 'a stillness such as I had never found before in my life. It was like a fruit I had never eaten before and was yet the most nourishing of all fruits; I had shut my eyes and was drinking it in' (*WP* 311; *NII* 251). The enjoyment of a secured environment without danger and without events is nevertheless disturbed by the coming of the accident, whose deferred advent was even more devastating: 'the stillness was as perfect as ever, but there was the continual threat of a disturbance at the door, about to break loose' (*WP* 311; *NII* 251). The threat of a catastrophic event signalled by the absent noise of delayed thunder disturbed the security of the rower, much as it did the burrower in his subterranean redoubt. The noise from without forced the rower to open his eyes: 'I rolled my eyes at it, this noise that was not there, I pulled one oar out of the rowlock, stood in the swaying boat, and made a threatening gesture into the void with the oar. All remained still for the time being and so I rowed on' (*WP* 310; *NII* 252). In many ways the inverse of Gracchus, who afflicted by the interminable accident sails on, the rower here after his act of defiance rowed on in the suspended moment of the coming of the accident.

In many ways these stories mark the limit of the healing vocation and of art – the doctor telling the patient to succumb at last to the accident, his vocation consists in saying it has arrived at last, need no longer be awaited or feared, has happened and can even be welcomed. Art serves both as the propitiation of the accident by letting it happen and recognizing its inevitability, but also as defiance of the coming accident by waving an angry oar at whatever seems to threaten the secured environment of the illuminated lake. But it can only defer the arrival of something that it cannot predict or control but that it knows is coming.

There is also the further option of increasing the light to force the accident to happen or inciting a crisis not just by illuminating the illusion of the world but by attempting to destroy it. This option is usually figured in terms of a breakout from the theatre, but in one variant the breakout itself becomes a performance. The wall of the cave, the glowing blue stone, is paper, a *mis-en-scene*: 'You must push your head through the wall. To do so is not so difficult since it is made of thin paper. But what is difficult is not to let yourself be deceived by the fact that there is already an extremely deceptive painting on the wall showing how you pushed your head through. It tempts you to say "Am I not pushing through it all the time?"' (*WP* 333; *NII* 339). The power of illusion seems enough to undo even the most determined act of defiance. It is this distinction between true and false defiance that runs through Gustav Janouch's memory of his conversations with Kafka and that unnerves some of the critics of this memoir. It appears in Kafka's refusal to allow his work to be read by in public by the *Protest* group,[12] his ambivalent identification with Ravachol and his close relation to Prague anarchist circles who 'attempted to realise the happiness of mankind without the aid of grace' (Janouch, 90). It also appears in his critique of Bolshevism and the October Revolution as 'little rehearsals for the great and cruel religions, which will sweep across the world' and the demonstrating workers who 'rule the streets and think they rule the world. In fact they are mistaken' (Janouch, 119) and of the Social Democractic leaders as '[t]he war profiteers of the class struggle' (Janouch,

135). Their defiance, however sincere, remained for Kafka a sham, 'for behind them already are the secretaries, officials, professional politicians, all the modern satraps for whom they are preparing the way to power … The Revolution evaporates, and leaves behind only the slime of a new bureaucracy. The chains of tormented mankind are made out of red tape' (Janouch, 119). The problem of true defiance involves both defiance and truth, and indeed Kafka will maintain that truth is the only true defiance and defiance truth. In an evocation of oral tradition, Janouch recalls his father – Kafka's colleague in the Institute – telling him the words that Kafka told him 'several times' that 'Without truth, which everyone understands, and to which therefore everyone willingly subordinates himself, all authority is naked force, a cage which sooner or later falls to pieces under the pressure of the need for truth' (Janouch, 120). The light of defiance is also the light of truth.

Defiant light

We have repeatedly returned to one of the most memorable if enigmatic of the Zürau aphorisms, the one where Kafka finds himself in 'a place I have never been before: breath comes differently, a neighbouring star shining brighter than the sun' (17th aphorism, *WP* 40, NII 117). What is the light of the star, Nietzsche's dancing star, that outshines the imperial sun? It sparkles in K.'s childhood memories, punctuating his struggles with the Castle, but most brightly in the inaugural act of the career of defiance that would bring him to the very foot of the Castle walls. K.'s memories cluster around the church as an assertion of the life of the community rather than the mausoleum for a dead God it had become in *The Trial* and *The Castle*. In a memory that came to him as he passed the village's abandoned church on his interminable and despairing march through the blinding snow led by the aspirant messenger Barnabas, K. recalls an 'old graveyard surrounded by a high wall' that he and other boys tried and failed to climb. K. remembers that 'It was not curiosity which urged them to do it, for the graveyard had no more secrets from them; they had often entered it through a small wicket-gate, it was only the smooth high wall that they had wanted to conquer' (*C* 469, 40). He recalls the defiant light that lit his success in finally scaling the wall: 'One morning – the empty quiet square flooded with light, when had K. seen anything like it either before or since? – he did it with surprising ease; he climbed the wall first time, with a little flag between his teeth, at a point where he had already often fallen back' (*C* 469, 40). Flag in mouth, young K. clambered to the top of the graveyard wall, provoking a small avalanche of stones anticipating the accident of his own fall that would soon follow: 'Stones were still rattling down under his feet, but he was at the top. He stuck in the flag, the wind filled the cloth, he looked down and around about him, then over his shoulders too at the crosses sinking into the ground, right here and now nobody was greater than he' (*C* 469, 40). The upsurge of life made possible by defying gravity and scaling the wall built by and containing the dead accompanied by a flood of light and the wind contrasts with the decay of the crosses and the dead in the graveyard below.

The burst of light and life released by K.'s defiance was immediately deflated by a chance accident. The *chance* arrival of a figure of authority and the boy's excessive haste to obey and descend the wall provoked the vengeance of gravity through an accident: 'By chance the teacher came by and forced K. down with an annoyed face; jumping down K. hurt his knee and made it home with difficulty, but still, he had been on the top of the wall . . .' (*C* 469, 40). As with the *Heimat* recollection 'Children on a Country Road', this memory too served as a *therapon* offering the healing light of a consolatory dream: 'that feeling of victory seemed then a victory for life, which was not altogether foolish, for it came now to help him after so many years on a snowy night on the arm of Barnabas' (*C* 469, 40–1). The healing light of the K.'s *therapon* parallels the dream of the children on a country road, but unlike the eternal return of the latter, his was an episodic light manifesting itself in moments of extreme need and strengthening his defiance.

Such defiant light differs from the light of the imperial sun, for instead of being held back by an obstacle, it outshines it. Another example of its eruption is also to be found in *The Castle* when one evening, on learning by chance from the new barmaid at the Herrenhof that Klamm was 'about to go, the sledge is already waiting for him in the courtyard' (*C* 538, 126), K. set off to intercept the official. Finding the gate open and the covered sledge waiting, K. got out his packed lunch and sat down to wait; as it grew colder and darker, K. heard the coachman growl 'it might be a long time yet', adding 'before you go away' (*C* 539, 128). The coachman then suggested they share a sip of Klamm's brandy from the flask in the door compartment, prompting K. to sit down in the cosy sledge. The brandy was a more subtle drug than mere alcohol, and as K. swallowed it there was a sudden illumination: 'Then – just as K. was in the middle of a long swig – everything became bright, the electric lights blazed on, inside on the staircase, in the corridors, in the entrance hall outside above the entrance' (*C* 540, 129). The courtyard had already been described as a theatre set, with one wall painted white against which the light reflected and now intensified as the scene lit up for the dramatic act of defiance and containment that followed.

The light served both domination and defiance: it exposed K. in the act of clumsily exiting the sledge and spilling Klamm's brandy, but it also set in harsh relief his prior resistance or refusal to move. Nevertheless K. is disappointed to see only Klamm's secretary Momus enter the stage and is angry with himself for not managing to surprise Klamm. However, in the bright light he refuses to move at Momus's bidding, initiating a subtle play of domination and defiance engaged between the two men in a gestural rather than verbal register: Momus says 'come with me' but 'not actually commanding, for the command lay not in the words, but in the slight and studiously indifferent gesture of the hand that accompanied them' (C 542, 131). K.'s response to the command is a defiant 'I'm waiting here for somebody', spoken 'no longer in any hope of success, but simply on principle' (C 542, 131). The gentleman's imperturbable 'Come' is met by K. emphatically shaking his head and adding, 'But then I would miss the person I am waiting for' (C 542, 131). In spite of failing in his objective of meeting Klamm, K. is left with the feeling 'that what he had achieved so far was something gained, that maybe he held only in appearance but that he must not relinquish' (C 542, 131). For the first time the unquestioned obedience that underwrote the dominion of the Castle was indeed put in question and the secretary instead of being unquestionably obeyed is forced to reason with K.: 'You'll miss him in either case, whether you stay or you go or' (C 542, 131), and then sullenly to digest K.'s refusal to be reasonable: "Then I would rather wait for him and miss him" said K. defiantly ...' (C 542, 131). Momus has no alternative but to retreat by closing down the failed scenario of domination; he orders the carriage put away, the lights extinguished and all trace of K.'s footprints in the snow erased.

K.'s sustained resistance, his unwillingness to cede ground de-accelerates the passage of time to the point of reversing the sequence of events that led to K.'s initial defiance: 'K. saw himself left behind alone, the sledge moved away in one direction while just as slowly the young man receded in the other, along the way he had come himself; both it was true very slowly, as if they wanted to show K. that it was still in his power to fetch them back' (C 542, 132). K.'s resistance literally holds him in stasis: 'He remained still, as one who held the field, but it was a victory that gave him no joy' (C 543, 132). Holding the stage, he enters a distended time in which gentleman and coachman slowly recede into the wings until at a certain point the former 'stepped into the hall, where he immediately vanished' (C 543, 132) and the coachman closed the gates 'and shut himself in the shed' (C 543, 132). At this point, as the lights went down, it seemed to K. that while he had gained a victory it was not full recognition. The dominator's response to his defiance was to reverse time and to return to a point before the defiance took place, leaving K. to languish in a future whose past had been almost wholly extinguished. His defiance has freed him, but he is left wondering where, when, for whom and for what?

Kafka closes this episode with a profound meditation on freedom and defiance. The extinction of the glaring stage lights left K. standing alone in the dark with only a slit of light slicing the darkness and thinking:

> [I]t seemed to K. as if all relations with him had been broken and as if freely he were freer now than he had ever been and could wait as long as he liked at this place otherwise forbidden to him and had won this freedom like hardly anybody else and that nobody could disturb, drive him away, or even speak to him, but – this conviction was at least strong – it was as if at the same time there was nothing more senseless, more despairing than this freedom, this waiting, this inviolability.
>
> (C 543, 133)

The ambivalence of K.'s defiantly won freedom testifies to the continued power of domination which, even when it loses a battle, will continue the war by minimizing the significance of the adversary's victory. Yet even Momus will concede that not all trace of the confrontation could be covered, for eventually when 'Klamm stepped out, he looked around him several times' (C 546, 136). Indeed, K.'s capacity to resist had been enhanced by the confrontation with Momus – he subsequently refused to attend the examination to make an official report on the episode, even when ordered by Momus 'in the name of Klamm'. And in one of the most beautiful moments of The Castle if not the whole of Kafka, he walks away, for the moment indifferent to the law and its officers. His freedom and acquired immunity prevail over the 'strong wind that was blowing' – ever the sign of past and future catastrophe in Kafka. Meeting the innkeeper on his way out of the Herrenhof, he explains that he no longer needs to obey the likes of Momus and his masters: he could stay or go – there was no necessity binding him to do one or the other – it was entirely up to him. Unlike his namesake Joseph K., he has fully understood the lesson of 'Before the Law' that court and castle 'want nothing from you. It takes you when you come and lets you go when you go' (T 193, 235), and he was just about to go ... Nevertheless, maybe, the innkeeper says, maybe he shouldn't have refused to stay and be examined, but anyway, 'seeing K. was silent, he added, whether to comfort K. or to get him to go away sooner: "Now, now then the sky won't rain sulphur for all that." "No," said K. "the weather doesn't look like it." And they parted laughing' (C 553, 145).

FINAL SENTENCE

A man from the country had the misfortune to stumble across a gateway guarded by a forbidding official. Once it happened there was no going back, nor any going forward. The gateway assumed an exterminatory necessity for him; it happened that he came upon it and then it turned out to be for him alone. Although he would later sometimes 'curse the unhappy chance' (*Er verflucht den unglucklichen Zufall*) that brought him to this pass, he remained convinced that there had to be a reason for his arriving there and waiting away his life under the indifferent gaze of the official. It must be because this is a gateway to the law, to the law that will explain why that gate stood open just for him and that would justify everything that had happened to him. It could not all just be a matter of chance, an accident? Yet it is only he who talks about the law, only he who imagines that this gateway might open to the law. The official or doorkeeper blocking the way at no point speaks of any law and indeed seems oblivious to its existence. He just says the man from the country cannot be admitted right now, that there are other more terrible doorkeepers beyond him. He allows himself to be bribed out of compassion, complains that the man from the country's questioning is insatiable and concludes that no one else could be admitted since this entrance was intended for him alone and he is about to close it. No mention of any *law* – only the man from the country is worried about the law, only he assumes it lies beyond the gateway. For it could not be that he stumbled across a gateway just by accident and that it was closely guarded for no reason, that he waited all his life for no reason and that it was closed upon him for no reason.

His being at the gate could not be an accident: he had to be there for a reason and what better reason than the law? In Josef K's discussion of the parable with the priest in the Cathedral, the final point of mutual incomprehension concerned this 'reason' and whether it belonged to the order of law or truth. The priest advises that 'one must not hold everything to be true, one must only hold it to be necessary', advocating the primacy of the law and its necessity over truth, against which K. protests '*Die Luge wird zur Weltordnung gemacht*' – this is to submit truth to necessity and make the lie a principle of world-order. And yet the gatekeeper never affirms or denies any law; he simply stands before a gateway that separates but also invites the man from the country to cross from one side to the other. The 'law' is but a story the man from the country tells himself and anyone who will listen about why he has been held up at this gate.

But if this gateway and its keeper are all there is, and if the law beyond the gate is but the man from the country's story about why he found himself arrested before it, what then is the light that radiates from the portal? The man from the country is unsure whether the world is darkening or his sight fading. We had just been told of his extraordinary eyesight, able to discern the fleas on the doorkeeper's fur collar, so the weight of interpretation seems to lie with the former, the darkening of the world. It is in this growing darkness that he now sees a radiant light flowing out of the 'gate of the law'. Was this the law itself shining out or was it the truth of the law? Was this the truth that before the law was the accident, that the accident did not just swerve away from the necessity of the law, but that the truth of law was the capture of accident by necessity? The radiant light allows the man from the country to formulate a final question for the doorkeeper – why was it only he who suffered the 'unlucky accident' of stumbling upon this gateway? And the truth of the law – confirmed by the doorkeeper's closing the gate – was that it had to happen to someone and this time it just happened to be him.

NOTES

Introduction

1 The question of how to understand the accident has been most recently addressed by Catherine Malabou (2012) and Paul Virilio (2012). Malabou returns to Kafka's *The Metamorphosis*, perceptively linking the accident to the hunt, while Virilio situates the accident in terms of its proximity and distance to the Aristotelian thoughts of substance and the automaton. My debt to and differences with their views will become quickly evident.

2 'The atmosphere at the airport confirmed all his misgivings: no monks, no red carpet, no girls strewing petals at his feet, but instead a sombre crowd, chanting slogans glorifying Angkar and the revolutionary army. "It was Kafkaesque", Sihanouk reflected afterwards. The smile frozen on my face must have looked ridiculous.' Philip Short, *Pol Pot: The History of a Nightmare*, John Murray, London, 2004, p. 331.

3 Pietro Citati's 1987 classic of Italian language Kafka scholarship regards his work as negative theology, an elusive and ever interrupted investigation of the One. Roberto Calasso's sophisticated reading of Kafka also declares its theological investments in departing from a suggestive pairing of *The Trial* and *The Castle* in terms of an ambivalence of 'election' – 'election and condemnation are *almost* indistinguishable' (Calasso, 5). This explicitly theological premise informs one of the most sustained and provocative global readings of Kafka's *oeuvre* but one that leaves little room for accidents.

4 Adorno's observation, 'His two great novels *The Castle* and *The Trial*, seem to bear the mark of philosophical theorems, if not in their details then in their general outlines . . .' (Adorno, 254), is unduly tentative – they *are* philosophical theorems.

5 '"And so you are looking for a leader you can hold on to, Disciple Kafka."' 'Conversations with Brecht', Benjamin 1973, 109.

6 This critical position is urged in the recent French language criticism of Casanova and Löwy that emphasizes the emancipatory dimension of Kafka's work.

7   See Löwy, 78, for the view that the first reception of Western Marxist readers was already sensitive to the implications of the distinction between power and domination in Kafka.

8   Emrich later defines 'universal' in terms of Hegelian *Sittlichkeit* or 'ethical life': 'The Universal is no "divine" authority; it is neither a superempirical, "Intelligible," or ideal sphere any longer, nor an absolute sphere in the sense of the classical period. It is the essence and sum total of everything that is lived, felt, thought, imagined and done by human beings . . .' (Emrich, 37).

9   Janouch recalls Kafka defending Plato's expulsion of the poets from the standpoint of domination (but in a way fully consistent with his anarchism): '"Poets try to give men a different vision, in order to change reality. For that reason they are politically dangerous elements, because they want to make a change. For the state and all its devoted servants, want only one thing, to persist"' (Janouch, 140).

10 Janouch's recollection of Kafka's subtle understanding of the necessity of the accident – whatever doubts may still cling to some aspects of his testimony – nevertheless rings true: '"Accident is the name one gives to the coincidence of events of which one does not know the causation. But there is no world without causation, but only here . . ." Kafka touched his forehead with his left hand. "Accidents only exist in our heads, in our limited perceptions. They are the reflection of the limits of our knowledge. The struggle against chance is always a struggle against ourselves, which we can never entirely win"' (Janouch, 92). The ostensibly epistemic definition of the accident locates it as an effect of the limited perception of causal connection while at the same time understanding that such limits possess a necessity that accidents expose and provoke a struggle against. Fiction is but one way in which the struggle to reduce the reign of the accident may be pursued.

11 I am indebted for this classification to Marcel Detienne's (1999) description of Ancient Greek culture in terms of the three masters of truth: the philosopher, the poet and the orator or politician and their respective words of truth, poetry and power.

12 Corngold et al., in their introductions to the translation of Kafka's selected *Office Writings*, properly insist that Kafka's position in the Institute between 1908 and 1922 was not that of the disaffected lowly clerk of literary legend but rather a senior executive. Dr Kafka or the Chief Legal Secretary of the Institute was an acknowledged 'innovator of modern social and legal reform in the Crown Land of Bohemia, "the Manchester of the Empire" – one of the most highly developed industrial areas of continental Europe' and responsible for publicly representing the work of the Institute and 'for dictating briefs of considerable intricacy and social importance' (*OW*, ix–x). Elsewhere, Ruth Gross has aptly described his occupational role as *concipist* in terms of 'what we would call today a technical or professional writer, a crucial figure in the modern business enterprise who articulates the rules and regulations that govern all activity. Accident prevention, Kafka's particular speciality, was important to the emergent industries of the early twentieth century, as it defined the rules for efficient production' ('Kafka's short fiction', in Preece, 82). For a historically oriented characterization of the role of *concipist* in the Austro-Hungarian bureaucratic hierarchy, see the introduction to the Frankfurt edition of the *Amtliche Schriften*, pp. 15–18.

13 This *Annual Report* also contains a contribution by Kafka in Czech that Kafka describes in his covering letter as the main reason for sending it to Blei, who had an interest in the Czech language. See Hermsdorf's speculations on this in his introduction to the Berlin edition of the *Amtliche Schriften* (1984, 28) and Paul Raabe's article 'Franz Kafka und Franz Blei' in Born et al. 1965, p. 13. Kafka also carefully pointed out to Blei that his contribution to the Annual Report ran up to page 22.

14 For the editorial challenges facing any attempt to attribute authorship to the archival remains of the Institute, see the Frankfurt *Amtliche Schriften*, p. 20. In the office, Kafka preferred to dictate or use a typewriter rather than, as in his night fictional work, write by hand.

15 Kafka detected the same tension at work in his relationship with Felice: 'The fact that mere accidents intervene to confuse our situation unnecessarily, that my telegram should arrive at your office when you are not there, that your telegram should be incorrectly addressed, and finally, as I now see, the fact that my letter to your parents should be delayed by one day (it was mailed on Thursday as the attached receipt shows) – all this is bad enough, but things between us have reached such a point that even the gravest accident cannot make things worse' (*F*, 21/3/1914, 501, 527).

16 This is why theological readings of Kafka framed in terms of being 'chosen' or 'selected' already operate at a second level; they attempt to make sense of the accident globally as well as to legitimate the fact that it happened to me. *De jure* legitimation even holds for the singularities of fiction where the law and its correlates of guilt and punishment continues to provide a powerful instrument for legitimating and making sense of why *this* accident had to happen to *me*.

17 After Kafka's death in 1924, Max Brod proceeded to publish the novels under pressure to secure financial assistance for Kafka's partner and family who were in debt after paying for his terminal medical care. He was forced by legal disagreements between Kafka's publishers – Kurt Wolff Verlag and Die Schmiede – to publish them in a different order to their composition. The Kurt Wolff Verlag had earlier published the first chapter of *America* – 'The Stoker' – as an independent novella and would not release the rights. Der Schmiede published *The Trial*, but *The Castle* and *Missing Person* were subsequently published by Kurt Wolff Verlag (see Unseld, 277–89).

18 Brod's title, 'Nature Theatre of Oklahoma', silently corrects Kafka's very deliberate misspelling of 'Oklahoma' as 'Oklahama'. For an extended critique of Benjamin and Arendt's interpretations, see Caygill (2011).

19 Her essay 'Franz Kafka, Appreciated Anew' begins with *The Trial*, moves to Kafka's 'second great novel *The Castle*' (Arendt, 98) and culminates with 'Kafka's last novel, *America*' (Arendt, 87).

20 The inquiry into the significance of Nietzsche for Kafaka intitiated by Malcolm Pasley in the 1960s (Pasley 1963 and 1966) was systematically pursued by Patrick Bridgewater in 1974. However, it is only in the work of Wagner and more recently Paul North (2015) that the full significance of Nietzsche's death of God for relieving Kafka of Brod's influential assumption that he was a religious and theological writer has begun to be appreciated.

Chapter 1

1 For a clear and precise statement of the unstable relationship between Kafka's manuscripts and the various editions of his work, see Osman Durrani's 'Editions, translations, adaptations' in Preece, 206–25.

2 Brod relates in the *Nachwort* to his 1925 edition of *The Trial* finding a folded note addressed to him in Kafka's writing desk instructing him to burn without exception all his unpublished writings and drawings.

3 Kafka prepares Pollak for the request to take care of a parcel of his writings by relating two parables. In the first, someone, whose voice resounds with that of 'life' in Nietzsche's *Also Sprach Zarathustra*, tells him 'You [*du*] will do nothing without others' and that since 'solitude is repulsive' he should 'lay [his] eggs out in the open and the sun will hatch them' (*L* 17, 8). The eggs are Kafka's embryonic writings that need to be hatched by exposure to 'others'. This thought or rather command is repeated in Zarathustrian style as 'better to bite into life than bite your tongue; honour the mole and its kind, but do not make it into your saint' (*L* 17, 8). This demand echoes Zarathustra's sleeping man waking to bite the head off the snake of *ressentiment* that had entered his mouth and modulates into a demand to reveal what had been written during the summer, framed parenthetically as a clever opening to a begging letter and leading to a second, much more ambivalent story. If the first parable is set in sunshine and present noon, the second takes place at the end of a long night. Confident that Pollak has understood the first parable of defiance and the greatest liberation, Kafka tells of domination and the greatest weight. He asks if Pollak understands the feelings of the horse that pulls the mail coach full of sleepers through the long night? Kafka can, for he is that horse, hobbling past the milestones with an eye on the road 'even though there is nothing on it but night' (*L* 8,

18). The horse dreams of awakening the sleepers if only he had a post horn, for he is not only pulling with him the sleepers, but also the post and even the very post horn that will awake them by announcing the arrival of the letters – including this one and others it promises. The sleepers have become the letters or writings that once again need to be exposed to the sun to hatch or have any chance of life, and Kafka has been pulling them along with him for too long a night.

4 See Judith Butler's subtle account of the difficult legacy of Kafka's manuscripts from Brod's rescued archive (Butler 2011).

5 The exception is the story 'Die stadtische Welt' that survived a larger, abandoned project of the same name and while ostensibly treating the same familial theme as 'The Judgement' handles it very differently from the juridical model dominating the later story.

6 For an analysis of the affinities between Kafka and Wittgenstein, see Ware 2015, chapter 5, and Schuman 2015. Paul North's proposal radically to rethink the 1917 writings by freeing them from assumptions such as their aphoristic character is salutary and thought provoking, but depends too much on isolating the 1917 *pensées* from the accident narratives that preceded and succeeded them.

7 See Greenberg (1971), especially the suggestive analysis of *The Castle* in terms of a 'dream story' and 'thought story' (257).

8 Richard T. Gray criticizes Hartmut Binder for regarding Kafka's aphorisms as an intermediate reflective and 'philosophical' stage located between the embedded fragments and notations of the diary and the free realm of the fictional writing. He also criticizes Walter Sokel's view that the aphorisms signify a change in Kafka's philosophical position from perspectivism to parable, an encoded reference to a shift from the significance of Nietzsche to Kierkegaard in Kafka's development.

9 Klemperer's diaries begin in pre-war Wilhelmine Germany and extend through the Third Reich into the German Democratic Republic.

10 Brod makes the unreliable claim that the diaries or rather quarto notebooks emerged from Kafka's 'little brown travel notebooks' and were sequels to 'our little notes on our journeyings'. More seriously he claimed it was 'well known that the short pieces in *Meditation* developed out of Franz's diaries; then came "The Judgement"' (cited Zilcosky, 10). While the diary genesis holds for 'The Judgement', most of the *Meditation* stories were written according to a different regime predating the diaries (see Brod, 106). Nevertheless, Brod's assertion is cautiously endorsed by Zilcosky as part of his otherwise compelling case for the importance of travel in Kafka's writing, and by Corngold who follows Brod on Kafka's early working methods and the hermeneutic through which he interpreted its results (Corngold 2004a, 19).

11 The publication of Meditation was largely brokered by Max Brod who introduced Kafka to the publisher and then ensured that he completed it and put it in the post.

12 'Our idea a poor one; to describe the trip and at the same time our feelings towards each other during the trip' (*D* 433); only one chapter, 'First Railway Journey', was ever published.

13 The gloom surrounding *Richard and Samuel* and the excitement of discovering Yiddish theatre intersect in the diary entry of 20 October 1911: 'The 18th at Max's; wrote about Paris. Wrote badly without arriving at that freedom of true description which releases one's foot from the experienced. I was also dull after the great exaltation of the previous day that had ended with Löwy's lecture' (*D* 80, 55).

14 Strangely, Kafka had anticipated a accident in Paris, but on the Place de L'Opera, in an entry on 15 December 1910 where he wrote, 'When I sit down at the desk I feel no better than someone who falls and breaks both legs in the middle of the traffic on the Place de L'Opera' (*D* 29, 81).

15 John Zilcosky compares the early style to 'a series of photographs placed down abruptly and juxtaposed before the eyes of the viewer' (Zilcosky, 12), and reads the 'Little Car Story' in terms of Kafka's move towards a 'telltale filmic idiom' or 'flowing narrative'. This assessment reverses Zischler's view that the direction of Kafka's fascination with photographic and filmic narrative moved from film *towards* photography (see Zischler 2003).

16 Pasley and Zilcosky both see a self-depiction in the vexed policeman failing to write up the accident at the end of the story, the latter noting that 'Kafka resembles the note-taking policeman' (Zilcosky, 12).

17 This has been perceptively linked by Benno Wagner to a conflict between thinking in terms of populations and individual events, a description of a struggle between the perspectives of Quételet and Nietzsche. After describing Kafka's university training in criminal and administrative statistics, Wagner comments, 'Against this background it is certainly no accident when Kafka makes the paradox of the statistically regular actions of the average person and the freedom of the individual the theme of his first extended attempt at narrative, the 1904/5 *A Description of a Struggle*' (Wagner in Koch and Wagenbach, 113).

18 Robertson concedes that his might be a 'premature judgement', but he remains perplexed by Kafka's compositional techniques. That Kafka did not 'plan' the accidental character of his narrative progression meant that he had to 'keep the narrative from rambling'. Indeed, he previously described the same tension between an accidental nexus of description and narrative action in terms of a tension between 'Flaubertian Naturalism' and the dynamic fractures of expressionism.

19 Kafka described extracting the stories for *Meditation* from the larger, abandoned narrative of 'Description of a Struggle' as 'quarry practice', cited by Unseld, 55.

20 In Nietzsche's words, 'What festivals of atonement, what sacred games shall we have to invent?' *The Gay Science*, § 125.

21 The distinction is obliterated in Brod's edition of 'Description of a Struggle', which conflates material from the two very different versions – his collage remains the basis of existing English translations.

22 They are seen panoramically passing under a vast sky and in close-up as *swaying* with respect to one another, an intimation of the theme of swaying (*Schwanken*) that will return as the moment of suspension characteristic of eternal return in the section extracted as 'Children on a Country Road'.

23 In Version A the hostess's movements provoke the emergence of dainty folds while in Version B her movements cause the folds to 'swing themselves' – the swinging will be transferred to the child at the outset of 'Children on a Country Road', which is the main addition to Version B. The creases return in an altogether more melancholy register in Chapter Three of Version A.

24 The story is notable for its attention to hands – hands withdrawn and advanced, hidden and disclosed, caressing, slapping and gesturing.

25 Bared chests recur throughout 'Description of a Struggle', the most erotically charged epiphany being the companion's 'quickly opening his overcoat and waistcoat and his shirt. His chest was indeed broad and beautiful' (*S* 49; *NI* 117).

26 In Version A the companion relates to Annie the cosmic analogy between the narrator's breathing and the starry sky. In B, all references to the celestial dome, horizons, fiery clouds and landscapes are deleted, leaving only the companion's oaths that he is not exaggerating the narrator's effect on him.

27 Except that the companion is said to have a 'fat face' in Version A, Chapter Three, which may make him a potential avatar of the fat man. It may be that 'der Dicke' is an allusion to the gym nickname 'Plato' – 'big bodied' or 'broad shouldered' (sometimes more apologetically 'broad forehead') that Diogenes Laertes in the *Lives of the Philosophers* claims the philosopher Aristocles adopted as his *nom de plume*. The repeated references in 'Description of a Struggle' to broad masculine chests seem to be playing with this etymology, although there is no evidence outside of the text to support this.

28 The ride in the celebrated 'Wish to be a Red Indian' from *Meditation*, probably contemporary with Version B, gallops into a void and experimentally deletes all the features of the 'unfinished region' by abstracting from spurs, reigns and even the horse's head leaving only the 'quivering', 'hardly visible', 'smoothly mown heath' (*glatt gemähte Heide*) across which the rider races. Most commentators have followed Walter Benjamin in locating the ride in the wild, overlooking the carefully described 'smoothly mown' heath that firmly sets the ride on a *race-course* and so links the desire to be a Red Indian with the pensive jockey of the previous 'Reflections for Gentlemen-Jockeys', who in an early incarnation of Kafka's reluctant artist participates in a highly organized and structured competitive spectacle.

29 The walkers in the mountains dressed in frock coats and Sunday best recall the strollers in the epigraph to Version A, except the latter are not last men on a fake Sabbath excursion but seriously sway under the great noontide.

30 This reduction of a chromatic to a tonal landscape anticipates the absence of colour that is such a striking feature of the winter world of *The Castle*.

31 For example, in Judith Ryan's observation that 'In *Betrachtung*, the opening piece (Children on a Country Road), treats the country city dichotomy through the somewhat whimsical eyes of a child . . .', 'Kafka before Kafka: The Early Stories', in Rolleston, 67.

32 Heidsieck persuasively locates the origin of these ideas in Gustav Lindner and Franz Lukas's *Textbook of Psychology* used by Kafka for his high school philosophy class (Heidsieck, 16). In addition, Kafka formally studied courses on the 'Fundamental Questions of Descriptive Psychology' in 1902 with Brentano's disciple Anton Marty and in 1904 the 'History of Modern Philosophy' with Emil Arleth, a student of Marti and follower of Brentano.

33 As when he distinguishes Kafka's neo-Herbartian position indebted to Fechner from Wundt's critique of Hebart framed in terms of willed apperception.

34 Heidsieck indicates the transition to philosophical fiction in his observation that 'Many of Kafka's works of fiction offer some observation regarding the dynamics of apperception and fatigue' (Heidsieck, 33). Kafka's aesthetic apperception emphasize the role of fatigue, relaxation and near sleep states in the removal of conscious obstacles to apperception, but never sees this as the outcome of willed concentration.

35 They comprise 'The Businessman', 'Absent-Minded Window Gazing', 'The Way Home', 'Passers By', 'Clothes', 'On the Tram', 'The Rejection' and 'Trees'. Two of these ('Clothes' and 'Trees') were extracted from the draft Version A of 'Description of a Struggle', while with the exception of 'The Rejection' – attached to a letter to Hedwig Weiler from the Autumn of 1907 and described as a '*eine schlechte, vielleicht ein Jahr alte Kleinigkeit*' ('a bad trifle perhaps around a year old') – the remaining stories left no manuscript traces.

36 *Hyperion* was a short-lived bi-monthly luxury literary journal managed by Kafka's friend Franz Blei. It succeeded two semi-pornographic journals also edited by Blei – *Amethyst* and *Opal* – to which Kafka subscribed. Apart from *Meditation*, Kafka also published two dialogues drawn from 'Description of a Struggle' in the Spring 1909 edition of *Hyperion*. He later wrote an ironic obituary for the journal in 1911, describing its fatal 'error' as aspiring 'to grant a representation, a great and vital one, to those who dwelled on the peripheries of literature' such as himself (cited in Unseld, 28).

37 The Prague German language newspaper in which Kafka previously published 'The Aeroplanes at Brescia' (29 September issue, 1909). Kafka was pressured by Brod to release the stories to the newspaper for their Easter 1909 literary supplement and did not approve the editorial change of *Betrachtung* to the plural *Betrachtungen*.

38 The others were 'Unmasking a Confidence Trickster', 'The Sudden Walk', 'Resolutions', 'Excursion into the Mountains', 'Bachelors ill luck', 'The Street Window', 'The Wish to be a Red Indian' and 'Unhappiness'. Kafka slightly changed the order of the stories in the final collection – ever since, the order has been wilfully changed by editors who, often inexplicably, do not respect Kafka's final decision.

39 There exists a third version, unchanged, published in the Christmas supplement to *Bohemia*, 25 December 1912, thus bringing this esoteric story a mass, newspaper-reading public.

40 The attention paid to sound paid in this story looks forward to the soundscapes of Kafka's later writings, for sensitive assessment of these from the soundpoint of sound-studies see Mowitt (2015).

41 The same dream of staying awake is central to *The Castle* and to the late story 'The Burrow'. The state of oneiric vigilance characterizes aesthetic apperception, as if being part of the audience in Plato's cave while remaining *aware* that what passes by on the walls is illusion.

42 It is tempting to follow the exaggerations of the existing translations 'Has something dreadful happened that can never be made good' (Willa and Edwin Muir) and 'Is it some specially awful, fatal disaster?' (Pasley).

43 In the manuscript the use of dashes instead of inverted commas forms part of a visually striking pattern of thick horizontal lines on the letters L, F and T that add peculiar urgency to the somnolent page (Kafka 1999, 61).

44 'Wedding Preparations in the Country' presents the compressed perception of the landscape experienced by travellers racing past in a train; for them our entire story is but a flash, a group of children waving momentarily at the train before slipping away into the distance. The reluctant traveller Raban sees something similar when he looks out of the train window and sees 'lights flitting past and others flitting away into the distance' (*S* 64), and 'all unexpectedly the tall railings of a bridge, outside the windows, were torn apart and pressed together it seemed' (*S* 65). His perceptions have no internal consistency; they are a catena of accidents like the passing appearance of a group of excited children waving beside the track. Yet there is an implied necessity to the perception intimated in

Kafka's reflection on Goethe's travel diaries that compare the perception of a landscape seen from a horse-drawn carriage on a 'country road' (*Landstrasse*) with the view from a train: 'Since the region offers itself unscathed in its indigenous character to the passengers in a wagon, and since highways too divide the country much more naturally than the railway lines to which they perhaps stand in the same relationship as do rivers to canals, so too the observer need to do no violence to the landscape and he can see systematically without great effort' (*D* 56, 33). Kafka describes this perception, from a slow moving standpoint embedded in the landscape as 'peacefully formed landscape thinking' (*D*, *T* 33) that Walter Benjamin will later formalize in terms of a distinction between *Erfahrung* and *Erlebnis*. The embedded character of *Erfahrung* is distinguished from the 'momentary observations' of *Erlebnis* and is a form of perception embedded within and indebted to a landscape. The latter, however, while appearing accidental, is in fact governed by a rigorous and technologically invested necessity.

45 Emrich is one of the few critics to attend to the question of fatigue in 'Children on a Country Road', linking it suggestively to Odradek and the world of parable: 'Children and fools here become parabolic images of a world that defies definition both with reference to orientation in time and space, and with respect to the laws of life. They never grow tired: they are "extraordinarily mobile and cannot be caught," as is the case with Odradek. They represent the only world that promises "liberation". In their world things and thoughts are liberated. Existence and imagining have become a perfect whole' (Emrich, 112). This Adornesque reading, thought-provoking and not necessarily wrong, is nevertheless incomplete and underestimates the ambivalence of this story. Emrich is too hasty to identify 'the only world that promises "liberation"' in the indefatigability of the children on the country road 'who never grow tired' – but they do eventually grow tired and return to their families, leaving the dreamer to seek another way to stay awake. This utopia of childhood that is never to be found in Kafka is also carried over by Emrich to *The Castle* where the officials undergo 'the sudden liberating change into a childlike state' (Emrich, 113).

46 It is probably the most commented on of all Kafka's stories, including *Metamorphosis* – see Flores 1977 for an early collection of essays. Richard T. Gray notes that 'The key position of *The Judgement* within Kafka's works corresponds to the key position that this text has assumed in Kafka research: no interpretation of his work as a whole can avoid this text and frequently its interpretation is taken as a point of departure for an interpretation of all of Kafka's work' (in Müller 2003, 12). The glaring exception as we have seen is Emrich's philosophical interpretation which shows scant interest in 'The Judgement', but this became cause for questioning his overall reading of Kafka. Sokel went so far as to claim, 'The complete omission of the text Kafka considered his most important "Das

Urteil" from Emrich's discussion of Kafka's *opus* appeared to me symptomatic of his tendency to miss what was essential to Kafka' (Rolleston, 42–3).

47 As in Ronald Spiers' retrospective judgement of *Meditation*: 'More radically than anything attempted in the *Betrachtung*, what "The Judgement" narrates is thus the imagined intersection of a strange, new disruptive form of movement with the familiar movements of natural and social existence, cyclical in the one case and goal-directed in the other' (in Lothe et al., 225).

48 Casanova notes that the time Kafka dedicated to anarchist politics in 1911 and 1912 was subsequently consumed by his passion for Yiddish theatre – nevertheless he insists that this was not a move from politics to aesthetics, but the pursuit of radical politics by other means (Casanova, 160 and 161–226)

49 Beck justly claims that 'The plays of Gordin clearly made a strong impression on Kafka, and he rightly judged Gordin superior to the other playwrights of the Yiddish theatre. Gordin was by far the best dramatist writing for the Yiddish theatre at the turn of the century, and *God, Man, and Devil* is one of his finest works' (Beck, 72), but adds less convincingly 'These many parallels in theme, character, action and technique show that Gordin's play provided an important source for Kafka's story' (Beck, 97).

50 Malcolm Pasley cites this passage as the 'best-documented example' of the improvised character of Kafka's writing, but does not draw attention to the wry '*dreht mir sich alles unter den Händen*'. This passage is not so much evidence of Kafka's improvisation as of his sitting down to write one thing and it turning out to be another. It is continuous with the celebrated Diary entry of 15 November 1911– also cited by Pasley – that evokes the same 'mishandling' of an initial inspiration: 'blindly and arbitrarily I snatch handfuls out of the stream ...' (*D* 118). See Pasley 108–10.

51 *Tumult* or uprising and *Menge* or crowd are translated by both the Muirs and Pasley with 'riot' and 'mob' – both conservative terms for an insurrectionary urban crowd that stress its irrationality – see Eric Hobsbawm, *Primitive Rebels*, and Christopher Hitchens, *King Mob* for critiques of this view. By the choice of word the translations incline to the point of view of the father out to repress what is to him irrational filial insurrection.

52 'George Bendemann and his friend in Petersburg incorporate two opposed reactions to the demands of bourgeois life: one opts for the flight from the institutions of bourgeois interaction the other for conformity with the power structures of bourgeois life' (Gray in Müller, 25).

53 The concept of reactionary suicide was developed in contrast with revolutionary suicide by the Black Panther Huey Newton in his book *Revolutionary Suicide*. Newton developed it with explicit reference to

Durkheim's sociology of suicide which contrasts the individual will to self-destruction with the statistical regularities of the population of suicides.

54 Kafka's description of the shared fate of the compliant Karl Rossman and the defiant Josef K. in the diaries (see below) corresponds to the Father's description of Georg at the moment of condemnation: 'An innocent child, yes, that you were, truly, but still more truly have you been a devilish human being! – And therefore take note: I sentence you now to death by drowning' (*S* 87). He is condemned both as dominated innocent (Karl Rossman) and as defiant devil (Josef K.).

55 For Beck, 'The "Urban World" is a work of transition: similarities in structure as well as in details of plot strongly suggest that it represents an early, unfinished version of "The Judgement" and despite its shortcomings as a work of art, it illuminates the development of Kafka's dramatic technique' (Beck, 59). This view is endorsed by Robertson: 'Die stadtische Welt is poorly constructed beginning too abruptly and then meandering on without real development' (Robertson, 1985, 28).

56 'The "Urban World" differs markedly from "Wedding Preparations" in the number of characters, their degree of complexity, and the methods by which their problems are conveyed. In the thirty pages that make up "Wedding Preparations" Kafka suggests a series of multiple relationships. In contrast "The UrbanWorld" introduces only three characters – Oskar, Father, Friend – all of whom are limited in function and interaction' (Beck, 61). This simplification is seen as the desideratum for Kafka's writing, rather than a temporary diversion or lapse of ambition.

Chapter 2

1 Hedwig was a student at Vienna University 'specialising in French, English, philosophy, and education' (*L* 32, 47).

2 Assicurazioni Generali was a Trieste based private insurance company then specializing in transport, fire and life insurance. It had a global network that made Kafka's fantasy of eventually representing the company in the Orient not entirely gratuitous.

3 'The "Accident Section" transformed the individual blows of fate into serial processes, the micro-elements of a statistical set into calculable insurance risks. The Institute administered the collisions between men and machines – shattered limbs, fatal falls, incurable industrial diseases belonged to individual cases that appeared only as statistics in the reports.' *Amtliche Schriften*, 34. The editors add that in 1909 the Institute registered 21,986 industrial accidents, a number that had risen to 26,206 in 1913. For Hermsdorf, Kafka's work in the Accident Department confronted him with 'the other side of the industrial epoch, namely the human costs of motorised technical progress' (Koch and Wagenbach, 43).

4   For Robert Marschner and his reforms, see Wagner *OW*, 36–8. Kafka got on well with Marschner, an unlikely boss who outside of the office was a published Goethe scholar with interests in Stirner and Nietzsche (Kafka 1984, 19).

5   Kafka's office career continued in the Appeals Department, with applications for pay rises, promotions and after his diagnosis with tuberculosis an increasingly extended period of sick leave (see Gilman). With the dismissal of his immediate superiors after the foundation of Czechoslovakia, Kafka continued to work, probably due in part to his competence in the Czech language. He was promoted to Chief Secretary in 1922 and on 30 June of the same year retired on the grounds of ill health.

6   Klaus Wagenbach's article 'Kafkas Fabriken' describes the forward-looking modernity of this region, celebrated for its large scale factory production and Gablonz famed for its 'American Style' skyscraper housing (Koch and Wagenbach, 15–17).

7   In his article on the history of the Institute in the 'Jubilee Report: Twenty-Five Years of the Workmen's Accident Insurance Institute', Kafka emphasizes the Prague Institute's commitment to accident prevention 'from the outset' and its role in imposing a preventative agenda on both government and trade inspectors (*OW* 311). Kafka refers to his own work on wood-turning machines, noting 'it was only the Institute's organisation of this initiative that led to favourable statistical results' (*OW* 316). He also refers laconically to problems with quarry safety – not so much with machinery as with the management of the excavation – insisting in the name of the Institute 'that caution be exercised continuously when it comes to quarrying, since the physical condition of any quarry also changes constantly as the work of breaking stones continues' (*OW* 316). This situation, Kafka notes, 'calls for constant supervision' (*OW* 316), without adding that such supervision was beyond the Institute's legal powers under the 1887 Act.

8   Both Hermsdorf and Wagner situate Kafka's work within sophisticated theoretical frameworks, the former in historical materialism, the latter with reference to Foucault's account of bio-power. Wagner's description of Kafka's 'job profile' is particularly illuminating: 'While accident prevention aims to optimize the interaction between bodies and machines risk classification calculates accident probabilities for different industrial branches' (*OW* 40).

9   For a thought-provoking meditation on Kafka, accident statistics and the connection between *Recht und Rechnung* (law and calculation), see Benno Wagner's article 'Poseidons Gehilfe: Kafka und die Statistik'. Wagner emphasizes Kafka's training in statistics, following courses in criminological, political and administrative statistics.

10 The Institute was required to produce Annual Reports on its activities since 1871. The editors of the Frankfurt *Amtliche Schriften* speculate on the wide readership and distribution of these reports, noting that the Prague Institute alone was responsible in 1911 for insuring 288,094 firms and 1,642,148 individual workers.

11 In his polemical newspaper articles on 'Workmen's Accident Insurance and Employers' of autumn 1911, Kafka encourages his readers to devote more attention to reading these reports, describing himself as a 'reader' of these 'sadly, not sufficiently perused' texts (*OW* 155) and offering lessons in how to interpret them, focusing on the second article – a reply to an employer's objections to the first article on a reading of the 1910 Annual Report. It offers a rare lesson by Kafka in how to read a text.

12 To these may be added newspaper articles defending the Institute's overall mission and Kafka's special interests such as the establishment of a psychiatric hospital for the treatment of shell shock and other mental disorders afflicting soldiers during the First World War.

13 'Fixed-rate Insurance Premiums for Small Farms using machinery' and 'Inclusion of Private Automobile "Firms" in the Compulsory Insurance Programme'.

14 Brod published an extract from this article in *Die Literarische Welt* 4, no. 18 as early as early as 1928.

15 Kafka reviewed the relationship between social insurance and accident prevention in an address read out by his boss Marschner to the Second International Congress on Accident Prevention and First Aid in Vienna in 1913. He dates the obligation to an official declaration of the Ministry of the Interior of 15 October 1889 and contrasts the legal discourse of accident insurance with the more technologically dependent discourse of accident prevention: 'A version of accident insurance will be adequate for some years, while accident prevention is in a permanent process of reformulation, since it must follow both the development of industry and machine technology as well as the developments of accident prevention technology' (*OW* 250).

16 The English translators' decision to translate *Gefahr* as 'potential risk' introduces a metaphysical concept of potentiality that is not present in Kafka's statistical understanding of the 'sphere of risk', which emphasizes less that accidents *may* happen than that they *will* happen. The 'sphere of risk' is not governed by the modality of possibility, but necessity.

17 Hermsdorf regards this article and its intersection of image and text as marking a 'paradigm-shift' in the literature of accident prevention; see Koch and Wagenbach, 2002, 62.

18 In 1918, Kafka was nominated by the 'Public Crownland agency for Returning Veterans' for an award in recognition of the merit of his work 'in the area of veterans welfare'.

19 The report on this incident under *Kleine Localnachrichten* in the Prager Tagblatt of 31 December 1899 is reprinted in Reiner Stach, 2012, 153.

20 See Corngold's judicious selection from some of the wilder reaches of criticism that accompanies his translation of *The Metamorphosis* (Corngold, 2004b).

21 As his mother tells the Chief Clerk, 'The only amusement he gets is doing fretwork. For instance, he spent two or three evenings cutting out a little picture frame; you would be surprised to see how pretty it is; it's hanging in his room . . .' (S 96, 105).

22 The link between 'Wedding Preparations in the Country' and 'The Metamorphosis' is usually understood in terms of Raban's fantasy about becoming an insect in bed instead of having to travel to visit his fiancée in the country. Zicolsky, however, suggests that Gregor is prefigured not so much in Raban as in the lachrymose professional traveller he meets on the train. He links this, perhaps fancifully, to the five-year incubation period for railway trauma.

23 Zilcosky convincingly diagnoses the symptoms of Gregor Samsa's metamorphosis – lassitude, nervous and physical agitation, bad dreams, blurred vision and anxiety – in the light of the proposition that 'The *Metamorphosis* begins precisely with the assumption that Gregor is "ill" from the same beastly rigours of professional travel that afflicted his author' (Corngold and Gross, 184). Zilcosky then draws back from this proposition, clarifying 'I am not claiming that Samsa's transformation is a direct result of train trauma. Such trauma cannot cause a man to turn into a giant bug' (Corngold and Gross, 194). Kafka himself, however, was very clear about the traumatic character of modern, technological experience and made a direct connection between it and shell shock when publicly calling for the foundation of a psychiatric hospital to treat the victims of shell shock (see OW 338–9).

24 The development of private accident insurance was also a response to the problem of real or perceived railway accidents, with accident insurance policies related to rail accidents issued in England in 1849 and Germany in 1853. See Peter Ulrich Lehner's comprehensive article on the development of Austrian accident insurance in Koch and Wagenbach, 101.

25 Zilcosky makes a suggestive link between the effects of the train and the vibratory *Apparat* or instrument of execution in 'In the Penal Colony'.

26 'Because the German railways became legally liable for injuries after 1871 – almost single-handedly creating Kafka's profession of accident insurance in 1884 (1887 in Austria-Hungary) – the legal medical debate about traumatic neuroses exploded by the fin-de-siècle. Doctors now had to distinguish between the truly injured and what Samsa's *Kassenartz* [insurance doctor] calls the "perfectly healthy" simulators' (Zilcosky, 188–9).

27 Perhaps the story is less about the 're-oedipalisation' of Gregor by the family (Deleuze and Guattari, 39) than the removal of an obstacle to the re-oedipalisation of the family itself after a season of paternal castration?

28 As noted by the editors of the *Amtliche Schriften*, 'Neither the objective precision nor the emotional conviction of Therese's narration of the death of her mother in an industrial accident on an unsafe building site in the fifth chapter of the America novel would be conceivable without the experience of his first year at work in the Institute' (*Amtliche Schriften*, 35).

29 Gerhard Kurz, 'Therese's Story in *Der Verschollene*', in Lothe et al., 100.

30 Schillemeit *Apparatband* to *Der Verschollene A*, 195.

31 Kurz perceptively identifies the ambiguity – 'one voice recounts the mother's death as a deliberate act, while another voice presents the death as an accident caused by clumsiness' – but too quickly resolves all doubt by deciding for suicide or the mother's 'determined pursuit of release from her situation' (Lothe et al., 102).

32 Durkheim showed that the peculiar modality of being forced voluntarily to take one's life is the most apt description of the stable suicide rates characterizing modern populations. In these cases the question of intent is by no means straightforward.

33 Kurz approaches Therese's narrative as a sub-plot or 'revealing variation of this pattern of inclusion and exclusion' (Lothe et al., 95) that he takes to characterize the novel. However, it seems more appropriate to situate this death within 'the ferocity of relations in a world of hunters and prey' (Lothe et al., 96) by which he later more insightfully characterizes the novel.

34 Kafka notes drily that the quarry would have received a favourable risk classification 'in total disregard of the actual conditions, as happened in so many other cases' had it not 'been the scene of a huge accident on April 1, 1911. According to the newspaper stories, one worker was killed and several other quarrymen suffered life threatening injuries. The accident was caused by the fall of a boulder, an incident that proved that the work was not carried out using terraces, that there were overhanging sections of rock, and that undercutting therefore also occurred; these facts had not only been passed over in silence in the report, they had actually been disclaimed' (*OW* 139).

35 In his review of the history of the Institute's work for the special 'Jubilee Report: Twenty-Five Years of the Workmen's Accident Insurance', Kafka refers to one of the strategies used by the Institute to circumvent the problem of being denied the right of inspection, namely voluntary unofficial or 'private' inspections carried out with the agreement of the owners, usually the 'largest firms'. These were carried out by the Institute 'within the limits of its agenda' on the mutual expectation 'that after a

private inspection of the firms – some before the decisions were issued and some during the appeals process – reclassification could be determined by mutual agreement' (*OW* 305).

36 Kafka's campaign to extend the independent surveillance capacity of the Institute was carried forward in two newspaper articles in the *Tetschen-Bodenbacher Zeitung* on 11 September and 4 November 1911. The first article rigorously criticizes the Institute's reliance on official statistics and on self-reporting for assessing risk and establishing premiums. He points out that dishonest businesses underreported their wage lists and were effectively free-riding at the expense of honest businesses. In the second article Kafka notes that 'in 1909 the reorganisation of the Institute's inspections was still in its infancy' (*OW* 155) and calls for more accident prevention work by the Institute.

37 Under the heading of 'Measures considered for Future Implementation' in the speech written for the Second International Conference on Accident Prevention and First Aid in 1914, Kafka systematically elides the forensic and didactic uses of photography in the phrase 'Typical accident investigations will be photographed and the pictures distributed' (*OW* 261). Photographic documentation of bad practice is used in accident prevention work but also as contributing to the evidentiary value of 'accident prevention statistics'. What is remarkable about the 1914 photographs is that they do not show accidents that have already taken place, but those that will take place in the future – they are photographs of accidents to come.

38 Advertised as 'Evenings for New Literature. Franz Kafka the writer who was awarded the Fontane prize last year, reads on Friday Evening November 10 in the Kunstsalon Goltz a previously unpublished novella, in the second half poems by Max Brod' (Unseld, 330).

39 In a newspaper review of the evening (Unseld, 166). For the sources and details of the reception of the novella, see Klaus Wagenbach's dossier *Franz Kafka In der Strafkolonie: Eine Geschichte aus dem Jahre 1914* (2010).

40 The stories and fragments of this writing campaign revive the philosophical ambition of the earlier stories and the reflective, philosophical style of *Meditation*. His working title *Verantwortlichkeit* (*Responsibility*), that became *A Country Doctor*, echoes the earlier collection and according to Unseld marked his return to 'the style of Meditation' (Unseld, 168). They definitely mark a return to explicitly philosophical themes also evident in the contemporary *Zurau Aphorisms*. In them and later *The Castle* the themes of accident, defiance, truth and enlightenment are explored in stories about the responsibilities incurred by the death, burial and mourning of Gods.

41 Zilcosky properly emphasizes the colonial location of the story, linking it with Mirabeau's *Torture Garden*, a deliberately Orientalist allegory of the hunt of Dreyfus and the erotics of colonial brutality that Kafka knew in translation: 'Kafka, like Mirbeau, proposes a deliberately perverse solution: he renders Old imperial sadism even crueller pushing it beyond its traditional limits, toward absurdity' (Zilcosky, 111). 'In the Penal Colony' indeed resounds with motifs from Mirabeau, ritual death through extended torture, execution by means of sustained vibrations – in Mirabeau's case an enormous bell – and an extended discourse by a grotesque executioner, but does not adopt Mirabeau's erotic focus on the sexual politics of the sadistic but sad Clara.

42 Politzer offers an extreme example of the critical fascination with the *Apparat*: 'In its centre emerges another "thing", an execution machine. The first sentence of the story introduces the machine as "a peculiar piece of apparatus", a formidable understatement indeed. Although this device is as dead as it is deadly, its presence so dominates the story that the human figures around it must be relegated to minor roles; they are not even accorded the privilege of having proper names' (Politzer, 98).

43 Kafka wrote to his publisher Kurt Wolff on 4 September 1917 describing the 'two or three pages shortly before the end' as '*Machwerk*' whose 'presence points to a deeper flaw, there is somewhere a worm who hollows out the completeness of the story' (*L* 136, 159).

44 Kirschberger, in spite of an endearing description of the Officer as 'a policeman and a handyman [who] steps in everywhere' (Kirschberger, 29) reads his suicide as confirmation of the old order through the argument that the Officer's release of the destined victim of the *Apparat* 'makes himself guilty of dereliction of duty, next to insubordination the most serious crime known to military codes' (Kirschberger, 34).

45 In *Capitalism as Religion*, Benjamin refers to the 'demonic ambiguity' of the word *Schuld* already noted by Nietzsche and evident in its translation as guilt, or debt, obligation, blame and even sin. Spanning economic, legal, moral and religious contexts, *Schuld* is a key to Benjamin's radicalization of Weber's Protestant ethic thesis in the fragment as well as later in the notion of 'Fetish Commodity' in the *Arcades Project*. Benjamin's proposal that capitalism creates *Schuld* can be understood in terms of its creating debt, liability, ethical wrong, responsibility and religious guilt. Weber of course focused on the role of religious guilt in the formation of the vocation that he sees at the origins of capitalism while Benjamin's condemnation of capitalism emerges from a combination of economic debt, moral responsibility for exploitation and religious guilt. His attention to the ambiguity of the term also allows us to situate Kafka's notion of absolute guilt more precisely. The 'larger movement' of capitalism that creates *Schuld* may also be understood in terms of the development of an economic and technical system that creates accidents, with victims who are innocent in intent but once touched by the event enter a context of absolute liability.

46 Richard Thieberger's 'The Botched Ending of "In the Penal Colony"' is representative of the underestimation of the messianic complications of Kafka's story: 'The story should end with this death. Its effect on the other characters, particularly on the explorer, could still be described at the same place. Instead the two pages devoted to the teahouse and to the explorers' embarkation destroy the unity of the work. The story begins in front of the intact torture machine; it should also end before the broken machine that has just spectacularly failed in its ultimate purpose' (Thieberger in Flores, 308).

47 The visit to the tearoom has irritated many readers of the novella. While Politzer is unusual in the attention he devotes to the scene in the teahouse, he does not grasp its significance although he is at least aware that there is one – 'Although the Explorer has a perfectly rational excuse for bending his knees, the reader cannot help feeling that here at last he pays his involuntary respect to the spirit of the Old Commandant' (Politzer, 113). Regarding the moment of messianic recognition, Politzer's intuition is sound, but his conclusion is 'A silent smile is the epitome of ambiguity; it may also be understood as a sign of amusement caused by the foreigner's obvious skepticism. It may even be the sign of an expectancy that is sure of its eventual fulfilment' (Politzer, 114). Emrich does not linger in the tearoom; the scene played out there is but the 'suspicion' of a foreigner and the subsequent chase an attempt by the condemned man and soldier to 'flee' with the Traveller. Pasley perceptively notes that the visit to the teahouse 'leaves the reader with a sense of foreboding' (301) but does not elaborate further.

48 See David Daube, *The Exodus Pattern in the Bible. (1963)*

49 Emrich cites among other examples Josef K.'s arrest, K.'s going astray in village and castle and the 'mistaken ringing of the night bell' in *A Country Doctor*.

50 Zilcosky observes very nicely that 'Gracchus refuses to accept the truly modern consequences of both a dead God and a frivolous colonialism. It is this nostalgia in spite of himself that sentences Gracchus to endless wandering, on the two metaphorical registers that structure the text: he is incapable of leaving *either* the religious "great stairway" *or* the historical "earthly seas"' (Zilcosky, 184).

51 At this point in the manuscript, Kafka deleted two references to a religious solution to the problem of Gracchus's guilt: the first, spoken by Gracchus, is an act of penance – 'I built a chapel to St Hubert' (the patron saint of hunters) – the second by the Mayor – 'I can ask the Priest. We too still have one [*ei*] [breaks off] (Kafka 2006, 34).

52 It is less likely to be 'a picture of Midas about to capture Silenus' that Bridgewater suggests in his reading of the Hunter Gracchus in terms of Nietzsche's *Genealogy of Morals* (Bridegewater, 125).

Chapter 3

1   Kafka's most extended reflection on the term occurs in a letter to Brod, 5 July 1922, where he asks, 'But how is it with *Schriftstellersein* itself' (B 384; *L* 333). He describes it as the predicament of living 'over a darkness from which the dark power emerges when it wills, and heedless of my stammering, destroys my life' (B 384; *L* 333) and the 'reward for serving the devil'. However, this statement echoes others dating back already to 1903 in his correspondence with Oskar Pollak.

2   One of Stanley Corngold's more speculative essays, 'The Ministry of Writing', understands *Schriftstellersein* by means of an analogy with Heidegger's 'analytic of *Dasein*' in *Being and Time* as an 'analytic of writerly being'. While allowing him to break down the wall between Kafka's office and bedroom writings, the claim that 'the world of Kafka's writing, both literary and official, is a single institution' (xv) reduces 'mode of being' to an institution.

3   Janouch recalls Kafka's obsessive drawing and describes his 'strange minute sketches, in which only the abstraction of movement was emphasised, of tiny men running, fighting and crawling, and kneeling on the ground' as 'the remains of an old, deep-rooted passion' (Janouch, 35). He recalls Kafka describing them as 'private ideograms' and himself 'still in Egyptian bondage' to external appearances; they contain a 'spark' of conscious life and are part of the effort 'to see the world as if revealed in a flash of lightning' that also characterizes his writing, *America* above all. The flash, he explains, illuminates the paradoxical 'condition of man's freedom' according to which the figures in his drawings, of which only a tiny proportion survive, 'come out of the dark only to vanish into the dark' (Janouch, 36). They are his attempt to provoke light – primitive magic he explains, like the lines drawn by Eskimos on wood before rubbing them to make fire.

4   In a newspaper article on the work of the Institute, Kafka described how 'The Institute also wants to have slides of illustrations of protective devices made and make these available for lecturing purposes' (*OW* 162, 267). The approach of commenting photographs in 'Accident Prevention in Quarries' is clearly grounded in the practice of a slide-lecture.

5   See Deleuze and Guattari use of photography as an entrance point to Kafka's work (Deleuze and Guattari, 3–4) and Duttlinger's comprehensive review of his applications of photography.

6   The ending of *The Trial* in a photographic pose was perceptively described by Carol Duttlinger as a contrast with the light of the law in the parable 'Before the Law': 'In contrast to the light emanating from the law in the Priest's parable, which is described as a continuous radiating glow, this light, taken by K. as a last, elusive sign of hope, resembles a photographic

flash capturing the protagonists death in a coldly revealing narrative snapshot' (Duttlinger, 205)

7   The editors of the Frankfurt *Amtliche Schriften* quite properly describe the 'pioneering medial extension of the perceptual apparatus of the Institute through photographs of the quarries . . .' (*AS* 877).

8   Kafka also attempted to stage industrial safety exhibitions contrasting good and bad practice at the Institute's premises. In this light the photographic sequence presents a miniature industrial safety exhibition with accompanying lecture.

9   Given the questionable legality of the undertaking, Kafka expressed himself indirectly: 'Allerdings konnten solche Aufnahmen auch nicht entfernt in dem Umfang vorgennomen werder' (*OW* 284, 395).

10   His envisaged 'lecture' on blasting that accompanies the photograph hints at his being physically present before it, above all with the references to colour that he adds to the black and white photograph. The model is an amalgam of four 'ideal quarries' of different stone with different textures and colour. Kafka places us beside him, behind the camera, when he says that 'The blasting charges are, following regulations, identified with black lettered signs, while the two signs with red lettering prohibit touching the exhibit' (*OW* 296). We of course cannot see the red letters in a black and white photo, and Kafka seems to mention them only to remind us that this is a model in an exhibit and to prevent us from becoming too absorbed. This fictional quarry, with its contrived history of misfired charges, with an emergency rope for workers who never existed 'to climb up and down the quarry wall easily and safely', is a fictional model of what the other 14 photographed quarries could become.

11   My thanks to Professor Benno Wagner for graciously providing me with scans of the photo-sequence.

12   Strangely obeying the theme of inversion that enters the sequence at this point, the English translation accidentally reverses the order of photographs V and VI, making the commentaries unintelligible and considerably disrupting the sequence of variations in lighting exploited by Kafka in curating his gallery of photographs.

13   Here the reproduction in the Frankfurt edition complicates matters by slightly cropping the lower edge of the photograph.

14   Stach reports that Kafka visited the latest Prague tourist attraction in the autumn of 1914, a facsimile of the trenches in which the young soldiers were fighting on the front.

15   Strangely, his posture resembles that of a graffiti artist in the act of writing the 'a' underlined on the wall.

16   Although the title *Der Verschollene* is better translated as 'Missing Person', I have retained the title *America* given it by Brod and by which the novel is more widely known in English.

17 Politzer intuits the presence of the photographic flash in the opening of the novel: 'Actually the first two sentences contain not so much the panorama of the of the city opening before the boy's eyes as a fixed image suddenly apprehended. The liner has slowed down and the light is "suddenly increased". The feeling is that of a flash photograph; the stream of life is interrupted by the light and recorded forever in its startled suspension. The vivid lifelessness of this passage suggests Kafka wrote it while actually contemplating a photograph of New York' (Politzer, 122). Politzer, however, tends to moralize justice and loses sight of the execution: 'The Sword of Liberty, however, is not drawn against the social injustices bred by America's capitalism; it is pointed against Karl Rossmann's conscience' (Politzer, 123). It should also be remembered that Kafka reports dreaming of the Holitscher photograph of New York which might also contribute to the oneiric quality of Rossmann's scene of arrival.

18 *America* dates from the autumn–winter of 1912–13, *The Trial* from the autumn–winter 1914–15. It began well, with Brod reporting in his diary on 29 September 1912 that 'Kafka in ecstasy, writing the whole night through, a novel set in America.' Oct 2 'Kafka continues to be very much inspired. One chapter finished. I'm very happy about it' (cited Unseld, 93). On 17 November he interrupts the novel to write 'The Metapmorphosis' and then loses momentum, eventually abandoning *America* in late January 1913 (see letter to Felice, 26 January 1913), only to return to complete the final chapter given the title 'Nature Theatre of Oklahama' by Brod while writing *The Trial.*

19 The Greenberg and Arendt translation unaccountably allows the 'guilty one' Josef K. to be pushed aside rather than struck down.

20 Kafka may have recalled Arthur Holitscher's description of nearby Ellis Island: 'This is Ellis Isle, the island of torment and judgement, where naked Fate and the unjust avenger are tolerated to an unacceptable degree. No Blake could have drawn or sung of the avenging angel who reigns over this island in a cloud of fear, whimpering, torture and blasphemy every single day that we spend in this country' (trans. Flores, 296).

21 They are certainly not as Adorno believed 'the stations of the epic adventure become those of a modern passion' in which 'The closed complex of immanence becomes concrete in the form of a flight from prisons' (Adorno, 265), for here there is no question of flight but only slow burial alive.

22 In a later reflection on the novel in the diary entry of 8 October 1917, Kafka understood retrospectively that his intention had been to 'write a Dicken's novel', citing the parallels with *David Copperfield* but noting that his story was more brightly illuminated and relied on sharper contrasts, in short was 'enhanced by the sharper lights that I took from the times and the duller that I should have taken from myself' (*D* 388).

23 Anna Fuchs in 'A Psychoanalytic reading of *The Man Who Disappeared*' noted the lost suitcase and its link to the lost umbrella and to the passport and family photographs (in Preece, 28–9). Her reading of the dazzle of the street and its 'glass roof' draws some fascinating conclusions about the role of light in Kafka's accident narratives: 'This perceptual confusion is further heightened by the light, which, as so often in Kafka's writing does not illuminate. Instead it disperses the boundaries of the objects until the human eye is completely dazzled' (in Preece, 31).

24 Janouch provides indirect independent testimony of Kafka's fascination with the figure of Lincoln when he recalls discussing with Kafka the 'poor prospects' of the Versailles peace treaty and the comment 'Nothing is final ... Since Abraham Lincoln nothing is finally settled unless it is justly settled' (Janouch, 131). The unfinished legacy of the American Civil War returns in connection with Janouch's memory of Kafka's gift of a translation of Whitman and accompanying comment on the 'war between the Northern and Southern states in America, which first really set in motion the power of our present machine world' (Janouch, 167).

25 The choice of Oklahoma is also well judged since it was settled at the expense of the Native American inhabitants by land runs and the frauds of the 1830 and 1907 laws that expropriated vast territories (see p. 333). It would later, however, host a vibrant African American culture and economy, but this post-dated Kafka in the 1920s.

26 Kafka had already reflected on the precarity of such work during Raban's train journey in 'Wedding Preparations in the Country'.

27 For a contrasting view of Josef K., as a figure of resistance, see Löwy, 97.

28 Thus Nietzsche cites Tertullian, pointing to the pleasure of the redeemed at the spectacle of the torments of the damned.

29 When he is escorted away to his death, K. recalls the image of dying flies, this time the agony of flies caught on flypaper.

30 The contrast of flares and constant light was previously used by Lenin in his organizational manifesto *What is to be Done* in order to distinguish passive 'trade union' from active 'revolutionary' consciousness.

31 Here it is less a question of becoming animal as Deleuze and Guattari believed (Deleuze and Guatarri, 40) than becoming prey.

32 In the manuscript, Kafka corrected 'extended' (*breitete*) with 'stretched' (*strekte*), emphasizing that the figure in the house may have been holding something in his hands (Kafka 1997).

33 In a first response to the images of torture and humiliation from the Abu Ghraib prison in 2004 under the title 'The Destruction of Morality', the *Independent* journalist Robert Fisk spoke of his realization of the role played by video and photography in torture. The filming of the 'brutal whipping of Iraqi prisoners by Saddam's security police' and subsequently the photographing of torture by the American prison guards did not merely document the treatment of prisoners, but was a constitutive part of their humiliation: 'But now I realise the videos were taken so that the prisoners could be humiliated. Their suffering, their pathetic pleas for mercy, their animal like behaviour was to be recorded – to add the final layer of degradation to their fate.' A similar rationale applied to the Abu Ghraib photographs: 'And now I realise, too, that the pictures of the Iraqis so cruelly treated – so tortured – by the Americans, were taken for precisely the same reason. Someone decided that the photos would be the final straw, the breaking point, the moment of capitulation for these young men.' *Independent*, 18 May 2016, http://www.independent.co.uk/news/world/middle-east/the-destruction-of-morality-a7033836.html (accessed 6 April 2017).

34 David Suchoff notes the proximity of land surveyor to messiah in Hebrew: 'The three letter Hebrew root that means "to annoint with oil" M-SH-KH ... and produces the word for "Messiah" ... also produced the Aramaic-Hebrew word for "land-surveyor" that is one letter apart' (Suchoff, 170).

35 As Adorno noted, there is already doubt about whether he was called or arrived by accident, and Adorno hastily decides K. 'cannot possibly have been summoned there' (Adorno, 247). For possible Nietzschean echoes in K.'s arrival scene, see Bridgewater, p. 90.

36 Barnabas, for example, the aspirant messenger, produces shoes by night for Brunswick who took over his father's dominant role in the economy of the village after the disgrace of Amalia's defiance of the sexual advances of the official Sortini.

37 Adorno's note on repetition focuses on Titorelli's landscapes and misses the emancipatory potential of repetition; for him, 'The social origin of the individual ultimately reveals itself as the power to annihilate him' (Adorno, 253) rather than to annihilate social origins themselves. He notes later that 'there is no eternity' for Kafka 'other than that of endlessly repeated sacrifice' (Adorno, 257).

Chapter 4

1 In a thoughtful reflection on *The Castle* in his *Hamletica*, Massimo Cacciari (2009) contrasts the closure of the *Schloss*, which forbids entry and exit, to the openness of the Castle as a mystical destination of the ecstatic quest: K. approaches the Closed as if it were a castle, home of the ecstatic arcanum. However, when viewed from the standpoint of the passage in the opposite direction, the *Schloss* is anything but closed; it is leaky and full of back doors and secret channels through which its messengers can reach the village.

2   Stanley Corngold is the most recent and persuasive advocate of this interpretive strategy, but of course complicating the Gnostic theology by an openness to the social and cultural, specifically of Kafka's work.

3   'We had insulted a messenger and driven him into a more remote bureau; what was more natural than for us to offer a new messenger in the person of Barnabas, so that the other messengers' work may be carried on by him, and the other messenger might remain quietly in retirement as long as he liked, for as long as the time he needed to forget the insult' (*C* 655).

4   In his effort to draw the parallel between Kafka's world and the Third Reich, Adorno errs in believing that the Castle officials 'wear a special uniform, as the SS did' (Adorno, 259); only the messengers wear uniform.

5   Olga's strategic assessment might be contrasted with the voice of the resistant to imperial domination in the fragment that begins 'One is ashamed to say by what means the imperial colonel governs our little town in the mountains' (*WP* 320). The assessment notes that the colonel's 'few soldiers could be disarmed immediately' and that help would not come 'for days, indeed for weeks'; he is consequently 'utterly dependent on our obedience' that is only tolerated 'because of his gaze' (*WP* 321). Occupying the old democratic 'council chamber', this colonel with assured imperial authority does not need to engage in performances of deference and delay – 'Ceremonial he does not care for, and any form of play acting even less' – and yet he performs insouciant confidence. He leans back smiling at the petitioner, scrutinizing him in the light of imperial authority. What is remarkable about this little noticed fragment is that it puts the colonel himself under the gaze of resistance; *its* strategic gaze, like Olga's scraps of intelligence about the inscrutable officials, is already an act of resistance.

6   The affinity of quarries and amphitheatres is made explicit in a fragment cited by Emrich: 'It sometimes happens (one has scarcely an inkling of the reasons for this) that the greatest bullfighter chooses for his scene of action the ruined arena belonging to a little town situated off the beaten track. Up until then the Madrid public had barely known the name of this town. An arena neglected for centuries – here with the grass growing exuberantly, a children's playground; there, burning hot with bare rocks, a retreat for snakes and lizards. Above, the upper edge of the arena long since demolished, a veritable quarry for all the houses round about – nothing left but a small bowl that will scarcely hold five hundred people. No adjoining buildings, above all no stables; but, worst of all, the railroad has not yet been constructed this far' (Emrich, 125).

7   *Der Bau* is more accurately translated as 'the building', shifting attention between the built object and the process of building; the burrow should be understood as both a noun – the creature's building – and a verb, its process of building.

8   The story concludes, 'That is also the reason why the city has a fist on its coat of arms' (115). It is often remarked that this is a description of the coat of arms of Prague, and the story linked biographically to Kafka's early comment about the impossibility of leaving Prague.

9   The words 'Ein Kommentar' precede the story in the manuscript and was assumed by Brod to be the title of the parable that follows. However, it is more probably related to Kafka's previous note on Rashi's commentary and does not necessarily have anything to do with the parable.

10 Janouch recalls Kafka's views on the 'repellent' character of the law and the paradox that 'the legislator produces, instead of order, a more or less visible form of anarchy' (Janouch, 181).

Chapter 5

1   Although Kafka is not explicit, it is probable that the light in the hall is lit by gas emitting a yellowish light and that of the kitchen by electricity emitting a bluish light The coexistence of two technologies of artificial light and their different light qualities was common in the European cities of the early twentieth century and is still to be found in Prague.

2   'This tremendous event is still on its way, still wandering; it has not yet reached the ears of men. Lightning and thunder require time; the light of the stars require time; deeds though done, still require time to be seen and heard. This deed is still more distant from them than the most distant stars – and yet they have done it themselves' (Nietzsche 1974).

3   The earliest aphorisms emerged from the Hippocratic medical school and were intended to provide practical maxims for the conduct of the healer. They focused attention on diagnosis, assessed whether a disease was treatable and if so what therapies might be attempted. The genre was revived in the eighteenth century with Lichtenberg and raised to perfection by Nietzsche and Kafka's contemporary Karl Kraus.

4   Kafka's interest in Kierkegaard predated his Zürau study of *Fear and Trembling*. He possessed Carl Dallago's short book *Über eine Schrift: Soren Kierkegaard und die Philosophie der Innerlichkeit*, published in 1914, as well as a copy of its original publication in the journal *Brenner*; in the early 1920s he was still thinking about Kierkegaard's distinction between the aesthetic and the ethical and gave a copy of Dallago's essay to Gustav Janouch (see Blank, 240 and Janouch, 81).

5   The phenomenological approach is present throughout the aphorisms, notably in aphorisms 11 and 12: 'Differences in the view one can have of things, for instance of an apple: the view of the little boy who has to crane his neck in order even to glimpse the apple on the table, and the view of the master of the house who takes the apple and freely hands it to the

person sitting at the table with him' (*WP* 39). Of course, given the preoccupation with the Fall already signalled in aphorism 3 and developed later in the reflections on the tree of the knowledge of good and evil and the tree of life, the perception and the gift of an apple is not an innocent example. The approach is exemplified in aphorism 59: 'A stair not worn hollow by footsteps is, regarded from its own point of view, only a boring something made of wood' (*WP* 44).

6 Jost Schillemeit's edition reads 'Einigkeit' – oneness – in place of Brod's reading 'Ewigkeit'. Yet the fragments immediately prior are discussing the 'endless space' and the experience of *Ewigkeit* and those that follow also address the theme. In addition, the manuscript is more plausibly read as 'Ewigkeit' (Kafka 2011, 24). For these reasons and for the internal consistency of the argument of the fragment, Brod's reading is in this case preferred.

7 Consistent with Kafka's fascination with Kierkegaard while writing the Zürau aphorisms, he here seems to be pondering the case of an Abraham without faith. If the mad voice tells him to kill his son, what would it mean to obey it in the absence of a faith in God?

8 What it reveals is the fugitive ugliness behind illusion: 'Our art is a way of being dazzled by truth: the light on the grotesquely grimacing retreating face is true and nothing else' (45). The light of truth exposes but also repels ugliness at the same time as disabling the vision of the one who looks. Aphorism 88 that followed this reflection in the notebook refers to 'Death in front of us, rather as on the school wall there is a reproduction of Alexander's battle' (*WP* 48). The role of art is not so much to illuminate as to obliterate this glaring image, leaving only a point where its truth can be perceived – 'The thing is to darken, or even indeed to blot out, the picture in this one life of ours through our actions' (*WP* 48).

9 'Josephine' and 'The Hunger Artist' present two figures of the vulnerable, transcendentally insecure artist.

10 This aphorism is put to fascinating use in Sloterdijk's *You Must Change Your Life (2013)* 63–65, but entirely removed from the context of the aphorisms that precede and follow it.

11 One of the entries in the notebook describes 'Evil as the starry heavens of the good' (*NII* 57) – the question being whether we are astrologers or astronomers of good and evil.

12 '"You must be mad!" he said to me. "A protest which is licensed and approved by the police! It is both absurd and sad. It is worse than real revolt, because it is only a sham outburst"' (Janouch, 82).

BIBLIOGRAPHY

Adorno, Theodor W. (1967). 'Notes on Kafka', *Prisms*, trans. Samuel and Shierry Weber. MIT Press, Cambridge, MA.

Allan, Neil (2005). *Franz Kafka and the Genealogy of Modern European Philosophy: From Phenomenology to Post-Structuralism*. Edwin Mellin Press, Lewiston, NY.

Alt, Peter-André (2005). *Franz Kafka Der ewige Sohn: Eine Biographie*. C.H. Beck, Munich.

Anderson, Mark M. (1989). *Reading Kafka: Prague, Politics and the Fin-de-Siecle*. Schoecken Books, New York.

Anderson, Mark M. (1992). *Kafka's Clothes: Ornament and Aestheticism in the Habsburg Fin de Siecle*. Oxford University Press, Oxford.

Arendt, Hannah (2007). *Reflections on Literature and Culture*, ed. Susannah Young-Ah Gottlieb, Stanford University Press, Stanford.

Beck, Evelyn Torton (1971). *Kafka and the Yiddish Theatre: Its Impact on his Work*. University of Wisconsin Press, Madison and London.

Benjamin, Walter (1973). *Understanding Brecht*, trans. Anna Bostock. NLB, London.

Benjamin, Walter (1992). *Illuminations*, trans. Harry Zohn. Fontana Press, London.

Binder, Hartmut (1967). 'Franz Kafka und die Wochenschrift *Selbstwehr*', *Deutsche Vierteljahrsschrift für Literatur und Geistesgeschichte* 41: 283–304.

Binder, Hartmut (1983). *Kafka: Der Schaffensprozess*. Suhrkamp Verlag, Frankfurt-am-Main.

Binder, Hartmut (ed.) (1979). *Kafka Handbuch*. Alfred Kroner, Stuttgart.

Blanchot, Maurice (1981). *De Kafka à Kafka*. Gallimard, Paris.

Blank, Herbert (2004). *In Kafkas Bibliothek*. Nakladatelstvi Franz Kafka, Praha.

Blumenberg, Hans (1984). *Arbeit am Mythos*. Suhrkamp Verlag, Frankfurt-am-Main.

Boa, Elizabeth (1996). *Kafka: Gender, Class, and Race in the Letters and Fictions*. Clarendon Press, Oxford.

Bokhove, Nils and Marike van Dorst (2011). *Einmal ein grosser Zeichner: Franz Kafka als bildender Künstler*. Vitalis, Utrecht.

Born, Jürgen et al. (1965). *Kafka Symposium*. Verlag Klaus Wagenbach, Berlin.

Bridgewater, Patrick (1974). *Kafka and Nietzsche*. Bouvier Verlag, Bonn.

Brod, Max (1974). *Über Franz Kafka*. Fischer Verlag, Frankfurt-am-Main.

Butler, Judith (2011). 'Who owns Kafka'. *London Review of Books* 33, no. 5 (3 March): 3–8.

Cacciari, Massimo (2009) *Hamletica*, Adelphi, Milano.

Calasso, Roberto (2006). *K.*, trans. Geoffrey Brock. Vintage, London 2006.

Casanova, Pascale (2011). *Kafka en colère*. Seuil, Paris.

Caygill, Howard (2011). 'The Fate of the Pariah: Kafka and Arendt at "The Nature Theatre of Oklahoma"'. *College Literature Arendt Special Issue* 38, no. 1 (Winter).

Citati, Pieto (1990). *Kafka*, trans. Raymond Rosenthal. Secker and Warburg, London.

Coetzee, J. M. (1981). 'Time, tense and aspect in Kafka's "The Burrow"', *Modern Language Notes* 96, no. 3 (April): 556–79.

Corngold, Stanley (2004a). *Lambent Traces: Franz Kafka*. Princeton University Press, Princeton, NJ, and Oxford.

Corngold, Stanley (ed. and trans.) (2004b). *The Metamorphosis: Franz Kafka*. Bantam Dell, New York.

Corngold, Stanley and Benno Wagner (2011). *Franz Kafka: The Ghosts in the Machine*. Northwestern University Press, Evanston, IL.

Corngold, Stanley and Ruth V. Gross (2011). *Kafka for the Twenty-First Century*. Camden House, Rochester, NY.

Daube, David (1963). *The Exodus Pattern in the Bible*. Faber & Faber, London.

Deleuze, Gilles and Felix Guattari (1986). *Kafka: Towards a Minor Literature*, trans. Dana Polan. University of Minnesota Press, Minneapolis and London.

Detienne, Marcel (1999). *The Masters of Truth in Archaic Greece*, trans. Janet Lloyd. Zone Books, New York.

Duttlinger, Caroline (2007). *Kafka and Photography*. Oxford University Press, Oxford.

Emrich, Wilhelm (1968). *Franz Kafka, A Critical Study of his Writings*, trans. Sheema Zeben Buehne. Frederick Ungar Publishing Co Inc., New York.

Flores, Angel (ed.) (1977). *The Kafka Debate: New Perspectives for Our Time*. Gordian Press, New York.

Friedländer, Saul (2013). *Franz Kafka: The Poet of Shame and Guilt*. Yale University Press, New Haven, CT, and London.

Friedländer, Saul (ed) (1977). *The Problem of 'The Judgement': Eleven Approaches to Kafka's Story*. Gordian Press, New York.

Gilman, Sander (1995). *Franz Kafka: The Jewish Patient*. Routledge, New York and London.

Goebel, Rolf J. (1997). *Constructing China: Kafka's Orientalist Discourse*. Camden House, Columbia, SC.

Gray, Richard T (1987). *Constructive Destruction: Kafka's Aphorism: Literary Tradition and Literary Transformation*. Max Niemeyer Verlag, Tübingen.

Greenberg, Martin (1971). *The Terror of Art: Kafka and Modern Literature*. Andre Deutsch, London.

Guattari, Felix (2007). *Soixante-cinq reves de Franz Kafka*. Nouvelles éditions Lignes, Paris.

Heidsieck, Arnold (1994). *The Intellectual Contexts of Kafka's Fiction: Philosophy, Law, Religion*. Camden House, Columbia, SC.

Holitscher, Arthur (1912). *Amerika Heute und Morgen: Reiseerlebnisse*. S. Fischer Verlag, Berlin.

Janouch, Gustav (1971). *Conversations with Kafka*, trans. Goronwy Rees. New Directions, New York.

Kafka, Franz (1984). *Amtliche Schriften*, ed. Klaus Hermsdorf. Akademie-Verlag, Berlin.

Kafka, Franz (1997). *Der Process, Historisch-kritische Ausgabe sämtlicher Handschriften, Drucke und Typoskripte*, ed. Roland Reuss and Peter Staengle. Stroemfeld Verlag, Frankfurt-am-Main.

Kafka, Franz (1999). *Beschreibung eines Kampfes. Gegen zwölf Uhr . . . Historisch-kritische Ausgabe sämtlicher Handschriften, Drucke und Typoskripte*, ed. Roland Reuss and Peter Staengle. Stroemfeld Verlag, Frankfurt-am-Main.

Kafka, Franz (2006). *Oxforder Oktavheft 2*, Roland Reuss and Peter Staengle, Stroemfeld Verlag, Frankfurt-am-Main.

Kafka, Franz (2011). *Oxforder Oktavheft 8*, Roland Reuss and Peter Staengle. Stroemfeld Verlag, Frankfurt-am-Main.

Kirschberger, Lida (1986). *Kafka's use of Law in Fiction: A New Interpretation of In der Strafkolonie, Der Prozess, and Das Schloss*. Peter Lang, New York.

Kittler, Friedrich A. (1986). *Grammophon, Film, Typewriter*. Brinkmann & Bose, Berlin.

Kittler, Friedrich A. (2003). *Aufschreibesysteme*. Fink, Munich.

Kittler, Wolf and Gerhard Neumann (eds) (1990). *Franz Kafka. Schriftvekehr*. Rombach, Freiburg.

Koch, Hans-Gerd (2005). *'Als Kafka mir entgegenkam . . .' Erinnerungen an Franz Kafka*. Verlag Klaus Wagenbach, Berlin.

Koch, Hans-Gerd and Klaus Wagenbach (eds) (2002). *Kafkas Fabriken*. Marbacher Magazin 100/2002, Marbach-am-Neckar.

Lothe, Jacob et. al (eds) (2011). *Franz Kafka: Narrative, Rhetoric, and Reading*. The Ohio State University Press, Columbus.

Löwy, Michael (2004). *Franz Kafka: Rêveur insoumis*. Éditions Stock, Paris.

Lukács, Georg (2006). *Journal 1910-1911*. payot-rivages, Paris.

Malabou, Catherine (2012). *Ontology of the Accident: An Essay on Destructive Plasticity*, trans. Carolyn Shread. Polity Press, Cambridge.

Mirbeau, Octave (2010). *Torture Garden*, trans. Michael Richardson. Dedalus, Sawtry, UK.

Moran, Brendan and Carlo Salzani (2013). *Philosophy and Kafka*. Lexington Books, Lanham, MD.

Mosès, Stéphane (2006). *Exégèse d'une légende: Lectures de Kafka*. éditions de l'éclat, Paris and Tel-Aviv.

Mowitt, John (2015) *Sounds: The Ambient Humanities*, University of California Press, Oakland.

Müller, Michael (ed.) (2003). *Franz Kafka: Romane und Erzählungen*. Philipp Reclam jun., Stuttgart.

Müller-Seidel, Walter (1986). *Die Deportation des Menschen: Kafka's Erzählung In der Strafkolonie*. J.B. Metzler Verlag, Stuttgart.

Newton, Huey (2009). *Revolutionary Suicide*, Penguin Books, New York.

Nietzsche, Friedrich (1974). *The Gay Science*, trans. Walter Kaufmann. Vintage Books, New York.

North, Paul (2015). *The Yield: Kafka's Atheological Reformation*. Stanford University Press, Stanford, CA.

Northey, Anthony (1991). *Kafka's Relatives: Their Lives and his Writing*. Yale University Press, New Haven, CT.

Page, Jack (2003). *In the Hands of the Great Spirit: The 20,000 Year History of the American Indians*. Free Press, New York.

Pasley, Malcolm (1963). *Introduction to Franz Kafka's Short Stories*. Clarendon Press, Oxford.

Pasley, Malcolm (1966). *Introduction to Franz Kafka: Der Heizer, In der Strafkolonie, Der Bau*. Cambridge University Press, Cambridge.

Pasley, Malcolm (1995). *'Die Schrift ist unveränderlich . . .' Essays zu Kafka*. Fischer Verlag, Frankfurt-am-Main.

Politzer, H. (1966). *Franz Kafka: Parable and Paradox*. Cornell University Press, Ithaca, NY.

Preece, Julian (ed.) (2002). *The Cambridge Companion to Kafka*. Cambridge University Press, Cambridge.

Robert, Marthe (1979). *Seul, comme Franz Kafka*. Calmann-Lévy, Paris.

Robert, Marthe (2012). *Introduction à la lecture de Kafka*. Editions de l'éclat, Paris.

Robertson, Ritchie (1985). *Kafka: Judaism, Politics and Literature*. Clarendon Press, Oxford.

Robertson, Ritchie (2004). *Kafka: A Very Short Introduction*. Oxford University Press, Oxford.

Rolleston, James (ed.) (2003). *A Companion to the Works of Franz Kafka*. Camden House, Rochester, NY.

Schuman, Rebecca (2015). *Kafka and Wittgenstein: The Case for Analytic Modernism*. Northwestern University Press, Evanston, IL.

Sloterdijk, Peter (2013). *You Must Change your Life*, trans. Wieland Hoburn, Polity Press, Cambridge.

Stach, Reiner (2005). *Kafka: The Decisive Years*, trans. Shelley Frisch. Harcourt Books, Orlando, FL.

Stach, Reiner (2012). *Ist das Kafka? 99 Fundstücke*. S. Fischer Verlag, Frankfurt-am-Main.

Stach, Reiner (2013). *Kafka: The Years of Insight*, trans. Shelley Frisch. Princeton University Press, Princeton, NJ.

Stach, Reiner (2014). *Kafka: Die frühen Jahre*. S. Fischer Verlag, Frankfurt-am-Main.

Stölzl, Christoph (1989). *Kafka's böses Böhmen: zur Sozialgeschichte eines Prager Juden*. Verlag Ullstein, Frankfurt-am-Main.

Sudaka-Bénazéraf, Jacqueline (2001). *Le regard de Franz Kafka*. Maisonneuve & Larose, Paris.

Sudaka-Bénazéraf, Jacqueline (2006). *Les cahier d'hebreu de Franz Kafka*. Retour à la lettre, Paris.

Unseld, Joachim (1982). *Kafka: A Writer's Life*, trans. Paul F. Dvorak. Ariadne Press, Riverside, CA.

Virilio, Paul (2012). '*Ce qui arrive*,' *La Pensée exposé: textes et entretiens*. Actes Sud, Arles.

Wagenbach, Klaus (1958). *Franz Kafka: eine Biographie seiner Jugend 1883-1912*. Franke Verlag, Bern.

Wagenbach, Klaus (1996). *Kafka's Prague: A Travel Reader*, trans. Shaun Whiteside. Overlook Press, Woodstock, NY.

Wagenbach, Klaus (2003). *Kafka*, trans. Ewald Osers. Haus Publishing, London.

Wagenbach, Klaus (ed.) (2010). *Franz Kafka In Der Strafkolonie: Eine Geschichte aus dem Jahre 1914*. Verlag Klaus Wagenbach, Berlin.

Wagner, Benno (2002). 'Poseidons Gehilfe: Kafka und die Statistik'. *Marbacher Magazin* 100: 115-19.

Wagner, Benno (2006). 'Insuring Nietzsche: Kafka's Files'. *New German Critique* 99: 83-119.

Ware, Ben (2015). *Dialectic of the Ladder: Wittgenstein, the 'Tractatus' and Modernism*. Bloomsbury, London.

Weber, Max (1978). *Economy and Society: An Outline of Interpretative Sociology*, ed. Guenther Roth and Claus Wittich. University of California Press, Berkeley.

Woods, Michelle (2014). *Kafka Translated: How Translators have shaped our Reading of Kafka*. Bloomsbury, London.

Zaslove, Jerry & Jeffries, Bill (2010) *The Insurance Man: Kafka in the Penal Colony* (exhibition catalogue), Simon Fraser University Gallery, Vancouver

Zilcosky, John (2003). *Kafka's Travels: Exoticism, Colonialism and the Traffic of Writing*. Palgrave, Basingstoke.

Zischler, Hans (2003). *Kafka goes to the Movies*, trans. Susan H. Gillespie. Chicago University Press, Chicago.

INDEX